**NOTHING
HERE WORTH
DYING FOR**

NOTHING HERE WORTH DYING FOR

TASK FORCE LION IN IRAQ

COL SETH W. B. FOLSOM, USMC (RET.)

Naval Institute Press
Annapolis, Maryland

Naval Institute Press
291 Wood Road
Annapolis, MD 21402

Library of Congress Cataloging-in-Publication Data

Names: Folsom, Seth W. B., author.

Title: Nothing here worth dying for : Task Force Lion in Iraq / Col Seth W.B. Folsom, USMC (RET.)

Other titles: Task Force Lion in Iraq

Description: Annapolis, Maryland : Naval Institute Press, [2025] | Includes index.

Identifiers: LCCN 2024037354 (print) | LCCN 2024037355 (ebook) | ISBN 9781682473252 (hardback) | ISBN 9781682473269 (ebook)

Subjects: LCSH: United States. Task Force Lion | Iraq War, 2003–2011—Personal narratives, American. | Folsom, Seth W. B. | Military assistance, American—Iraq. | Iraq—Armed Forces—Training of. | United States. Marine Corps—Officers—Biography. | United States. Marine Corps—History—Iraq War, 2003–2011. | Iraq War, 2003–2011—Campaigns— Iraq—Anbār (Iraq : Province) | Iraq War, 2003–2011—Biography. Classification: LCC DS79.766.F65 A3 2025 (print) | LCC DS79.766.F65 (ebook) | DDC 956.7044/342092 [B]—dc23/eng/20241107

LC record available at https://lccn.loc.gov/2024037354

LC ebook record available at https://lccn.loc.gov/2024037355

♾ Print editions meet the requirements of ANSI/NISO z39.48–1992 (Permanence of Paper).
Printed in the United States of America.

9 8 7 6 5 4 3 2 1

All maps created by Pete McPhail.

For my eighty-five pipe-hitters . . .

task force: [task fôrs] English, *noun*
    1. An armed force organized for a special operation.
    2. A unit specially organized for a task.

الأسد: [al ə-sad] Arabic, *noun*
    the lion

lion: [līən] English, *noun*
    A large, tawny-colored cat that lives in prides, found in
    Africa and northwestern India. The male has a flowing,
    wshaggy mane and takes little part in hunting, which
    is done cooperatively by the females.

CONTENTS

AUTHOR'S NOTE

This was a difficult book to write.

The source materials were there, and it was a story I had to tell, but obstacles and roadblocks thwarted me each time I attempted to put fingers to keyboard. I began drafting my manuscript several months after Task Force Lion returned from Iraq in 2018, but work and life got in the way. My assumption that the Marine Corps would show me the door after I returned from abroad proved false. Instead, in the years after my time with the task force, I took on a series of challenging jobs that limited my free time. So much for "work-life balance."

Perhaps more important, after many months away from my family I was reluctant to absent myself voluntarily after being gone so long. That was no surprise. I drafted my first book in 2004, before my first daughter was even born. As my children grew older, I found myself with less and less time to focus on writing. And so, as the years passed, with each new book I faced the realization that time and energy I put toward a writing project ultimately took away from my precious family time. It's not something I regret . . . it just explains why each book has taken longer to write and edit than the last.

This was also a difficult book to write because, even more than five years after our 2017–18 deployment, my feelings are still conflicted about the mission, our team's accomplishments, the challenges we faced, and the ultimate results. As a young captain in 2003, I never imagined our nation would still be so deeply involved in Iraq two decades later. In the years after Task Force Lion's departure, as the situation in Iraq and Syria continued to devolve—and periodically escalate—I often struggled to make sense of my team's role in the interminable mess that the Middle East remains in two decades on.

Hopefully this book, and the story it tells, will shed some additional light on how we got to where we now are in Iraq.

A note for readers regarding our interactions with the Iraqis. Despite high-minded aspirations early in the war, the Marine Corps—and the Department of Defense, for that matter—never fully developed the deep pool of fluent Arabic speakers it envisioned. As a result, throughout the Long War that followed the events of September 11, 2001, we had to rely on interpreters to facilitate our relationships with our Iraqi partners. Our 2017–18 deployment was no different. Although some of our partners spoke fluent English, in most cases we spoke to them almost entirely through interpreters. Readers should understand that, for simplicity's sake, the back-and-forth dialogue between Americans and Iraqis in this book is written in English. Additionally, numerous spellings of Iraqi leaders' names exist. In many cases, military documents and media reports often conflicted with my own personal notes and records. I have attempted to keep the spelling of their names as accurate as possible, but there will no doubt be errors.

A note on the story's characters. Throughout our deployment, Task Force Lion's numbers fluctuated, from a low of 2,300 to a high of almost 3,000. While every element of the task force contributed significantly in some degree or another, my focus in telling this story is the task force command element, which centered around a core team of eighty-five U.S. Marines and sailors. In previous books, I included details about scores of men and women in my units; later critiques often pointed to the difficulty associated with keeping track of all the different names, ranks, and billets. And so, for the sake of brevity and flow, I have focused on the key leaders who led and represented the task force's various units and elements. I wish I could have included everyone, as it was truly a team effort.

As this is a modern military story, it is naturally jargon and acronym-heavy. I have attempted to limit my use of acronyms as much as possible, but they are unavoidably intertwined with the story. I recommend readers take the time to review the glossary at the book's end to understand the alphabet soup that is part of everyday military life. Otherwise, at least for nonmilitary readers, the story will likely amount to little more than a confusing jumble of undecipherable hieroglyphics. The story is also heavy on tactical and operational terminology—something readers of military stories often thirst for, but which similarly confuses nonmilitary readers. My advice is simple: focus on the story and try not to get lost in the details. The story, after all, is why I wrote this book in the first place.

Finally, I should underscore that this story is my recollection of events. As with previous books, I relied heavily upon notes from my daily journal, after-action reports, and operational briefs and summaries. In many cases, to meet the DoD's strict security and policy guidelines, it was necessary to water down or gloss over some details. Most important, it is a tale told from *my* perspective. Others will certainly remember things differently, and that's fine . . . that's why it's called a memoir. Regardless, and as always, any mistakes or opinions are my own.

MAPS

CAST OF CHARACTERS

Task Force Lion Command Element

Col Seth Folsom—Task Force Commander

LtCol Tom Merritt—Task Force Deputy Commander

SgtMaj Alex Leibfried—Task Force Senior Enlisted Advisor

Maj John Kelly—Task Force Intelligence Officer

Maj Aaron Awtry—Task Force Operations Officer

Maj Greg Duesterhaus—Task Force Assistant Operations and Future Operations Officer

Capt Robert (Bob) Jankowski—Task Force Plans Officer

Maj Christopher (Chris) Julian—Task Force Fires and Effects Coordinator

Maj Lindsay Mathwick—Task Force Logistics Officer

Maj Roberto Falcon—Task Force Communications Officer

Task Force Lion Coalition Partners

Lieutenant Colonel Neil Bellamy—Commander, UK Security Force (2 Rifles)

Lieutenant Colonel Jesper Momme—Commander, Danish Contingent (Team 6)

Lieutenant Colonel Terje Bruøygard—Commander, Norwegian Task Unit (Team 1)

Lieutenant Colonel Brandon Payne—Commander, Task Force Slugger, U.S. Army (3-89 Cavalry)

Iraqi Security Forces

Combined Operations Command

Staff Lieutenant General Abdul Amir Rashid Yarallah—Deputy Commander

Staff Major General Adil—Chief of Plans

Jazeera Operations Command
Staff Major General Qassim al-Muhammadi—Commanding General
Staff Brigadier General Athir—Commander, JaOC Commandos
Colonel Ahmed—Senior Advisor

Iraqi Army 7th Division
Staff Major General Numan Abdul-Zawbai—Commanding General
Brigadier General Kiffa—Fires Officer
Staff Brigadier General Firas—Commander, 7th Division Commandos
Staff Brigadier General Qutaiba Muwafaq Assad—Commander, 28th Brigade
Staff Colonel Ali Saaud Fandi—Commander, 1st Battalion, 28th Brigade
Lieutenant Colonel Adnan Ali Mirza—Commander, 1st Battalion, 27th
  Brigade

Anbar Operations Command
Staff Major General Mahmoud al-Falahi—Commanding General

Iraqi Army 8th Division
Staff Major General Abdul Hussein Saud Suwadi—Commanding General

PROLOGUE

September 20, 2017

Dulce et decorum est pro patria mori
—Horace, *Odes (III.2.13)*

The air conditioner General Qassim al-Muhammadi promised wasn't working. The clock had just passed 0900, and the yellowing container our Iraqi partner had provided for our command post was heating up like a fiberglass oven. September had reached its midpoint, but with the sun's rays bouncing off the Al Anbar desert sands it felt like the middle of summer. There was plenty of room in the prefab structure for the Marines, the Iraqis, and all the communications equipment. But between the adrenalin of the last few days, the oppressive heat, and the failing air conditioner, the command post was a sour cocktail of unwashed feet, armpits, and crotches. I wiped beads of sweat from my forehead, put a fresh plug of tobacco in my mouth, and cracked open a can of Rip It. If the excited chatter squawking from the radio was any indication, things were about to get sporty.

At dawn, the leading edge of the Iraqi Army 7th Division had stepped off northwest toward Anah, a congested city along the banks of the Euphrates River. Rumors abounded that my Iraqi partner was personally invested in

Anah's liberation. Over the years, the city had become a retirement community for senior Iraqi military and government leaders, and Qassim may have envisioned a post-military life for himself there. His future plans aside, one thing was certain: liberating Anah from the occupying Islamic State forces would be a good thing for Qassim's brand.

With his lead formation closing in on the city, Qassim seemed to have the mission in the bag. That morning, 28th Brigade, the same Iraqi army unit I had embedded with as an advisor nine years earlier, had begun moving north along the highway to join one of its subordinate battalions. The two units pushed out through the desert, west of the heavily mined highway, and from there set up a blocking position southwest of Anah, overlooking the urban sprawl. As the two 28th Brigade elements provided overwatch, three other Iraqi units left their battle positions north of the town of Rayhanah and sped toward the next objective.

Before the advancing soldiers could push into Anah, bursts of rifle and machine-gun fire from an apartment complex anchoring Anah's southeast corner stopped them in their tracks. A handful of darkly clad Islamic State fighters, darting from building to building, were having an outsized effect on the much larger advancing force. In minutes, the enemy defenders had ground the attacking Iraqis to a halt just short of the city's perimeter. We watched it all unfold on the command post's scrolling video feed, powerless to do anything.

Qassim's mounting frustration, which bubbled to the surface earlier when he learned his soldiers weren't moving fast enough, boiled over with the report of the logjam at the apartments. The kink in the plan the ISIS (Islamic State of Iraq and Syria) fighters had created was understandable, if not somewhat expected. But the slow movement of Qassim's soldiers was his own fault. His men hadn't eaten in two days, and they either couldn't muster the energy to move, or they were sitting on their packs and *refusing* to move. In his zeal to get across the line of departure, Qassim had focused only on the tactics of the fight—not the logistics of it. Napoleon's supposed saying, "An army fights on its stomach," was playing out right in front of us. I stared at a table across the room. Untouched Iraqi food, delivered by Qassim's orderlies, filled the platters, the day's first flies alighting on the grilled lamb and its congealing fat. The Americans behind the lines were eating the Iraqi soldiers' food, not the *jundis* (soldiers) actually in the fight.

Qassim bellowed something in Arabic, banged a meaty fist on the table, and stormed out of the sweltering command post.

"Whoa-whoa-whoa," I said, flipping a thumb toward the door. "Where the hell is *he* going?"

"He's pissed off that his men aren't getting fed," our interpreter replied. "He's heading out to see what's going on."

I shook my head and looked at my operations officer.

"We going with him?" the major asked.

I glanced at the video screens projecting drone feeds and the array of radios and phones linking us to Al Asad and Baghdad. As much as I wanted to accompany my partner to the front, my place was now at the tactical command post—not chasing Qassim across the desert.

"Hell no," I said. "We have no idea where he's going or how long he'll be gone. We can control things better from here."

The major mumbled something unintelligible and went back to work. I knew what he was thinking: he wanted to be out with Qassim, not cooped up in our dusty, trailer park-ish command post. But we had bigger fish to fry. Our team was there to help the Iraqi Security Forces (ISF) defeat the Islamic State. We weren't there to do the fighting for them. But it was turning out to be more difficult than any of us had imagined.

Jesus wept, I thought, rolling my eyes. *How the hell did I end up here?*

PART 1
TASK FORCE AL ASAD

June 2016—August 2017

You forget what you want to remember,
and you remember what you want to forget.
—Cormac McCarthy, *The Road*

There will come a time when you believe everything
is finished. That will be the beginning.

—Louis L'Amour, *Lonely on the Mountain*

In this life, we have to make many choices. Some are very
important choices. Some are not. Many of our choices are
between good and evil. The choices we make, however,
determine to a large extent our happiness or our unhappiness,
because we have to live with the consequences of our choices.

—James E. Faus

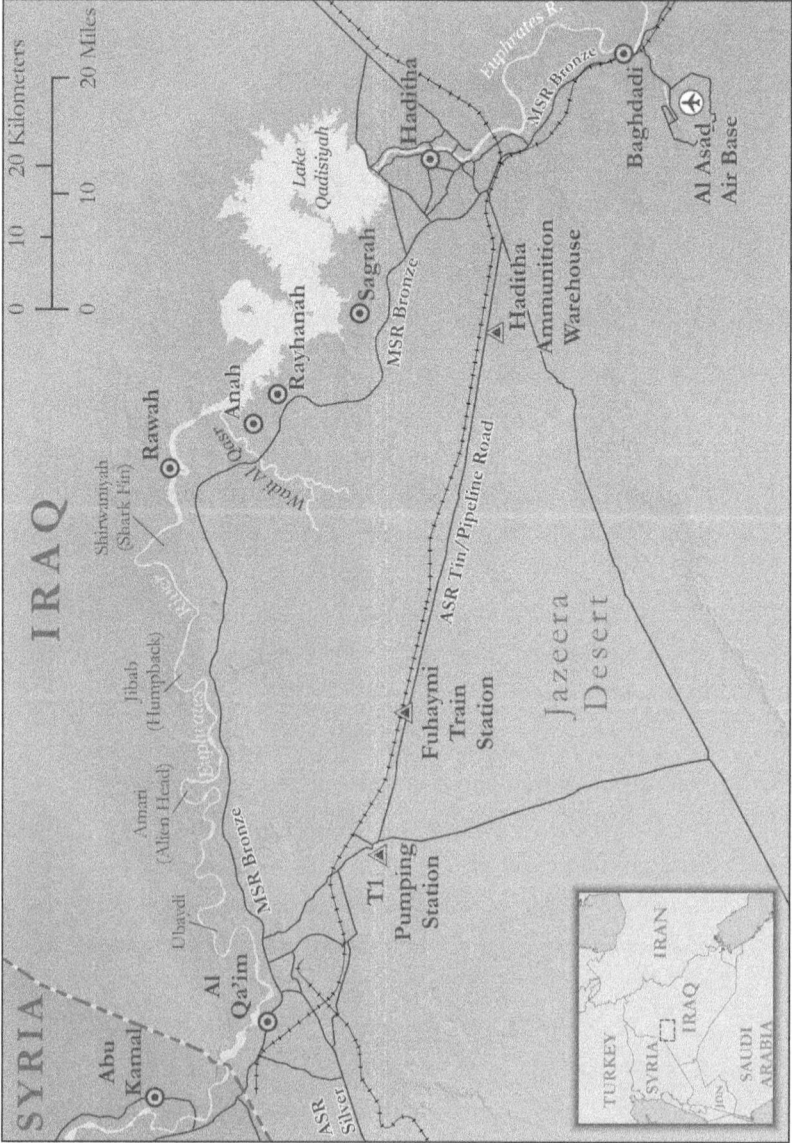

Map 1. WESTERN AL ANBAR PROVINCE, IRAQ

1

THREE OPPORTUNITIES

IN THE SPRING OF 2016, not long before leaving my job in the Pentagon basement, I received an email from the chief of staff at I Marine Expeditionary Force (I MEF). The note, addressed to me and two other colonels heading to the MEF, informed us we were on the short list to lead the next Task Force Al Asad rotation. The implication was clear: we had the option to volunteer before one of us was "voluntold." I was familiar with the general background of the task force. In the opening months of the campaign to defeat the Islamic State, Combined Joint Task Force–Operation Inherent Resolve had requested advisor teams to partner with Iraqi army units garrisoned at the Al Asad and Al Taqaddum air bases. With its historical ties to Al Anbar Province, the Marine Corps ponied up both teams, which deployed within weeks of notification. My knowledge of the mission pretty much ended there.

Months earlier, a similar note from Col Tom Savage, a longtime friend and mentor who was in Camp Lejeune, North Carolina, had offered a similar opportunity.

2nd MarDiv is looking for a team OIC [officer-in-charge] for the Iraq mission at Al Taqaddum. Last two commanders have been either sitting in O-6 command or waiting to take it. BGen Castellvi asked if I knew anyone that would be good for the job. I immediately thought of you. He snapped at it and asked me to write you immediately to see if you were interested. Let me know what you think.

The recruitment was both flattering and confusing. As a colonel in 2008, Robert Castellvi had been the senior advisor to the Iraqi army's 1st Division during the same period I was advising 3rd Battalion, 28th Brigade in the border district of Al Qa'im. By the time I returned to 1st Marine Division later that year, he had taken over as the chief of staff. Our most meaningful interaction had been him chewing my ass after I made a snarky comment to the commanding general during a staff meeting. With that memory still fresh in my mind, I couldn't understand Castellvi's enthusiasm for me to take this new job in Iraq.

Regardless of how the opportunity materialized, it interested me. But the timing couldn't have been worse. The previous week, an orthopedic surgeon had rebuilt my right shoulder after a lifetime of Marine Corps abuse. Even high as a kite on OxyContin, I had enough self-awareness to accept that I was in no shape to jump into a strenuous training cycle. It would be many painful months before I would be physically ready to deploy. But that wasn't the only thing holding me back. Joining the mission would mean leaving Virginia early, training with a team I didn't know, and shipping out in December. That would involve moving my family to Camp Lejeune—a post none of us knew—and leaving them to fend for themselves while I whipped through a fast-paced workup and then deployed for nine months.

In earlier years, I might have accepted this opportunity as an obligatory part of the job. But I had been in the military for more than twenty years, and I was no longer as willing to demand such sacrifices from my family. The "Global War on Terror," or the "Long War," or "Overseas Contingency Operations," or whatever the hell else they were calling our interminable conflict that began on 9/11, was in its sixteenth year—old enough to drive and becoming more obscure by the day. The war's unpopularity, and the turmoil it caused the families of service members who had spent a lifetime in uniform, made the notion of repeatedly deploying to strategic sinkholes like Iraq and Afghanistan similarly unattractive. Nevertheless, the requirements for warm bodies continued unabated. And the conventional wisdom within the service was that career professionals like me should be thankful for the *opportunity* to deploy . . . just as I should be thankful the Marine Corps had promoted me to colonel.

I didn't buy into that. One way or another, I didn't have many years left in uniform, and I wanted to ensure I still had a family left to go home to when the music stopped. Plenty of friends, colleagues, and mentors had ground themselves into dust pursuing specious and often unobtainable promotion and command goals—advancements the service's senior leaders typically meted out to officers who were preordained early in their careers while the rest of us jackasses were still trying to figure everything out. So, I politely declined the Al Taqaddum assignment and thanked Savage for recommending me.

Three months later, after receiving the Al Asad email from I MEF, I was equally unenthusiastic about the timing. My interest in the assignment had grown, but volunteering would mean similar hardships for my family. The only difference would be moving them across the country to California rather than to North Carolina before abandoning them for the training workup. To be sure, our strong support network from previous southern California assignments would lessen the challenges, but—again—it didn't seem right. And, quite frankly, I still didn't know if I was physically up to the task. As an infantry officer on the wrong side of forty-four, I was burning out quickly—thickening around the middle, slowing down each year on my physical fitness test, and now the proud owner of a bum shoulder with a second soon to follow. Playing Marine in a combat zone is a job for the young, and those days were far behind me. But I wasn't quite ready to be put out to pasture.

I had questions about the mission, though I should have known the answers. After all, in my current job on a small team in the Joint Operations Directorate–U.S. Central Command Division (JOD-CENT), I had helped plan the operation in 2014. We had crafted the official orders sending U.S. troops back to Iraq, and we briefed the Chairman of the Joint Chiefs of Staff and his directors on each new request for forces that filtered up from United States Central Command (CENTCOM). Hell, we had even *named* the damned thing: Operation Inherent Resolve. "The way we are running this operation is neither inherent," quipped one of my frustrated teammates, "nor does it demonstrate any resolve whatsoever." I wanted to name it "Operation Event Horizon." As far as I was concerned, getting involved in Iraq again meant the United States would be crossing the point of no return.

After a hesitant start, the campaign to defeat the Islamic State gained steam, as did the monolithic buildup of U.S. and Coalition combat power in the region. As the campaign evolved, so too did the adversary's name. First referred to as the Islamic State of Iraq and the Levant, and then *Da'esh*, it eventually became known as the Islamic State of Iraq and Syria—ISIS. Now, with a genuine enemy and a mission to defeat them, everyone wanted a piece of the action—a role in the Islamic State's extermination. Despite the general revulsion for war my experiences in Iraq and Afghanistan had imbued in me, I found myself among the saber-rattlers screaming for ISIS blood. The summer of 2014 at the Pentagon had been one of the worst of my professional life, with soul-crushing sixteen-hour days, seven days a week frequently the norm. My family never knew if I was coming or going. More often than not, the sound of my phone buzzing with messages recalling me to work interrupted weekend mornings. It eventually reached the point where, whenever the phone chimed during breakfast, my wife Ashley would roll her eyes and simply say, "Bye. . . . See you when we see you."

The JOD-CENT summer from hell was not just writing deployment orders and building the perfect PowerPoint slides for the generals and admirals on the Joint Staff. From our isolated workspace in the bowels of the Pentagon, my colleagues and I also viewed footage of Islamic State fighters running rampant across Iraq's countryside. They terrorized civilians, they burned people alive and crushed them with rocks, and they murdered members of the U.S. and international media alike. One night, an Army colonel, who seemed to relish being the world's biggest asshole, strode into our cubicle farm. Holding a compact disc aloft, he announced, "I've got the James Foley video."

I had no desire to watch a high-definition snuff flick. And yet, as we stared at the ritual decapitation of Foley and a line of other terrified victims, my urge to eliminate ISIS grew. The militants were thugs, animals that were perverting Islam and trampling what was left of Iraq's fraying culture. What was unfolding in Mesopotamia wasn't the same war I had talked my way into in 2003 and again found myself in five years later. Nor was it the swirling cesspool the war in Afghanistan had become. This time, the Iraqi government had asked for our help . . . no, they had *begged* for it. Above all else, the Islamic State fighters were enemies that deserved killing. The more I understood about it, the more this seemed like a war worth fighting.

After all the contemplation and mental anguish on my part that second time around, I didn't get the assignment. Instead, I joined the MEF headquarters in a new version of my previous job on the Joint Staff. In my first weeks there, my boss made an announcement to the collection of colonels sitting in his office. His words echoed the email I had received from the chief of staff months earlier.

"Pretty soon we'll have to select someone to take the next Al Asad rotation. You are the only three who have combat arms backgrounds. In all likelihood, one of you will get selected."

We gulped the Kool-Aid, believing we would indeed be *lucky* to get the job. Even when I considered the extensive experiences of the other two officers, I believed my qualifications were more aligned. At its heart, the task force was an advisor mission, and I had done a previous tour with 7th Division. I even had the relatively new—and generally maligned, if not flat out ignored—Foreign Security Force Advisor military specialty to certify my experience. But no one who made the decisions seemed to care. When the time came to select the next leader, all three colonels wanted the job, and the MEF's decision makers didn't want to select *any* of us. Marine colonels were in high demand, and apparently the task force job wasn't important enough to waste a set of silver eagles.

At the same time, I was cautious about putting my hand in the air because I had a family to consider. They were no strangers to deployments. Ashley had endured four of them in the first ten years of our marriage, and our daughters had likewise suffered through two. The idea of volunteering to leave them again troubled me. We were a close quartet that enjoyed each other's company, whether it was hanging out on the beach or relaxing on our slowly collapsing couch, eating pizza while binge-watching episodes of *Doctor Who*. As the head shed deliberated, I decided not to hide it from Ashley. Doing so would have been pointless, anyway; she could read me like a book.

"What do you want to do?" she asked.

"Well," I hesitated. "You see, the thing is . . ."

"Is this what you *want* to do?" she asked, her tone more direct.

"Well, if there's one thing I am more than qualified to do, this is it."

"Right, but do you *want* to do it?"

"I don't want to leave you and the girls behind."

"This is not about *us*," she said. "This is about *you*. *You* need to decide if you want this. Do we *want* you to go? Of course not! But this is *your* decision to make. If you truly want to go, then you can't say you don't; you will resent us for it later. And you'll be impossible to live with."

"Yes," I finally admitted. "I want to do this."

"Okay then," she replied. "That's what we'll prepare for."

After nearly a year, and two previous opportunities, the job was now mine. But it was a dubious honor. As it turned out, my selection was based less on my qualifications and more on my role as the staff's most expendable colonel. It wasn't exactly an ego-booster, but I didn't care. The Marine Corps had already signaled its plans for me—or lack thereof—the previous summer when I didn't make the cut on the command selection board. So, I didn't have much to lose. The bottom line was, by the beginning of 2017, I would be building a team from the ground up and deploying to Iraq later that summer. The dreariness and quiet desperation of life as a staff officer faded as I looked forward to the daunting task ahead of me.

2

SEEKING GUIDANCE

WITH THE TASK FORCE about to start its fifth deployment rotation, the name Paul Nugent had become synonymous with Task Force Al Asad. A colonel I had known for many years, Nugent had relinquished command of 1st Marine Division's Headquarters Battalion more than a year earlier, and he cycled through Al Asad from April to December of 2016 during the unit's third rotation. Paul was respected throughout the infantry community, and the Army general commanding the Coalition had credited him with taking the task force to the next level during his deployment. Word of his team's accomplishments reached halfway around the world. One day, in late 2016, the MEF operations officer asked me, "Have you been reading Task Force Al Asad's sitreps? Man, they have turned into a killing *machine*." After hearing that, I made a point to attend Nugent's debrief to the commanding general and his staff. What I heard put my jaw on the floor.

We had barely heard a peep about the task force's successes in the press or within Marine Corps circles. Yet in Nugent's nine months at the helm, the task force conducted more than six hundred kinetic strikes. In the process, his team removed close to a thousand bad guys from the battlefield and enabled 7th Division to regain long-held territory from ISIS along the Middle Euphrates River Valley—the "MERV." Altogether, their operations supporting the Iraqi army stretched from Baghdadi to Haditha, which was the home of 7th Division's corps-level higher headquarters: the Jazeera Operations Command (JaOC). All the news from Iraq, however, had focused on the brutal fight in Mosul. Back home in southern California, it was as if Nugent's team had never existed.

Nugent got everyone's attention with the kinetic details of his deployment, but there was more to his debrief than just an ISIS body count.

"The task force is not simply an advisor team," Nugent told the "Council of Colonels" sitting around the conference room table. "The Marines and sailors assigned to this mission form the core of a command element for a combined, Joint, and Coalition task force. *One* of its key tasks is 'advise and assist.' But it does much more than that. It trains and equips the Iraqis; it runs and protects Al Asad; it manages the airfield and all the ISR [intelligence, surveillance, and reconnaissance] platforms. It is responsible for everything that happens aboard the base, which is growing by the day."

As the discussion returned to the topic of the team's advisor mission, Nugent took it a step further.

"It's not just working inside the wire. 'Expeditionary advise and assist' is now an enduring task, something that requires appropriate personnel *and* a mobile command-and-control capability to be successful. Future rotations should develop that capability for the upcoming MERV campaign."

Nugent had been the first to take a Marine advisor team outside Al Asad's secure boundaries to Haditha—an act that threw the senior U.S. leaders into a frenzy of handwringing and teeth-gnashing. The mission had practically required the Pope's blessing to execute in the risk-averse operating environment at the time.

"Who told you to take your team outside the wire?" the general asked, looking down over his glasses at Nugent. "Where did you get the authority?"

"We initiated the plan ourselves," Nugent replied. "And we briefed it all the way up our operational chain for approval."

That should have closed the matter, but it did not. The implication was clear: the general didn't seem to dig what Paul had been doing. He was wary of commanders shopping around for missions in CENTCOM, lest it create a demand signal for more MEF forces in theater.

The conversation around the table shifted.

"What about the Shi'a militia groups?" one officer asked. "Once the MERV campaign is over, will they fill the post-ISIS vacuum? I mean, what's the end state?"

"The reality is," the general answered first, "there is no end state."

Nugent's brief resonated with me so much that I made it a priority to seek him out as soon as I learned of my selection to lead Rotation (Roto)-5. His advice was simple, and it set the tone for my team's training workup and the eventual deployment itself.

"Train your Marines as a battle staff capable of working across all warfighting functions," he said. "Remember what I said: your team is the core of a command element for a combined, Joint, and Coalition task force. Only *one* of its key tasks is advise and assist. You'll have plenty more responsibilities than advising the Iraqis. Just ask Fred; you will have dozens of units and a couple thousand people working for you. If anyone says you're 'just an advisor team,' tell them to pound sand."

"Fred" was Col Fridrik Fridriksson, an infantry officer I had known since my first days in the fleet as a second lieutenant. Our paths had intersected several times over the years, and he'd become one of my closest colleagues in an organization where you don't look for friends unless you want to spend your life getting disappointed. He was an upbeat guy who always sported a broad, toothy grin. If something was bugging you, somehow you couldn't help but feel better after talking with him. His positive outlook had not waned during his time in Iraq, but he was quick to convey the realities of the mission. His video teleconference update to me echoed Paul Nugent's brief to the MEF staff, and he added that the mission's scope and scale had only grown since Nugent's departure.

"You will be a task force commander responsible for everything aboard Al Asad," Fridriksson told me. "That's 2,200 people and sixty-five different units."

Despite the tinny, sterile medium of the video conference, I sensed the same frustration in him that Nugent had exhibited weeks earlier.

"We aren't getting credit for what we're doing out here," he said. "We have control over more ISR assets than the entire Marine Corps. We literally have lance corporals on our team dynamically re-tasking theater-level ISR on a daily basis. *Lance corporals!* No one believes me.

"Advise and assist is the easy part; managing this air base is the hard part. I gotta tell you, man, I shouldn't know this much about medical waste incinerators and sewage treatment plants."

I laughed, and after he vented a while longer the conversation turned toward future operations.

"The Iraqis need another infantry division to execute the MERV campaign. Seventh Division is stretched to its limits from Hit to Haditha. We're anticipating movement west by fall, but it will depend on what's happening in Mosul. That fight is sucking all the oxygen out of the room, and it's wearing out the Iraqis.

"The Coalition wants ISIS defeated in Syria by August. I'm here to tell you that's not gonna happen, but don't worry about that. You'll have your hands full enough when you get here."

My recent promotion to colonel had introduced me to a new world in the Marine Corps, one where people automatically assumed I knew what I was talking about just because there was a set of silver chickens on my collars. Truth be told, with my varied, somewhat checkered background, I was more than a little surprised I had survived the Corps' vicious selection process for that rank. Not long after pinning it on, I sat down with Maj Gen. David "Stretch" Coffman, the MEF's deputy commanding general. A brilliant helicopter pilot who was famous for piloting his aircraft to ground in Iraq in 2004 after being shot through the face, he had an intense, sometimes frenetic personality. As far as I could recall, my meeting with Coffman was one of the few times a senior officer had taken the time to sit me down and tell me what was expected in my new position. The hour I spent with him was invaluable.

"Remember this," he said. "You are essentially at your terminal rank. The competition is over; colonel is the officer rank where everyone catches up with each other. The only people you need to worry about now are your peers who are running scared because they want something else: to become generals. And most of them are guys you don't want to have anything to do with anyway.

"You are now part of the 'Senate of the Marine Corps,' and your reputation among the senators is as important as your reputation with the emperor. You should be aiming for positive, aggressive leadership.

"You need to remember your alignment with and loyalty to the institution. You're one of us now, and it's your responsibility to carry the boss's decision. The 'break-line' rank for constant grousing or being a wild man is when you're a major.

"But it's also your responsibility to speak truth to power and be an effective leader. You must protect the rank and police your peers. Believe it or not, a lot of them are fucked up."

He then addressed my role with the task force.

"Do not underestimate the importance of your position as a commander. Start with 'commandership,' and *then* focus on the mission. Take care of your Marines and their families. Task organize to fit the mission, and be self-sufficient. You must be decisive and engaged in everything you do. The team will pace to your leadership. And it's important that you build connections with your higher, adjacent, and supporting units.

"Just remember, generals are desperate for competent, effective leadership among their subordinate commanders. They automatically expect that from colonels. If you ever have to ask your boss how to do your job, you can expect to be fired."

After filling several pages in my notebook, I thanked him for his counsel.

"I never regret 'kneecap-to-kneecap' time," he said. "And neither will you. My entire career has been like *Schindler's List*: I wish I had done more; I *could* have done more.

"Man," he said. "I wish *I* was a colonel again."

Even with Coffman's mentorship and vote of confidence, a list of questions remained about the mission that lay ahead. I hoped for answers from Lt. Gen. Dave "Smoke" Beydler, the commander of the Tampa, Florida–based Marine Corps Forces Central Command (MARCENT)—the component command for all Marine units in the CENTCOM theater. He would be the senior Marine I reported to while leading the task force, and he insisted I travel to Tampa for an in-call with him and his staff before deploying. The previous two team commanders had urged me to do the same. *You don't want to get on MARCENT'S bad side early,* one cautioned, *or your life will be a living hell while you're in theater.*

Beydler had been my boss on the Headquarters Marine Corps staff in 2009. Along with his reputation as a prickly leader, he was infamous for his endless rounds of "stump the chump" with any poor bastard foolish enough to brief him unprepared. Since we had already worked together, I had an idea what I was getting myself into. I didn't dislike the guy, despite his reputation and my occasional misfortune to be on the receiving end of his grilling. Nor did I disagree with most of his positions as the MARCENT commander. However, his perpetual sense of disappointment with everyone—including me—was frustrating.

As we sat in his office in March of 2017, he told me that his focus for the men and women under his charge was readiness, standards, and core values.

"Marines must be ready to deploy at a moment's notice," he said. "I have directed my staff here in Tampa to be prepared to deploy within ninety-six hours. I won't let them get too comfortable when we have people in harm's way downrange."

He insisted the Marines must remain ready for the next hard thing, especially in the dynamic setting of Iraq. "The environments out there may get harsher. We're getting indications that Coalition forces may move west soon," he told me. "Simply put, you may *start* your deployment at Al Asad, but you may not *finish* there."

Standards were everything for Beydler, and he demanded that Marines adhere to them. "Hammer home discipline," he warned, "or bad things will happen."

He emphasized the importance of core values, saying I should demand good decisions from my Marines based on those values. "When an organization begins to stray from its own culture and core values, when it ceases to enforce them," he prophesied, "the end is near."

A senior member of Beydler's staff later echoed his guidance in private.

"Smoke has no tolerance for bullshit," he said. "He will visit you at least twice while you're deployed, and he *will* scrutinize your Marines. Prepare accordingly."

Beydler's emphasis on readiness, standards, and core values was a platform upon which we could both agree—to a point. I had witnessed firsthand the fraying at the edges that sixteen years of war had done to the fabric of the institution, and I knew you could never go wrong by enforcing standards of good order and discipline. But it *was* possible to overdo it.

As a colonel commanding Marines and sailors, I believed I had earned the trust and confidence to enforce standards and accomplish the mission based on commander's intent. I thought my previous experiences leading Marines in Iraq and Afghanistan validated that. But the generals at the MEF and MAR-CENT didn't see it that way. Rather than being granted the authorities that traditionally accompany command, I was designated as an "officer-in-charge," with essentially no command authority. My fiscal powers were limited, as were my administrative and legal authorities. I could not impose nonjudicial punishment, nor could I convene a special court martial, as other colonels commanding infantry regiments and Marine expeditionary units (MEUs) were empowered to do. I was not alone in this regard; similar restrictions had been placed on the command authorities of my four task force predecessors.

One thing Beydler and I could certainly agree on during our first meeting was a mutual sense that the Marine Corps was distancing itself from the conflict in Iraq.

"The two task forces represent the *only* conventional Marine Corps units officially designated to deploy in support of Inherent Resolve," he told me. "The Special Purpose MAGTF [Marine Air-Ground Task Force] is doing great things in CENTCOM, and Task Force 51/5 has achieved complete Navy–Marine Corps integration in Bahrain. But your team is one of only two which are *solely* dedicated to the fight in Iraq."

"The Corps is focused on readiness recovery and the pivot to the Pacific. There is tension among the geographic combatant commanders and the service chiefs over whether we should focus on today's fight or on readiness for the future fight. My job is to shape thinking for the service headquarters, and I'm focusing on today's fight. Your task force is part of that. Make no mistake: you are the main effort. Act like it."

You are the main effort. Act like it.

Now *that* was something I could get behind.

3

FORMING THE TEAM

THE EIGHTY-FIVE-MEMBER TEAM that would form Roto-5 was not an organic element pulled from a single unit. Instead, it would be a "purpose-built" task force, composed of Marines and sailors from thirty-five different commands across the MEF. Previous rotations had formed around core teams of twenty-six advisors, and the first four teams relied upon the Kuwait-based Special Purpose Marine Air-Ground Task Force–Crisis Response–Central Command (SPMAGTF-CR-CC) to augment them with personnel to fill critical enabling roles. However, the so-called "enablers" had not trained with the core teams in the United States prior to deploying. That, coupled with muddled reporting chains and frequent unit rotations in and out of theater, created significant cohesion issues and unity of command concerns within the teams. In one case, during the task force's third rotation, SPMAGTF had ordered a critical set of enablers to redeploy to Kuwait just as the Iraqis were launching a major operation.

After joining the MEF in 2016, I participated in an operational planning team (OPT) at MARCENT, where we drafted the manning document for the different ranks and specialties necessary to complete the purpose-built task forces. Once MARCENT and Headquarters Marine Corps agreed on the manning document's composition, the MEF went about sourcing the personnel for each billet. The purpose-built task force model emerged just as Fridriksson's Roto-4 was training for its deployment, and the service intended to implement the model fully during Roto-5's forming period in February of 2017.

Almost from the moment of my selection to lead the task force, parallels to my previous advisor tour surfaced. Just as it had been in 2007, when my first advisor team formed, there was little enthusiasm among the different parent units providing personnel for Roto-5. The men and women assigned were referred to as individual augments (IAs), and after sourcing four previous task force rotations, the MEF was deep in the throes of "IA-fatigue." By design, military advisor teams are rank-heavy. Additionally, the enabling functions of the new purpose-built teams demanded critical-specialty Marines, such as intelligence analysts, joint terminal attack controllers (JTACs), and network operators. Many commanders were reluctant to give up high-quality personnel from low-density specialties for jobs that would take the Marines away from their units for close to a year and a half. The same phenomenon had occurred in the war's early years, when deploying units often went without key personnel because of the endless stream of IA requirements that trickled down from CENTCOM and the Pentagon.

By the time my first team formed in 2007, the well of talent was nearly dry. A similar situation faced me in 2017. The never-ending operations in Iraq and Afghanistan, both of which had earned reputations as "troop sumps," were no longer a priority for the Marine Corps. Instead, fighting a future war against peer or "near-peer" competitors such as China, Russia, or North Korea was now the singular focus. Just as I had learned a decade earlier, it didn't take long to understand that my team's manning situation would be a case of "you get what you get, and you don't get upset." Any requests to swap personnel or obtain mission-essential equipment for the deployment would be met with skepticism at best, or finger-wagging and lecturing at worst.

Among the first to join the team was Maj Aaron Awtry, one of my action officers on the MEF staff who would become the task force operations officer, or "OpsO." A quiet, unassuming prior-enlisted infantry officer from Odessa, Texas, he had been a junior Marine in 1st Light Armored Reconnaissance Battalion with Fred Fridriksson and me when we were lieutenants two decades earlier. Awtry and I hadn't known each other then, but our mutual experiences in that unit, as well as his tour as a lieutenant in 3rd Battalion, 7th Marines (3/7) nearly a decade before I took command, gave us common background.

Even though he rarely spoke, he was a skilled planner and briefer who had graduated from the Marine Corps' prestigious School of Advanced Warfighting (SAW). His voice and mannerisms transformed every time he briefed an audience; no one listening to him would ever guess he preferred to stay silent if given the opportunity. He was an interesting, if somewhat mysterious, character—a somber, almost dour officer who seemed to get more joy out of long, solitary runs and studying videos of his son playing baseball than just about anything else. I referred to him as "Llewelyn," Cormac McCarthy's tight-lipped protagonist in *No Country for Old Men*, and I often reminded him that he was an anomaly: a Texan who shunned cowboy boots, huge belt buckles, and Stetsons.

Awtry was an enigma. His serious demeanor, guarded humor, and enduring scowl made me think he would just as soon kill you as look at you. While he was a lieutenant in 2004, his company had had a rough go of it in the Iraqi border town of Husaybah. Later, in 2011, he commanded a rifle company in Musa Qala, Afghanistan—certainly no garden spot—across the Helmand River from my battalion. During our time working together, I spoke with several officers who had seen him in action in Iraq and Afghanistan. Despite his quiet nature, Awtry was, by all accounts, a ferocious combat leader.

In our initial discussions, he didn't hide the fact that joining the team was not his first choice. Instead, he wanted to move on from the MEF to be an infantry battalion executive officer (XO), which was what I had wanted as a major on the 1st Marine Division staff in 2007. With his face bunched up in a contemplative grimace the way it did whenever he disagreed with something, he wondered the same thing I had a decade earlier upon learning of my advisor assignment: *Does this shit job mean "career advancement stops here"?*

All I could tell him was what I knew from Task Force Al Asad's sitreps: it was the most interesting and relevant thing out there. U.S. conventional operations in both Iraq and Afghanistan had transitioned to a "by, with, and through" approach, which focused on our Iraqi and Afghan partners confronting the enemy. For the most part, the Americans were supporting the indigenous forces from inside the wire with intelligence and fire support rather than pulling triggers with them on the battlefield. He eventually warmed to the idea of deploying as the team's OpsO, and he threw himself into planning our pre-deployment training and preparing us for the role we would assume at Al Asad.

The scope and scale of operations at Al Asad, which included corralling the growing Joint and Coalition community aboard the air base, necessitated assigning a sergeant major to the task force. My time in company and battalion command had validated for me the critical role a senior enlisted advisor plays in a commander's job. In both tours, mine had gone everywhere with me, whether it was vehicle patrols, foot patrols, or key leader engagements (KLEs) with local civilian, government, and military leaders. We had formed tight bonds that centered on mutual respect and concern for our Marines' welfare. Our difficult deployments in combat zones had further solidified those connections. I wondered how anyone would ever stack up to the men who had served with me in the past.

In other words, the bar was perhaps unreasonably high for the next guy. When I met SgtMaj Alex Leibfried, my first thought was *Man, this dude's so short he can't even* reach *the bar.* And that was unfair. He may have been short, but he was in damn good physical shape and could run the pants off me. He had volunteered for the job, something I soon learned was rare on the team, and he was committed to the professional development of the men and women under his charge. He didn't shrink from his responsibility to tell me when he thought I was wrong, but he always had enough tact to do it behind closed doors.

Leibfried drew from a deep pool of experience, having served as an artillery cannoneer, a supply Marine, and a drill instructor during his twenty-five years of service. A teacher at heart, he was completing his college degree so he could return to instruct at his hometown high school in Washington. He was not shy about telling me, his fellow staff noncommissioned officers (SNCOs), and the junior enlisted team members that he had been a tremendous screwup as a young Marine. He redirected those dodged bullets into learning points for the men and women who still had their entire military careers and adult lives ahead of them. The two of us had that much in common. Once we got to know each other, I often regaled him with tales of how jacked up I had been as a junior officer. And as a company grade officer. And as a field grade officer.

A career full of missteps wasn't the only thing we had in common. We also shared emotional scar tissue from Afghanistan's Sangin Valley, where in 2012 he had been a company first sergeant in 1st Battalion, 7th Marines—the unit that replaced my battalion. We both had lost Marines in the valley, were pretty screwed up in the head when we returned home to our families, and still harbored deep resentment for the endless void the Afghanistan war had become. But Leibfried was a personable, engaging leader who was as devoted to his Marines as he was to his family, and he tended to treat his subordinates as peers. He also had a terrific sense of humor. When he found something funny, he never tried to hold back his emotions. Instead, he would squint his eyes into tiny slits and unleash a loud staccato burst of laughter with a grin that stretched from ear to ear. It was that sense of humor I would rely on to keep me sane in the months ahead.

Among the phone calls I received from prospective team members was one from LtCol Tom Merritt, who was the staff judge advocate (SJA) for 1st Marine Logistics Group. I was as anxious about who would be my deputy as I was about the selection of my senior enlisted advisor. My time as a battalion commander had also proven the value of a good XO—the second-in-command who keeps the trains running *and* takes charge in the commander's absence. I had convinced myself that my XO in Afghanistan would be a tough act to follow. It was only because he had been so good at his job and could work seamlessly with my operations officer and sergeant major that I was able to patrol outside the wire with the battalion's rifle squads so often.

Preferring a combat arms officer for the job, I balked when I learned a lawyer would become my deputy. Hell, I would have even taken an *aviator* over an ambulance chaser. It was difficult to envision a lawyer doing the kinds of things expected of us at Al Asad. But I had little say in the matter, so I tried to stay positive and hope for the best once I met Merritt. He did not disappoint. Originally from New Hampshire, he was tall and handsome in a classic, early 1960s way. With gently graying hair and a perpetual five-o'clock shadow, he was a bizarre hybrid that physically resembled *Mad Men*'s Don Draper and exuded the terminal cheeriness of *The Simpson's* Ned Flanders. "Fantastic" was his favorite word to express pleasure or approval, and between his upbeat nature and old-fashioned vocabulary, I wondered if he would eventually throw in a "golly" or "gee-whiz" to prove how square he was. But still waters run deep. Behind his prim, chipper persona was a bizarre sense of humor, and occasionally he would utter something so outrageous and profane that it could make a sailor blush. He was a health-conscious, avid runner, yet he was not averse to having a drink or a smoke when the urge struck him. To be sure, the latter trait was handy when dealing with the Iraqis, who were serial chain-smokers.

A true Renaissance Man, Merritt possessed more varied life experiences than anyone I had ever known, and he was the closest thing we had on the team to "The Most Interesting Man in the World." Each time Leibfried and I sat down to a meal with him, he unearthed another bizarre tale from his cosmopolitan personal history. He had lived in France, studied in Spain, and taught English at a private school in Japan. He was fluent in Portuguese, French, and Spanish, and he would later use his linguistic skills to communicate with our NATO colleagues in Iraq—an act that put our Coalition partners at ease and endeared him to them.

As I got to know Awtry, Leibfried, and Merritt on a personal level, I developed a deep sense of trust, admiration, and respect for these three men. Each was committed to excellence, and they took their roles as my trusted agents seriously. I also sensed in them a degree of war fatigue similar to what I struggled with daily. I hadn't yet been on the ground in Iraq for this new conflict, but that didn't stop me from feeling like our country was a rudderless ship in the roiling waters of the Middle East and Southwest Asia.

As Marines and sailors from across southern California assembled in the last week of February 2017, my previous experiences in command compelled me to get in front of the team and set my expectations early. Major General Coffman's mentoring session had been a pivotal moment in my continuing education as an officer, and I took his advice to heart. I believed my days leading large formations of Marines were over, and my assignment with the task force would likely be the last time I was in command. I was determined not to make the same greenhorn mistakes that had plagued me in company and battalion command, and so I formulated how I wanted to lead the team. It wasn't going to be easy. The group's task-organized nature made adopting a single, unique identity difficult. As the commander, the responsibility for creating that identity fell on my shoulders, and I struggled to find a solution.

I knew there would only be one chance to make a first impression, and with everyone coming from such varied backgrounds, it would be vital to deliver an unmistakable message up front. But I no longer resembled the meat-eating, jingoistic warfighter I had tried to be for years. I had mellowed as the decades passed, enjoying quiet time with my family or a good bourbon more than the pursuit of my craft as an infantry officer. Perhaps being the father of two daughters and husband to a business-minded transformation coach had done that to me. Or maybe I had accepted the reality that I'd spent much of my career fighting in losing wars. And so, when I stood in front of the new team for the first time, I was content to be myself. There was no need to hide behind flag-waving, chest-thumping bullshit.

"Something you need to know about me," I told the group. "Although I use a lot of sports analogies and metaphors, I am not a sports fan. If you want to get on my good side, don't bother talking to me about sports. I appreciate a good movie reference more than hearing about the starting line-up of the New York Yankees." The skeptical expressions on the faces of the Marines seated in the room sent a clear message: *Who the hell is this guy?*

"Who volunteered for this assignment?" I asked. A few hands went up. "Who was 'voluntold'?" More hands raised, outnumbering the others.

"Okay, who has deployed to Iraq before?" Some hands lifted again. "Who has deployed to Afghanistan?" Several more. "And who has been an advisor before?" Almost all the hands dropped. "Roger that," I said.

It was worse than I expected. Few people had been in combat, and while just under half the group had deployed to either Iraq or Afghanistan, only a fraction had previous advisor experience under their belts. The officers and SNCOs accounted for the bulk of the team's operational experience. Otherwise, it would be the first deployment for more than a third of the unit. And, while more than half had volunteered, an equal number had learned of their assignments less than a month before reporting for duty.

Although the dearth of experience was concerning, I was happy to be working with young Marines and sailors again. I had always valued youthful energy and initiative, which is to say I had no patience for those with rank and experience but no motivation to work as part of a team. As far as advisor experience was concerned, it really wasn't an issue if most of the team had none. One lesson I had learned about advising was universal: it doesn't matter how much training, cultural instruction, or foreign language immersion you receive. If you are an asshole in the United States, you will be an asshole as an advisor anywhere else.

As I provided an overview of the task force's background and mission, the looks on their faces told me many had no idea what they had gotten themselves into. I then announced my expectations.

"Discipline and accountability are two hallmarks of the Marine Corps. Flexibility, adaptability, and resilience are the hallmarks of advisors. I expect that from everyone. We must become subject matter experts at our jobs; lives will depend on it. You must also understand the significance of our mission: we are an independent unit with an operationally important mission. Our performance must reflect as such.

"This is what you can expect from me: firm, fair leadership. I believe in standards, and I'm not afraid to enforce them. Trust me, if you need a haircut, I will tell you.

"I have an open mind and open ears. If you have a better idea, open your mouth. But before you do, know the difference between voicing a disagreement and being an asshole. It's okay to disagree; it's not okay to be disagreeable.

"I have a sense of humor. The best, most effective teams are ones who laugh a lot. I don't take myself seriously, but I do take my responsibility as a Marine, an officer, and commander seriously."

I closed with some final thoughts.

"From here on out, I need everyone to focus on *the team*—something bigger than yourselves. We are the leading edge of the Marine Corps. We are going to be so goddamned good that ISIS won't know what hit them. Make no mistake, we are MARCENT's priority, but we must be humble about it. We must be the epitome of quiet professionals."

I later conveyed a similar set of expectations to the officers and their senior enlisted chiefs.

"My first priority is to form our team as a functioning battle staff that operates across all warfighting functions," I said, echoing Paul Nugent's guidance. "We're at a disadvantage as an IA-sourced, purpose-built task force. We have to form from scratch and incorporate the best practices we have all learned from our parent commands.

"Because we come from so many different units and backgrounds, we need to focus first on building the team. Mastery of individual and collective skills will come later. We don't have much time before deploying, so there is no room for boredom or inactivity. We must integrate everyone into daily operations.

"It is important that you know the difference between my priorities and 'paying the rent.' My priorities will focus our operations and resource allocation to enable us to accomplish the mission. 'Paying the rent' is what good, competent units do automatically—things like personnel and gear accountability, timely and accurate reports, and mundane paperwork. In other words, tedious things that take care of the unit and the Marines. Let me be clear: to paraphrase Chris Rock, 'You don't get credit for just doing your job.'

"Here's the bottom line," I closed. "Moving forward, we need to keep the ship tight. Our success or failure in Iraq begins and ends with our professional reputation. At the end of the day, that is how everyone will judge us."

I was unsure how the staff took my words of introduction, but there was no doubt about my expectations. And yet, even though I was confident in my position and with the Marines assigned to me, the uncertainty of what lay ahead remained. With the team formed, we now had five months to train and prepare for that uncertainty.

For the most part, once the non-volunteers got over being voluntold, they embraced the mission. Eventually, everyone came together and trained as a single entity. As the team gelled, I tried to absorb details of their personal backgrounds. It was a talented and diverse group of Marines and sailors. One woman was an amateur bodybuilder and personal trainer. Another woman had been born in Soviet Lithuania, immigrated to the United States, and later married a SEAL team operator. One youthful officer, a career student and athlete who had attained a bachelor's degree with multiple majors and minors, as well as a master's degree, had worked with both a Washington, D.C., brokerage firm *and* the United Nations World Food Program before volunteering for Officer Candidate School. The team even had an amateur rodeo rider among its ranks.

There were Marines who had served during the 2003 invasion of Iraq. There were others who were not only on their first deployment, but also had not yet been born when I joined the service in 1992. Just a handful had served as long as I had. Most were so young they could be my sons and daughters; others were junior enough to be my younger brothers and sisters. It was challenging not to dwell on their lack of experience. In Afghanistan in 2011, more than half my battalion had fought there before; the number of Iraq combat vets on that deployment was even higher. It had spoiled me, and in 2017 I had to remind myself repeatedly that the task force did not have a direct combat mission. By design, we would not personally engage the enemy—that was the Iraqis' job—but we would still be in a combat zone with all its inherent dangers.

Our pre-deployment training was haphazard at best. In 2007, my advisor team had attended classes in a run-down building nicknamed "the crack house." However, even with its fractured, peeling walls, unfinished floors, and intermittent plumbing, the crack house had been a palace compared to most of the facilities the MEF now offered the task force. Our home in 2017 was a second-floor wing of a dilapidated building down the street from the MEF command post. I shouldn't have complained. In 2007, my team didn't even *have* dedicated office space; we had borrowed spare rooms to conduct planning, and we did much of our work from our own cars.

While there was some dissatisfaction with the office spaces the MEF had provided us, the facility down the street where we received most of our actual training in 2017 was the pits. Once a schoolhouse for corporals, the building was now a condemned shell with no running water, no heating or air conditioning, and no dignity. Yellowing photographs depicting chiseled instructors and proud graduating noncommissioned officers (NCOs) plastered the walls at crooked angles. Fading posters drooped from their mounts or rested in crumpled, neglected heaps on the moldering carpets. Access to the second floor was forbidden out of fear the Marines would plunge through the rotten flooring. Anyone needing to relieve themselves had to trek outside to a line of Port-A-Jons formed up on the road. The highlight of each day's instruction was the arrival of the "roach coach," a silver food truck that supplied the Marines with overpriced snacks and energy drinks. *If this is what being the main effort looks like,* I often thought, *what does it look like for everyone else?*

Some training events were invaluable. Other elements failed to meet muster. Some were nothing less than colossal wastes of time. The cultural instruction, which arguably should have been among the most important training we would get, was nothing but a joke. On more than one occasion, during our week of receiving erratic survival-Arabic language and cultural instruction by a nervous, unprepared contractor, I felt compelled to stand up in the middle of the class and clarify what the instructor was saying. In some cases, I outright contradicted him. The most we gleaned was that you should never curse in front of Iraqis; you should never talk about women or sex; and if you encounter a tribal sheikh in a robe with gold piping, you have hit the KLE jackpot. All three dictums would turn out to be total bullshit. Our Iraqi partners never cared if we used foul language because they used it too. We would also discover that, once we had developed close relationships with the

Iraqis, they talked about women all the time. And, although I encountered more than a couple of sheikhs with gold-trimmed dishdashas, there was never any indication they were the most important people in the room.

Our most valuable training focused on basic Marine combat skills and rehearsing the tasks we would employ once we were in Iraq: tactical vehicle operations, communication systems training, and fire support coordination drills in our combat operations center (COC). Whenever we went to the field, Marines issued operations orders to the entire team around terrain models. I was constantly on everyone's case about individual and continuing actions, pre-combat checks and inspections, and developing standard operating procedures—actions and skills that I knew from hard experience could mean the difference between a Marine coming home standing up versus in a rubber bag. My greatest enforcers of this demand for "brilliance in the basics" were Major Awtry, Sergeant Major Leibfried, and SSgt. Ken Rick, the senior enlisted leader of my personal security detail (PSD). All three men had spent many months patrolling the ground in Iraq and Afghanistan, and they knew the cost of inexperience, inaction, and apathy.

The team's lack of basic combat skills expertise exasperated me, and the staff poked fun at what they perceived as my perpetual disappointment in them. Maj John Kelly, the team's intelligence officer, was the ringleader when it came to such ribbing. Known for his running commentaries, where he would adopt a Lowell Thomas voice straight out of 1940s *Movietone News* clips, he also borrowed heavily from Ken Burns documentaries. "It's hard going, leading this purpose-built task force of misfits," Kelly would say in a southern drawl. "I miss my boys in the infantry."

A Jacksonville, North Carolina, native and the elder son of Gen John Kelly, he never led with the fact that his father was one of the most revered general officers in modern Marine Corps history. It was hard to connect John with his father, who had risen through the ranks to become the commander of U.S. Southern Command and the secretary of Homeland Security. Instead, he was almost the antithesis of a Marine officer, with a baggy uniform, horn-rimmed glasses, and a slight paunch accentuated by his hunched-over, slope-shouldered carriage and gait. Involuntarily designated as a supply officer when he was a lieutenant, Kelly later transferred into the intelligence field at his first opportunity. He was an eclectic, cynical officer—in many respects a square peg in a round hole. Every now and then, when I called him out on his surliness, he would shrug his shoulders and reply, "Sorry, sir . . . twenty-third job choice."

He was acutely aware of his father's stature and following. On the rare occasion when he mentioned him, he simply referred to him as "Dad," and the things he talked about were father-and-son matters that anyone with a Y-chromosome could relate to. The general's later selection to become President Trump's chief of staff would catch John off guard as much it did the rest of us. He almost plotzed when he saw his father's face on the cover of *Time* magazine.

Kelly was a capable intelligence officer in his own right, and our rigidly scheduled yet chaotically executed training cycle frustrated him to no end. With an S-2 (intelligence) shop that accounted for more than a quarter of the team's manpower, he faced the same challenge as everyone else: his Marines came from many different units. To add to his frustrations, the long list of pre-deployment requirements did not account for the collective intelligence training his shop needed to function. Consequently, and despite Kelly's best efforts, the S-2 shop's first opportunity to work together as a cohesive entity would only come once we were on the ground in Iraq.

Like Awtry and Leibfried, Kelly had served in the Al Qa'im District in the war's early years. His memories were not fond ones. His bubble had been burst early, first with his disappointment at not making the cut for the infantry, and later by the brutality that defined daily existence in western Al Anbar in 2004 and 2005. He embraced his self-appointed role as my staff's outlier, the officer with no reservations about challenging assumptions and speaking truth to power. If there was one Marine on the team who filled the role of the Roman slave whispering in my ear, "All glory is fleeting," it was him.

4

BOULEVARD OF BROKEN DREAMS

IF ONE PLACE SERVED as a monument to the Marine Corps' interminable campaign in Iraq, it was Al Asad Air Base. Originally built by a Yugoslavian company for the Iraqi Air Force in the 1980s, it had been a thriving aerial hub that boasted numerous aircraft hangars, storage warehouses, and office buildings. Several taxiways wound south from the low ground of the base's center to a series of parallel, east-west running runways, and steel-reinforced trapezoidal bunkers blossomed like monstrous, concrete mushrooms. The Marines first occupied the outpost in 2004 to run the campaign in western Al Anbar, and the Multinational Force (MNF)-West headquarters eventually moved there from Camp Fallujah to control operations throughout the entire province.

By the time my first advisor team passed through Al Asad on our way out of the country in 2008, the base signified much of what had gone wrong with the American war in Iraq. Everyone had begun referring to the place as "Camp Cupcake," and rightly so. To support the nearly 10,000 service members and contractors who lived and worked there, it provided a stable of amenities that rivaled American military outposts across the world. There were fast food restaurants, post exchanges (PXs), and bazaars specializing in cheap, useless shit that screamed *I deployed to Iraq and never left the wire or spoke to an actual Iraqi citizen.* During those dark days there were salsa nights, belly dancing lessons, and a movie theater. There were dining facilities (DFACs) run by handsomely paid employees from contractors such as Kellogg, Brown, and Root (KBR). Nearly everyone lived in air-conditioned containerized housing units (CHUs), alternately known as "cans." And, despite the base's location in the middle of the desert, there was no shortage of running water and ice.

In 2008, as I rode across the base with a gunnery sergeant who had picked up my team at the flight line, I watched crowds of young men and women shuffling up and down the streets. Many held hands or wrapped arms around each other's waists or shoulders. We had already heard the rumors.

"What kind of trouble are Marines getting into around here?" I asked, watching a gaggle of young men and women on a street corner. They were smoking cigarettes, drinking tall cans of Monster Energy, and clutching white plastic PX shopping bags.

"You name it," he said, shaking his head. "Any way they can get in trouble in CONUS [continental United States], they are doing it here. And any*thing* they can get there, they can get here. Booze, drugs, gambling, prostitution . . . it's all happening right here at Camp Cupcake."

The whole scene had disgusted me. Back then, the war was in full swing. American men and women were still dying, but you would never know it at Al Asad. There was little to remind everyone they were in a combat zone, and few policed each other. Basic standards of good order and discipline had flown the coop, and the thirst for creature comforts had taken priority. As an example, the Marines running the base had spent countless tax dollars and man-hours refurbishing an Olympic-sized indoor pool on the base's northern wing. One day in 2008, as my team waited in the sweltering passenger terminal for a flight home, I decided to venture across the base for a swim. The journey involved a two-block trek to a bus stop, a fifteen-minute ride in an air-conditioned bus driven by a Russian-speaking contractor, and then another two-block stroll to the pool itself. To prove a point about how far off the deep end things had gone, I made the entire trip clad only in shorts, t-shirt, and shower shoes. I had no weapon on me, no identification, no rank insignia; I carried nothing but a towel and sunglasses. And no one said a damned word to me about it the entire time.

The nonsense of Camp Cupcake vanished when the Marines vacated in 2010. With the bottomless wallet of U.S. dollars gone, the bastion of Little America rapidly disintegrated. During the years they occupied Al Asad, the Americans had erected a fortress of canvassed, sand-filled Hesco barriers, massive concrete T-walls and Jersey barriers, and prefab wooden structures known as "SWA" (Southwest Asia) huts. When the Marines departed, they turned everything over to the Iraqi military, but it was an unsustainable gift for the cash-poor Iraqis. The Iraqi Air Force maintained control of the air base, and 7th Division likewise continued to occupy the base's northwestern corner, but both units could only preserve the immediate areas within their respective cantonments. The rest of the post was left to rot in the unforgiving heat, wind, and choking dust of the Anbar desert. When the Marines from SPMAGTF landed in late 2014 to secure the airfield and establish Camp Havoc for the task force, little but sandblasted ruins remained.

When we arrived in 2017, we found not much had changed since 2014. Although the task force and its battalion of support personnel and contractors had grown exponentially, most people still resided in Camp Havoc at the base's center or along the Coalition-run sector of the airfield. In its first three years, the task force expanded Havoc's perimeter to accommodate the influx of personnel and equipment accompanying the increased tempo of the counter-ISIS campaign. However, there was no accompanying expansion into the northern half of the base. Russian-built SU-25 fighter jets and Mi-24 attack helicopters flew missions from the southern runway, and a largely hidden contingent of Chinese, Russian, and Iranian maintainers supported Iraqi airfield operations. The presence of our strategic adversaries was a sore point for the Coalition leaders, but one they were unable to affect.

Relics of the Russian arms sales program, such as ancient MiG-21 fighters and Mi-17 transport helicopters, sat neglected in various states of decomposition in odd locations across the vast outpost. In earlier years—perhaps before the start of Desert Storm in 1991 or before the 2003 American invasion—the Iraqi Air Force had evacuated many of its aircraft from the flight line and plopped them down in the dunes at the farthest reaches of the base. Throughout our deployment, each time we passed by one of those disintegrating hulks in the rolling desert, I wondered how the hell the Iraqis had managed to get the airplanes out there.

Traveling along Wassam Street, the main road running east to west across the base's northern half, was like driving through ground zero of a neutron bomb detonation. Runners of sand spilled from decaying Hesco barriers onto the streets and buckling sidewalks. Wood SWA huts, dried into fragile tinder by Anbar's scorching sun, threatened to spontaneously combust in the summer heat. Rows of cannibalized vehicles, heavy equipment, and generators, all in various states of rusting disrepair, sat abandoned in overgrown lots. Countless empty plastic water bottles—the new national flower of Iraq—littered the base. Wassam Street, which at the war's height had been a bustling concourse showcasing the might of the American war machine, was now a ghost town—an embarrassing legacy of the U.S. effort in Iraq. I later started referring to that dismal stretch of road as the "Boulevard of Broken Dreams," not in reference to the Gottfried Helnwein painting or the Green Day song, but rather as a reminder of what once was—and what it had become.

There were historic elements to Al Asad most people didn't know about. The Iraqis had constructed Camp Majid—7th Division's headquarters— around Abraham's Well. According to legend, the well was an oasis Abraham had visited during his journey through the desert to Canaan. Al Asad had also become a symbol of the Iraqi army's resolve. When the Islamic State cut through Al Anbar like a hot knife through butter in 2014, routing the majority of the Iraqi army in the process, 7th Division's soldiers never surrendered their positions. Throughout the campaign's early years, they fought off several attacks against the base. Even when ISIS forces occupied the nearby garrison town of Baghdadi, effectively isolating the air base, 7th Division held firm.

Camp Havoc's heavily guarded interior perimeter surrounded the "green zone," where U.S. and Coalition activity was unrestricted. Miles of asphalted roads and repurposed taxiways attracted avid runners and Coalition members who had brought bicycles with them to Iraq. Although there was still an indirect fire threat—the base had received several volleys of rocket fire earlier in the summer of 2017—life was pretty safe inside the green zone. Every hundred meters or so, concrete bunkers swaddled in sandbags waited to provide safety in the event of another rocket attack. Based on the heaps of trash routinely removed from them, the bunkers served less as readily available protection from indirect fire and more as clandestine spots for Al Asad's inhabitants to smoke cigarettes, drink Monster Energy, or hook up—probably all three.

The area between Havoc's perimeter and the base's outlying boundary, which members of the Iraqi Air Force and the 2nd Anbar militia guarded, was the "amber zone." Movement into the amber zone required detailed planning, coordination, and mission briefing. U.S. and Coalition service members were compelled to don body armor and travel in armored vehicles whenever they ventured into the amber zone for KLEs with Iraqi forces at either Camp Majid or the Air Force headquarters.

Everything beyond the outer perimeter was the "red zone"—hostile territory—and movement outside the wire was a significant emotional event for conventional units such as ours. Although Colonel Fridriksson had continued Colonel Nugent's program of expeditionary advise-and-assist missions to the corps headquarters in Haditha, there was still a great deal of scrutiny each time his team signaled its intent to leave the wire.

Two giant, tethered aerostat balloons hovered over the base day and night, complementing an assortment of mast-mounted cameras and ground sensors scanning the immediate area of the red zone beyond Al Asad's perimeter. A more advanced version of the surveillance system that had supported my battalion in Afghanistan, the balloons sported a suite of cameras and sensors that surpassed those I had grown accustomed to seven years earlier. Although designed to protect the base, the balloons were also handy when it came to investigating hijinks aboard Al Asad. One system the balloons carried, called the Kestrel, recorded in a 360-degree arc and could rewind up to a month in the past. On more than one occasion, the task force leaders credited the Kestrel's archival footage with nabbing thieves, vandals, and other hard cases. In one case later in our deployment, the Kestrel would identify a group of soldiers who had taken it upon themselves to steal the Norwegian unit's battle colors. In one tragic episode, the Kestrel would produce footage of a troubled young American soldier as he sat down in a nearby bunker, put his rifle barrel in his mouth, and blew his brains all over the concrete walls.

Although Al Asad was no longer Camp Cupcake, there were indications it was inching back in that direction. Fridriksson and his predecessors had worked hard to provide everyone the basic amenities that make service members happy: a respectable gym, a DFAC inside an old warehouse at center camp, and a laundry service. The Danish contingent's contribution to Al Asad's creature comforts was a café known as "the Kuffen," where a pair of matronly Danish women brewed coffee and baked goodies each day for those who stopped in for a much-needed break. In general, if you had no idea where someone had disappeared to, there was a strong likelihood they were hiding out in the comfort of the Kuffen. There was also a sizeable PX that, Fridriksson noted, sold the four "eens" all growing Marines needed: caffeine, nicotine, protein, and creatine. Before long, the PX would expand to meet the needs of the air base's exploding population, and it soon boasted the highest monthly sales in Iraq. I guess everyone needs to be proud of something.

Contractors were everywhere, yet there still weren't enough to meet the daily demands of the base. When Fridriksson asked the lead KBR manager why he couldn't fill the empty billets, the contractor replied that Al Asad was a hardship post and therefore not attractive to potential employees.

"How do we fix that?" Fred asked.

"Well," the contractor said, "authorizing a Green Bean coffee shop to operate here would help."

"Tell me where to sign," Fred replied.

Overnight, the empty slots filled once word spread that Green Bean was on the way. Fridriksson took a lot of heat for that decision, including barbed comments implying that he was rewinding the clock to the bad old days of Camp Cupcake. But he held fast. He was forward-thinking enough to know that the base's population would continue to swell, and he needed to lay the foundation of contract support to accommodate it.

———————

We left our families behind in the early morning darkness of Camp Pendleton on the last day of July, a ritual countless units had performed over the previous sixteen years. At sunset, we boarded a flight run by Atlas Airlines, another in a long list of carriers no one had ever heard of that the government contracted to ferry troops to the Middle East. As the team queued up to load the aircraft, we watched a maintenance crew tape one of the engine doors shut.

"That," one Marine said, "does not inspire confidence."

"Reminds me of *Major League*," I replied. "You know, where the team gets stuck with the shitty plane, and they see the pilot duct-taping one of the propellers before taking off?" No one laughed.

It was a typical flight operated by the lowest bidder: rundown and shabby on the inside, with mismatched seat cushions and video entertainment technology that was probably state of the art in the 1970s. The flight included a team of maintenance personnel who moved back and forth throughout the passenger cabin, working on the inside of the plane during the entire trip. As I plopped down next to Sergeant Major Leibfried for the journey, I craned my neck around to survey the cabin.

"Man, they really rolled out the red carpet, huh?"

"We might die on this flight," he replied ominously, donning a set of headphones.

The flight attendant crew was a collection of oldsters who had a harried, almost paranoid look about them, as if they were running away from something. As they yelled at everybody to get to the back of the plane—*all the way back*—they offered little in the way of sympathy for the planeload of Marines heading to a combat zone. The only bright star among the black hole of customer service was an overly friendly, slightly creepy flight attendant. With wisps of thinning hair that swayed back and forth and devilish eyes that stared through your soul, he offered trays of refreshments to the Marines, leaning in much too close with a mischievous smile as he asked, "*Snacks?*" He made a significant impression on Major Kelly. For the remainder of the deployment, Kelly would often pantomime holding a tray in front of him, twist his mouth into that disturbing grin, and say, "*Snacks?*"

We landed at dusk at Germany's Frankfurt-Hahn Airport, where a procession of buses shuttled us across the airfield to the same faded, Cold War–era holding terminal I had waited in during my return from Afghanistan in 2012. As the Marines pulled out their phones and searched for a Wi-Fi signal, they gravitated toward the bar. Leibfried turned to me.

"You gonna let them drink?" he asked.

"Any reason I shouldn't?" I replied, looking around at the imploring, hopeful eyes blazing holes in me.

"The other Marines on our flight aren't allowed to," he said, pointing to a group of deflated-looking men and women nursing soft drinks and cups of coffee.

Everyone was acutely aware of CENTCOM's infamous General Order Number One, which had been in effect since 1990. At its core, the order boiled down to "no sex, no drugs, no booze, and *no fun.*" I understood its original intent, which was to minimize friction while U.S. forces were operating in the Middle Eastern societies that forbade alcohol. And to be sure, even though Marines and soldiers in Vietnam had grown accustomed to wrapping up a hard day with a lukewarm can of Budweiser, alcohol-related discipline problems had been a significant issue back then. Hell, alcohol-related incidents were *still* a significant issue in 2017. However, we had reached the low point in our long war where Marines could no longer count on basic privileges like enjoying a beer or two *before even setting down* in a combat zone. It had been the same in 2011 as I headed to Afghanistan; the standing policy prohibited Marines from consuming alcohol on their way into theater. I never learned the rationale behind the policy; I just assumed some asshole had gotten shit-faced and screwed it up for everyone. That was how it always was. That was why, as the saying went, we couldn't have nice things. I considered all this, and the wait in Hahn was shaping up to be much longer than we anticipated. I turned back to Leibfried.

"Two-beer limit; no liquor," I said. "And for Christ's sake, tell everyone to be adults about it."

Later, as I watched the revolving door of Marines and sailors rotate between the bar and the smoke pit outside, it was obvious most had snaked more than two drinks. There was no way to control it without posting an officer or a SNCO at the bar, but it didn't matter anyway. Our long wait for the plane to refuel had busted the aircrew's rest timeline. After midnight, the buses returned to drive our team an hour and a half across Germany's darkened countryside to a hotel in Frankfurt.

5

THE *STAR WARS* CANTINA

OUR GERIATRIC 747 TOUCHED DOWN at Kuwait International Airport just before dawn, and a sense of déjà vu enveloped me as uniformed handlers herded our team into a fenced-in holding area near the flight line. It was the same pen where, in 2003, my men and I had stood in the freezing darkness, drinking coffee, smoking cigarettes, and anxiously waiting for transportation to our cantonment area south of the Iraqi border. This time it was the peak of summer, and Kuwait's oppressive heat hit us the moment the sun appeared. The temperature soared as we passed through the U.S. Army's Camp Arifjan, and it continued to climb once we arrived at Ali Al Salem Air Base several days later. The heat was a cruel constant. The moment you left the air-conditioned comfort of indoors, beads of perspiration popped out on your forehead, sweat ran down your back in clammy rivulets, and your fingers tingled with pins and needles. I had no idea what it was like walking on the surface of the sun, but this had to be close.

There were no aircraft available to carry us into Iraq, and we spent days at Ali Al Salem's passenger terminal, waiting for expected flights that never came or were inexplicably cancelled. As everyone passed the time watching bootleg episodes of *Game of Thrones* on hard drives bursting at the seams with pirated media, Maj Lindsay Mathwick attempted to find anything smoking that could lift us out of the Kuwaiti furnace. The daughter of two retired naval officers, Mathwick was a San Diego native and graduate of Penn State who had joined the team as our logistics officer. Her experiences in Iraq between 2006 and 2009, leading and participating in hundreds of convoys and supporting Camp Fallujah's closure, uniquely qualified her to return to the country as the leader of the task force's S-4 (logistics) shop. An upbeat, charming, and determined officer, she had attended the Defence Academy in Shrivenham, England, where she earned a master's in defense studies from King's College London. She was also an outdoors enthusiast and amateur photographer. Each Friday during our workup, when I asked about her weekend plans, she would outline a long list of activities that usually included camping and hiking in austere destinations like Joshua Tree National Park in southern California's high desert.

Lindsay had landed in a unique position. Although not the team's only woman, she *was* the only female among the collection of testosterone-filled male majors who formed my primary staff. Early in our time together, after witnessing her exposure to several team members talking shit about inappropriate topics, I pulled her aside to seek assistance.

"I have worked with women before," I told her. "Several were attached to my battalion in Afghanistan. But that was a different time, and I wasn't very good about working with them. I probably wasn't very responsive to them or their circumstances. I regret it, and I don't want to make the same mistake again.

"I could use your help. You are the senior woman on this team, and I need you to be my directed telescope. If there is something going on that adversely affects the women, I need you to let me know about it. Everyone deserves to be here, and everyone deserves to be treated with dignity and respect."

She was more than willing, and in doing so, she became a true asset to the entire outfit. As it turned out, there was no need for me to worry. The team's women were more than capable of holding their own among the men, and Lindsay shined in that regard. After many weeks of working together, the staff developed into a strong-willed clique that made dishing out jokes, barbs, and carefully crafted insults a regular part of their daily routine. Lindsay could give as good as she got. The other officers often teased her about how she wore her long auburn hair, which she pulled into a tight bun. She routinely parted it in different places, sometimes straight up the middle of her head, other times with the part angling off to one side. Sometimes it went in a zigzagging pattern. Where and how the part in her hair pointed signified different degrees of what she referred to as "spiciness." When the staff ribbed her about it, she would flash a broad grin, pat the design in her hair, and say, "Pretty spicy today."

Our C-130 Hercules touched down at Al Asad in the middle of the night on August 7. Sweat-soaked and disoriented, everyone was exhausted after more than a week of disappointing starts and stops. Fred Fridriksson and his team met us in the radiating heat of the darkened airfield, and they spirited us to our quarters so we could get our heads down for the night. We had lost most of the week designated for the turnover between the two teams, and our now-compressed schedule left little room for wasting time. Everyone would need a good night's sleep before the long days ahead.

My new home was a can in Camp Havoc's "VIP" quarters: a collection of CHUs surrounded by high concrete T-walls that was a short walk from the task force command post. I dropped my gear on the floor in a dusty heap and looked around at the stark surroundings. There was a bed, a desk, a chair, a wall locker, and four white walls. Ever the host, Fred had stocked the room with bottled water and fitted the mattress with fresh sheets. Twenty feet away outside was a pair of modular shower and toilet cans. Space was a premium in both, with toilets so cramped that the heavy nylon curtain covering each stall draped down over your knees and into your lap as you sat on the commode. To add to the discomfort, the low-flow nozzles in the shower stalls did little more than dribble water on you. Signs in English, Danish, and Arabic implored prospective bathers to take "combat showers."

In other words, *turn on water, get wet, turn off water, lather up, turn on water, rinse, turn off water, get the hell out*. Despite routine warnings about water shortages, I grew convinced that the only time anyone took a real combat shower was if someone else was present to keep them honest.

Some people had complained that life at the air base was too hard. I surveyed my room again. An actual bed, with an actual mattress and clean sheets. An air conditioner. Running water and flushing toilets just around the corner. In 2011, home was a mud hut cave in Afghanistan. In 2008, I lived in a dry-rotted, flyblown wood hut in Iraq, and I shat in plastic bags every day. In 2003, I went without a shower for more than a month, sleeping in shallow dirt trenches and crapping in holes I dug myself. I had no idea what all those people were complaining about at Al Asad; as far as deployments go, this was the best I ever had.

Most of the team lived in a rickety, sheet-metaled aircraft hangar dubbed "CHU City-1." In the years since its construction, the hangar had deteriorated in Anbar's brutal climate. When the winds picked up around the base, great scabs of aluminum siding affixed to the hangar's walls rattled and flapped, threatening to break loose, fall to earth, and split some unsuspecting bystander in half. Sometime after the first task force rotation occupied Al Asad, a team of contractors cleaned out the bird-shit-spattered hangar and installed rows of CHUs inside the shelter. It was a valiant effort, but it didn't stop the endless showers of droppings that rained down from the squadrons of pigeons roosting in the rafters. And, despite the solar protection the hangar provided, it did nothing to guard against the dust storms that plagued the region. Each time a *shamal* blew through Al Asad, CHU City-1 filled with an impenetrable haze that choked its inhabitants and reduced visibility to a glaucomatic blur. Despite all this, the place had become a small community, with flags and unit crests adorning the walls, laundry hanging on lines, and bicycles parked in corners. The place smelled like a college dormitory, minus the alcohol vapors.

The task force command post was an oblong, one-story concrete building at the heart of Camp Havoc. Its flat roof bristled with an array of antennas and sensors that supported the team's collection and targeting efforts, and its shotgunned interior hosted a suite of office spaces and conference rooms.

There was still an eerie sensation to the place, and reminders of Saddam Hussein's legacy were everywhere. Two doors down from the commander's office was a long, narrow room that would become Lieutenant Colonel Merritt's workspace. With a sloping tiled floor that led to a drain at the back of the room, it had all the look and feel of a Ba'athist execution chamber. There was also an old morgue across the street, which one of the Coalition units had occupied. I avoided the place for the entire time I was at Al Asad.

Planning and analysis occurred in the office spaces branching out from the command post's main corridor, and it all came together inside the COC. Rows of makeshift wooden tables filled the long, rectangular room, each supporting computer terminals, radio handsets, and twisted bundles of wiring and power cables. JTACs, uniformed and contracted ISR tactical controllers, and radio operators manned the terminals, occasionally glancing up at the head of the room, where a projector flashed graphics depicting the current operating picture. Flanking the projection on both sides were large, flat-screen televisions displaying aerostat and surveillance camera footage. The screens also live-streamed grainy video broadcasts beamed from orbiting unmanned aerial systems (UASs) far out in the battlespace.

Overlooking the workstations on a raised platform were terminals for the watch officer, watch chief, and current operations officer, or "COPsO." Behind them, on a higher platform, were chairs and a table for the Iraqi liaison officers and their interpreters. The tiered room buzzed with radio transmissions, chatter among the watch team, and the din of the Iraqis shouting into their cell phones. Boxes of pogey bait—candy, chips, and other goodies sent by flag-wavers back home—filled the corners. A coffee maker churned out black stuff, and half-filled plastic water bottles of dip spit or chewed-up sunflower seeds littered the tables. The COC was the team's nerve center, and it was where the task force had done what it did best: kill enemy fighters.

We jumped into the relief-in-place with Fridriksson's team the morning after our arrival. The brief that most interested us was the current enemy situation. It was ominous. The intelligence data estimated that close to 2,500 Islamic State fighters remained in Al Anbar Province. More than half that number

were believed to be in Abu Kamal, Syria, just across the border from Iraq's
Al Qa'im District. Enemy forces controlled the Middle Euphrates River
Valley eastward from Al Qa'im to the towns of Rayhanah and Anah along
Highway 12, which everyone still referred to as Main Supply Route (MSR)
Bronze from the war's early days, and ISIS exerted significant influence south
from Al Qa'im along Highway 20—Alternate Supply Route (ASR) Silver—to
the southwestern town of Akashat.

For months, the Iraqi army had controlled Route Bronze from Sagrah, a
town twenty kilometers southeast of Anah, to the population centers of Hit
and Kubaysah southeast of Al Asad. The Iraqis also controlled Highway 1
(MSR Mobile) and Highway 11 (ASR Michigan) from the far western desert
settlement of Rutbah east to the Al Anbar capital city of Ramadi. Battle-
hardened fighters had barricaded themselves in the urban sprawl of the
towns they controlled and seeded the battlefield with obstacle belts.

Dozens of Popular Mobilization Forces (PMF) units—the predominantly
Shi'a militia organizations ostensibly controlled by the Iraqi prime minister—
operated in Al Anbar Province. Among them were a collection of Shi'a militia
groups (SMGs) that Iran influenced, supported, and equipped. It took some
time for us to understand that all SMGs were considered PMF forces, but not
all PMF units were SMGs. The terms were not interchangeable, and when
discussing the issue with senior Coalition officers you conflated the two at
your own peril. There were several SMGs in western Al Anbar that concerned
us, and they concentrated most of their efforts west along Routes Mobile and
Michigan toward Akashat. Operating in pickets along the two highways,
the SMGs were, by default, securing the southern boundary of the JaOC's
expansive battlespace. Until now, they had not presented much of a problem
for Coalition forces. However, a unit of Kata'ib Hizballah (KH) fighters had
established an overt presence at Al Taqaddum Air Base, and they flew their
signature yellow and green flags in plain view for Coalition units to see.

There were few issues in Iraq as politically charged as the SMGs. To ease
the tension, the Coalition's senior leaders would insist that we use less con-
frontational terms such as "noncompliant PMF." But observing the militia
groups do as they pleased and gradually take control of large chunks of Iraq

was like watching a slow-motion train wreck. Many units were little more than rebranded versions of the same groups of angry young Shi'a fighters who had fought Coalition forces between 2004 and 2011. They weren't shy about broadcasting their goals to expel the Americans from the country and secure an Iranian land bridge through Iraq to Syria and Lebanon.

What alarmed us most about the SMGs was their overt *and* clandestine activities against U.S. forces. Our sister task force at Al Taqaddum reported regular overflights by KH-controlled drones, and the militia fighters standing posts there were openly hostile to the Americans. The SMGs were also notorious for rolling into areas the Iraqi army had secured, and then taking the credit for the ISF's victories. Deep down, I think we were all waiting for the day when Iran would finally give the order for the SMGs to engage Coalition personnel. They were light, mobile, and deadly, and they employed an impressive arsenal. Although most SMG units sped around in pickup trucks mounted with heavy machine guns, they also had armored vehicles, missiles, and even artillery pieces. They weren't going to let anyone push them around, and the presence of the heavily armed Americans didn't faze them.

Despite the Coalition's general distaste for the Shi'a militia groups, there could be no disagreement about their accomplishments, their battlefield efficacy, and the pivotal role they had played in pushing back the Islamic State in the war's early months. When the uniformed Iraqi army all but evaporated in the face of the invasion, the PMF—and especially the SMGs—had rallied. They inflicted significant losses on the marauding enemy fighters and, in doing so, secured their part in the future of Iraq's internal security.

Until the summer of 2017, the recapture of Mosul had been the Coalition's priority, and Task Force Al Asad's operations were an economy of force effort. But that had shifted following the arrival of the U.S. Army's 1st Armored Division, which would serve as the new headquarters element for Combined Joint Forces Land Component Command (CJFLCC). Al Anbar was now the deep fight, and the overall Coalition headquarters in Kuwait had directed 1st Armored Division to ramp up operations in the task force's battlespace.

"The time is coming," Fred told me, echoing his words from our conversation the previous February. "The final Iraqi operation to clear the MERV will probably happen on your watch. The hard decision you're gonna have to make is whether you will be a battlespace owner or fill an A3E [advise, assist, accompany, and enable] role like General White has talked about.

"If you're gonna advise and assist, that's fine . . . you have everything you need here. But you also have everything you need to run the battlespace. And if it's a division-level fight for the Iraqis, then you'll need Coalition battalion commanders to partner with the ISF brigades. You could bring in the infantry battalion from SPMAGTF; you can also have the Norwegian team do it. Then *you* can focus on command and control. You can tell your ISF partner if he wants to command and control, he'll do it from here . . . and then you don't need to sit on a firebase somewhere. You could do that, but your ability to command and control would be much greater from Al Asad.

"So, like I said, you're gonna have to decide; you're gonna have to choose how you employ the task force. Will you be a battlespace owner, or will you be an advisor? Because I don't think you can do both."

On top of it all, I was also supposed to assume all responsibilities as base operating support-integrator (BOS-I) aboard Al Asad. It was no small task. Throughout our turnover, Fridriksson spent more time talking about his headaches managing the base's logistics than he did discussing how his team supported the Iraqis. He was not properly resourced to run the base, but he continued to accomplish the mission. That was why successive Coalition commanders had such an affinity for the task force: the Marines didn't complain; they just made things happen.

Fridriksson had a point: the BOS-I responsibility, onerous though it was, could not be ignored. If the air base was not managed properly, the increasing numbers of American and Coalition personnel flooding it would quickly become a problem. People across the CENTCOM theater were already referring to Al Asad as the "*Star Wars* cantina" due to its rogue's gallery of different nationalities, uniforms, grooming regulations, and weapons carriage. Left unmanaged, the base could earn a reputation like another infamous aspect of Tatooine's Mos Eisley spaceport: a wretched hive of scum and villainy.

As our turnover continued, I gained a greater appreciation of the task force's size and diversity. Its numbers, which grew each day and were rapidly approaching three thousand, included members of four uniformed military U.S. services, representatives from more than ten Coalition nations, and a small army of contractors. Fortunately, Fridriksson had three subordinate commanders to lead the bulk of the people on the base. Once our turnover was complete, I would inherit those three commanders.

Lieutenant Colonel Jesper Momme, the Danish contingent (DANCON) commander, led the build partner capacity (BPC) team composed of soldiers from Denmark, the United Kingdom, Latvia, Lithuania, Estonia, and the Czech Republic. He had been a colonel back in Denmark, and he believed so much in the mission to rebuild and professionalize the Iraqi army that he had accepted an administrative demotion to enable him to lead the effort. A genial, almost grandfatherly officer with a silver stubble of a beard and a warm, broad grin, Momme led his soldiers with kindness and respect. Above all else, he believed in taking a generational approach to training the Iraqis by building relationships with them, empowering them, and arming them with the basics they needed to survive as soldiers. In time, the two of us would spend many hours together comparing ideas on how best to train the Iraqi recruits who mustered for training.

In the years since the program's inception in 2014, the different teams that had rotated through Al Asad had trained more than eight thousand Iraqi service members. The recruits were always a mixed bag, with wide variations in ages, literacy, and personal motivations. And, in most cases, the units came from regions far from the base. Momme and I agreed that the primary training audience for the program should be *local* soldiers and border guards. He was convinced such a methodology had a substantial force protection component to it. He believed that, if Iraqi soldiers received dignified, respectful training from professional instructors co-located with their units—as the task force was with 7th Division—they would be less likely to turn their guns on the trainers. Momme's pleas to the Coalition to align Iraqi training audiences with their local partners typically fell on deaf ears, and it would become a source of continuous frustration for us both.

As the Iraqi army prepared to clear the MERV, Momme's BPC contingent would play a critical role. Combat casualties, desertion, and the natural attrition woven into the culture of the Iraqi military had taken a toll, and there was more demand in theater to train and refresh the Iraqi Security Forces than there were proper resources. Iraqi soldiers weren't the only ones who would need training before the operation began. Once the ISF had cleared the way to Al Qa'im and the Syrian border, someone would need to guard the 150-plus miles of porous border territory that ISIS fighters were transiting with impunity. The Iraqi army might be able to hold the positions temporarily, but they were not a long-term solution. That was the Border Guard Force's responsibility, and there were not enough units to do the job yet. The training mission would likely fall to Momme and his Danish team.

Lieutenant Colonel Neil "Bells" Bellamy, a self-described erratic skier and enthusiastic but average wine taster, commanded 2nd Battalion, the Rifles—a British regular army unit quartered in Northern Ireland. His battalion, augmented by Danish and U.S. soldiers and a detachment of SPMAGTF infantry Marines, formed the core of the base security force (SecFor). They performed one of the most critical—and thankless—missions aboard the post. Responsible for both internal and perimeter security, Bells spent most of his waking hours trying to figure out how to secure the exposed airfield and its fleet of exotic aircraft and armed drones. Al Asad had grown into the busiest aerial port in Iraq, processing nearly 20,000 tons of cargo and 11,000 passengers in the previous six months. It had also launched and recovered close to two thousand aircraft missions, making it a juicy target for any committed Islamic State fighters who might want to score an easy media victory. The 2012 Taliban attack on Afghanistan's Camp Bastion airfield had left an indelible impression on Bellamy. It had ended with two dead Marines, eight damaged or destroyed AV-8B Harrier jets, and an enormous black eye for the Marine Corps. He believed it was only a matter of time until ISIS attempted the same thing, and he insisted on routine base-wide drills to ensure his SecFor personnel were prepared to respond to any incursion.

The units Momme and Bellamy commanded were, by Danish and British national caveats, restricted to operating within the confines of Al Asad. Momme's soldiers trained the Iraqis in a secure, cordoned area within the amber zone, and Bellamy's platoons manned guard towers and entry control points (ECPs) across the base. They also conducted perimeter patrols to search for breaches in the barrier system and maintained the array of ground sensors the Marines monitored from Bellamy's base defense operations center. The national caveat preventing his soldiers from going outside the wire frustrated Bells to no end, and once he got wind that future operations would require U.S. movement beyond the wire of Al Asad, his discouragement skyrocketed. The Danish and British missions went back to the earliest days of the task force, and whatever the next move was going to be, Bells wanted in on it.

A new arrival earlier to Al Asad that summer increased the task force's capability dramatically. Lieutenant Colonel Terje Bruøygard, the commander of Norway's Telemark Battalion, was the leader of the Norwegian Task Unit (NOR TU), a battalion headquarters that had been repurposed to support the Iraqi army at the brigade level. In our first meeting, Bruøygard, who was a graduate of two of the Marine Corps' professional military education schools, was quick to inform me that the Norwegian Ministry of Defense (MoD) had earmarked his unit to work solely with 7th Division's 28th Brigade. The Norwegian army had outfitted his team with a remarkable suite of equipment and cutting-edge technology to support their operations—they even had freeze-dried blood to treat battlefield casualties—but there was one problem: although the entire unit was aboard Al Asad, not all their equipment had arrived, nor would it be fully operational for at least a month. At the time of our turnover with Fridriksson's team, there was no operational timeline pressing us, so the Norwegians' readiness problems interested me only mildly. The cultural rivalry between the Danish and the Norwegian teams fascinated me more. Both groups claimed to be descendants of the original Vikings—DANCON had named their cantonment Camp Valhalla; the Norwegians had christened their new site Camp Midgard—and each time Bruøygard referred to his team's "Viking" call sign, Momme would roll his eyes.

6

WOODEN BOYS

DESPITE THE COALITION'S FOCUS on the battle for Mosul, which devoured aviation and fire support resources across the theater, Fridriksson and his team had put the wood to the Islamic State. In their nine months at Al Asad, they had conducted over two hundred kinetic strikes, killing more than three hundred enemy fighters in the process, and they had supported numerous small-scale ISF operations—all while managing the base's daily operations and planning and supervising its physical expansion. Despite all the good work the outfit continued to do, it still received little recognition from the Marine Corps writ large. The service considered it a drain on resources, and most senior leaders who knew anything about it didn't seem to consider Fred or his predecessors to be full-fledged commanders. But the responsibility the task force leaders had shouldered since 2014 was enormous. And, Fred lamented, while the Coalition was quick to laud the task force for its countless tangible contributions to the campaign, the disconnect between his team, the Coalition, and the different Marine Corps chains of command was gaping.

"You could cure cancer out here," he concluded, shaking his head, "and you wouldn't even get an 'Atta boy!' from the Marine Corps."

It was easy to read between the lines: colonels who were formally selected to lead traditional units such as infantry regiments, aircraft groups, and MEUs were, in the eyes of our superiors, the only true commanders in the Corps.

"They're the *real* boys," Fred added, the irritation in his voice palpable. "We're just wooden boys."

However, the message we received from MG Pat White, USA, CJFLCC's gravel-voiced commanding general, was completely different. He made one thing clear during our first meeting together at Al Asad on August 10: he considered me and my counterpart at Al Taqaddum as full-fledged commanders, equivalent in authority and trust and confidence to the U.S. Army brigade commander leading operations in northern Iraq's Nineveh Province. With that in mind, he wanted Task Force Al Asad to command and control the coming MERV campaign, beginning with the clearance of Rayhanah and Anah in the first weeks of September—less than one month away.

His announcement perplexed me. I had known White briefly in my JOD-CENT days, when he directed the J-5 Pakistan and Afghanistan Coordination Cell just down the hall in the Pentagon basement. An armor officer through and through, he wore his hair cropped closely to the skin, and he dipped Copenhagen like a fiend. He was passionate about exercise, especially burpees, and he was probably the most physically fit soldier in 1st Armored Division. At Fred's urging, my staff and I had spent a week with his division headquarters in Fort Bliss, Texas, the previous spring to participate in their pre-deployment mission rehearsal exercise. As we war-gamed vignettes for the western Al Anbar campaign, White had conveyed the same intent: our team would be the ones to finish the job alongside the Iraqi army. Even though I had a pre-existing, albeit limited, relationship with White, it didn't make sense to me. I couldn't understand how a U.S. Army general had enough faith in my abilities to hand me control of the Coalition effort to support an Iraqi corps, yet my own service's chain of command wouldn't recognize me as an actual commanding officer, much less arm me with the administrative tools necessary to exercise command authority.

Before he departed, White gave me his final guidance.

"Listen, you guys just need to keep working yourselves out of a job," he said. "We've got one goal here: Iraqi self-reliance. Fridriksson's team was an economy of force mission; yours is not. You have to continue to generate will for the Iraqis to fight; you have to look deep. To export violence, we've got to break away from this place.

"So, I need you to determine what it will take to split the task force away from Al Asad—what it will take for you to shed your installation responsibilities. And I need to know what it will take to re-position your team to command the campaign from a forward position. General Qassim needs to get off the ISR crack; he needs to get out in the battlespace and lead from the front.

"I don't know what I don't know," he grunted. "But I do know your partner can't command the fight from here."

As he stood to leave, he turned back to me. "Hey, look, I'm an armor guy, so I'm into call signs and all that shit. What's yours?"

"Lion-6."

"Lion-6, huh?" he said with a crooked grin.

"Yes, sir. *Al Asad* is Arabic for 'lion.'"

"Alright, Lion-6 it is," he said. "Good to have you and your team aboard."

<hr />

White's moral support was helpful, but three main concerns overshadowed the coming operation. Sunni-Shi'a tensions still existed among the Iraqi units, and no one had solved the riddle of what role the PMF would play in the river valley's clearance or, for that matter, in Al Anbar after the Islamic State was no longer a threat. Sunni and Shi'a leaders were tabling historic tribal, ethnic, and religious feuds, and they were striking deals all over the country to face down the enemy. They were holding the hands of the devil they saw in each other to cross the bridge to defeat ISIS, and few Coalition members were willing to discuss in public what we all knew to be true: the campaign to defeat the Islamic State was only the beginning. Once the Iraqi government declared victory, and the Sunni and Shi'a forces no longer needed each other, the situation would likely revert to the Hatfields and McCoys across the country. When asked what would happen once the smoke cleared and the country returned to the status quo ante bellum, one tribal leader allegedly promised an Arabic prediction similar in tone and tenor to "There will be blood."

There was a critical shortage of resources necessary to support Iraqi army operations in Al Anbar. The Mosul campaign had drained the coffers, and our partners were at the end of the line as far as the Iraqi Ground Forces Command was concerned. There were challenges getting the Iraqis fuel, spare parts, and ammunition, and the JaOC relied on the task force to facilitate their requests for the materiel they required. The Iraqis would also be leveraging *our* resources for the operation, namely strike and attack aviation platforms and indirect fire systems. Equally important, the coming operation would consume precision-guided munitions (PGMs) such as laser-guided Hellfire missiles and GPS-guided ordnance like 155-mm Excalibur artillery rounds and guided multiple launch rocket system (GMLRS) rounds for the high-mobility artillery rocket system (HIMARS). Mosul had consumed so many Hellfires and GMLRS rounds that CENTCOM was now rationing them throughout the theater. There was, after all, still a war going on in Afghanistan.

Perhaps most concerning was the continued possibility of enemy attacks in the rear area. The Iraqi army had secured the urban centers along Route Bronze from Hit and Kubaysah all the way north to Sagrah, but it was a shallow defensive line. To maintain its presence, 7th Division had picketed the highway with checkpoints and fortified outposts, a tactic that consumed soldiers and equipment. The defensive line was only as strong as the motivation and discipline of the individual soldiers manning the pickets. Multiple infiltration routes—ancient desert trail networks referred to as "rat lines"—pointed to the urban centers along Bronze. It was only a matter of time until a committed enemy team penetrated the Iraqi defenses with a suicide vehicle. Such an attack would shake the confidence of both the Iraqi army leadership and the local population. A similar attack against Al Asad could be devastating.

By 2017, the Special Operations Forces (SOF) world had built up a heavy presence aboard Al Asad. The real operators lived in a sequestered compound on the base's eastern side, and it was easy to spot them roaming around among the rest of us *untermenschen*. Most wore baseball caps and perfectly tailored combat fatigues, with shirts untucked and trouser cuffs unbloused around their commercial hiking shoes. When they went outside the wire, they sported lightweight body armor, high-speed chest rigs, and hand-painted carbines adorned with exotic optics devices. They also had souped-up rides. The mine-resistant, ambush-protected all-terrain vehicle (MATV) was their armored car of choice to roll around outside the wire. Many of the SOF teams had heavily modified their vehicles and painted them in outrageous camouflage schemes that broadcast *Look at me . . . I'm an operator!* to anyone who was even remotely paying attention.

And then there were the beards. Oh, yes, the beards. At some point in their history, someone had decided relaxed grooming regulations were necessary to blend in with the local populace or the proxy forces the operators were supporting. That, of course, was bullshit. There was no way for Americans, with all their whiz-bang gear, to blend in anywhere, no matter how man-tastic their beards were. But the operators wore their facial hair with pride. Many of the Coalition SOF (COALSOF) members were even more flamboyant, sporting not only the obligatory beards but also long, flowing manes tied in exquisite man-buns and top-knots. Some of them, several of us would later admit, were truly beautiful men.

As our two teams neared the transfer of authority, Fred cautioned me about the task force's interactions with Al Asad's SOF contingent, which Special Operations Task Force (SOTF)–West managed. A SEAL team with the call sign "Trident" that Special Operations Command had beefed up into a formidable action arm, SOTF-West had its fingers in everything in Al Anbar.

"The relationship with the Iraqi commander is yours," Fred said. "You are his primary partner, and you are the battlespace owner. Trident's mandate is to work with the Sunni TMF [Tribal Militia Forces]. There are a couple of groups they work with more than others, but at the end of the day, Trident takes a lot of direction from your partner. If a particular tribe gets sideways with him, he will all but forbid the operators from working with them until that group is off his shit list."

The most challenging thing about the relationship between SOTF-West and the task force, Fridriksson explained, were the different authorities and chains of command under which the two organizations operated.

"Trident works for CJSOTF [Combined Joint Special Operations Task Force]," he explained. "They don't work for General White, and they'll be quick to remind you of that. The COALSOF teams—the Danes, the Spaniards, the Aussies—all live in the SOF compound and have similar mission sets. But COALSOF doesn't work for Trident; they work for CJSOTF. However, Trident supervises them and plays the role of 'den mother' for all operators at Al Asad."

Some of the friction, he continued, had to do with notification for operations. Although the SOF teams were not required to gain the task force's approval to operate in our battlespace, they *were* obligated to notify us before an operation commenced. The reason was clear: if a SOF team was snooping and pooping in the desert without informing us beforehand, we—or the Iraqis, for that matter—might mistake them for the enemy and call in a strike. It behooved the SOF teams to incorporate the task force into their plans, coordinate with us, and keep us informed. The opposite was true, as well. After hearing all this, my head spun. Navigating and understanding the special operations architecture was becoming as difficult as understanding Al Anbar's tribal networks.

Trident's problem, Fridriksson explained, was that they hadn't always kept their word when dealing with the Iraqi commander and the tribal militias. And, he added, the SOTF-West team often made promises they were unable to keep.

"Despite all the compliments Qassim heaps on the guy in public," Fred told me, "he doesn't trust the outbound Trident commander."

"Huh," I said. "Really?"

"Yeah, it's pretty simple, man," he said, leaning in. "Even though she says otherwise, the prostitute doesn't actually love you."

With all the local dynamics to consider, we couldn't lose sight of the task force's requirement to maintain its advise, assist, and enable effort with the

Iraqi army. That was, after all, our raison d'être. If we couldn't capitalize on the gains the previous teams had made, we would be dead in the water. The challenge with advisor teams was universal: whenever turnovers occurred, the new team was starting from zero with the foreign partner. Previous advisor experience was certainly important. But at the end of the day, the Iraqis at Al Asad and Haditha didn't know us. And because they didn't know us, they didn't trust us. The feeling was mutual.

To complicate things further, we still had not actually *met* our partners. During our pre-deployment site survey earlier in the spring, Fridriksson had kept us away from the Iraqi leaders. An operation was under way at the time, and he didn't want to distract or confuse his partner. He said the same thing once we arrived in August; he planned to introduce us to our new partners at the conclusion of the relief-in-place. I trusted Fred's judgment, but his decision to sequester us until the very last day irked me. With all the talk about the MERV operation's timeline accelerating, we wouldn't have much time to build relationships with our Iraqi partners. My partners, of course, were General Qassim and General Numan Abdul-Zawbai, the commanders of the Jazeera Operations Command and the Iraqi Army 7th Division.

7

NEW PARTNERS

HEFTY, GRAYING AT THE TEMPLES, and the proud owner of a luxuriant mustache worthy of national acclaim during Saddam Hussein's era, Staff Major General Qassim al-Muhammadi was every bit the quintessential Ba'athist strongman. He had indeed been a card-carrying member of the Ba'ath Party under Saddam. With his rich baritone and frequent over-the-top theatrics, he was a larger-than-life character who commanded everyone's attention the moment he entered a room. An immaculate dresser, he wore uniforms that were always spotless, crisply pressed, and superbly tailored. Even in the heat and dust of the Anbar summer, his tan Chelsea boots were buffed to a high-gloss shine, and he completed his ensemble with an olive-green canvas cartridge belt securely fastened around his bulging mid-section.

During pre-deployment training, our team had interacted with Iraqi-American role players filling the parts of our partners. Most of the actors were unshaven, slovenly, and clad in dirty, rumpled, and mismatched camouflage uniforms. My experience with the Iraqi army in 2008 reflected the opposite, and I made sure to tell everyone in 2017 that the role players were not an accurate representation of our future counterparts.

"They'll be better dressed than you," I said during a debrief. "Trust me, Iraqi officers wouldn't be caught dead in a filthy uniform."

Qassim was more than pressed fatigues and spit-shined boots; he was also a controversial figure in the Iraqi army. He had joined the service in 1983, and he fought during the bloody war with Iran in the 1980s. He had been a battalion commander in Mosul during the 2003 American invasion, and he headed home to Fallujah after the Coalition Provisional Authority's disastrous decision to disband the army. He returned to service in 2008 and assumed command of 7th Division's 28th Brigade just months after I left Iraq. Within five years, he became the division commander.

Something happened while Qassim was commanding 7th Division that cemented his deep distrust of Iraq's central government. As the story goes, he was transporting captured Syrians to the border town of Waleed. Understanding the dangers associated with traveling along Iraq's unpatrolled highways, he requested helicopters to support the mission. The request was denied, and his convoy promptly ran into an ambush. The detained Syrians died in the attack, and the blame landed squarely on his shoulders. Iraqi government officials jailed him, tuned him up good, and allegedly sentenced him to death. Following the intervention of Iraq's Shi'a leader, Ayatollah Ali al-Sistani, the government released him from prison and dismissed him from the military. Later, in 2014, the Ministry of Defense recalled him after purging the generals who had allowed the Islamic State to blow through the country uncontested.

Upon his recall, Qassim assumed command of the Ramadi-based Anbar Operations Command. A car bombing wounded him less than a year later. He recuperated and resumed his duties in 2015, and several months later he was wounded again in a mortar attack. But his inability to get along with senior Iraqi officers at Baghdad's Combined Joint Operations Center (CJOC) led to the MoD firing him after he requested additional soldiers and resources to battle ISIS forces in Ramadi. Not long after—and likely with the endorsement of several senior Coalition officers with whom he had developed close ties—he assumed command of the Jazeera Operations Command in May of

2016. Apart from the appearance that he had nine lives, one other thing was certain: Qassim rubbed a lot of people the wrong way, and he had paid the price for it many times throughout his checkered career. Nevertheless, he was the definition of the "right man at the right time" in Al Anbar Province, and he had a loyal following within Baghdad, the JaOC, and 7th Division.

A chronic chain-smoker who was forever calling to his hapless aide to fetch his laser pointer, his iPad, and another pack of cigarettes, he often burst into outrageously loud fits of bronchial hacking and coughing. Between his pre-emphysema symptoms, his persistent insomnia, and a swollen belly that spilled over his cartridge belt, he was anything but the epitome of health. Eating with him was a horror show. He would repeatedly jam his hand up to the wrist into piping hot beds of rice and lamb, stuffing great gobs of food into his mouth as I feebly attempted to keep up. Between his overeating, smoking, and sleeplessness, I eventually grew genuinely concerned about his health, fearing he would have a debilitating stroke or a John Candy–level heart attack.

Qassim was a natural orator who was obsessed with mugging for the camera, and he frequently repeated the "three pillars" of his Anbar campaign plan. He insisted the key to controlling the province was securing the routes and population centers, sealing the border with Syria, and then continuing to hunt the Islamic State in the desert. His oft-repeated mantra was "ISIS started in the desert, and we will finish them in the desert." He was not shy about telling everyone that his strategy depended on support from the Coalition and the Sunni tribal militia forces, who were technically part of the PMF and deemed essential to Iraqi army operations. Because the tribal units were lightly armed, mobile, and genuinely lethal when let off the leash, Qassim employed them as his own maneuver arm. He could corral them and control their actions because he had made promises about the new world order that would emerge in Al Anbar following the Islamic State's defeat.

Fridriksson had paved the way for me with Qassim, talking me up and relaying my experience before I showed up at Al Asad, and so our first meeting was a smooth one. In a visit not long after our arrival, Major General White reinforced Fred's messaging campaign by singing my praises to Qassim while I was in the room.

"*Sayidi* [sir], this is your man," White said, pointing to me. "*Aqeed* [Colonel] Folsom is your partner now; he and his team will go with you all the way to Al Qa'im."

Qassim was visibly pleased to learn much of my staff had experience in Iraq, and he was delighted when I assured him my principal advisors—Leibfried, Awtry, and Kelly—had each spent significant amounts of time in Al Anbar in the war's early years. If Al Qa'im was the eventual goal, I explained, we certainly had the right people in the room. From that point forward, he automatically expected those three men to accompany me to our frequent meetings.

Qassim was also overjoyed that I would smoke with him. I was, he pointed out, the only Marine colonel he had *ever* seen smoke cigarettes.

"Great men have great flaws," I winked.

As we stood smoking outside the command post, Qassim asked if I had any children. Iraqi men were immensely proud of their sons. I had known American officers who, to build rapport with their counterparts, only referred to their sons and not their daughters. One culture instructor had even *recommended* we take that approach. I had no sons—only two beautiful daughters whom I was convinced had hung the moon.

"I have two girls," I said, pulling out my phone and showing him pictures.

"What is your older daughter's name?" he asked. I told him, and he then said, "From now on we will refer to you as Abu Emery."

"That means 'Father of Emery,'" my interpreter said.

"Yeah," I replied, smiling at Qassim. "I got it."

It didn't take a rocket scientist to figure out that General Qassim's shadow was Staff Major General Numan Abdul-Zawbai, the commander of 7th Division. The two men rarely went anywhere without each other. With his thinning, slicked-back hair, bushy mustache, and gold-rimmed glasses that narrowed his red, rheumy eyes into slits, Numan was not the friendliest-looking person you ever met. During the cold winter months, his slightly menacing appearance grew even more sinister when he alternately donned either a waist-length, rich brown leather jacket or a heavy, green woolen overcoat redolent of Soviet Russia. When I first met him, he seemed as tight-lipped and introverted as Qassim was boisterous and extroverted. When he was with Qassim in public, Numan would clam up and let his boss do the talking and soak up the limelight. Because 7th Division was the JaOC's only organic infantry division, Qassim micromanaged the hell out of it. Despite this, Numan always remained silent in Qassim's presence. However, when Qassim wasn't around, Numan would talk a mile a minute.

One look at Numan and you knew the guy had street creds. Originally from Baghdad, he had joined the army the same year as Qassim. Between 2005 and 2009, he had served as 7th Division's chief of staff; from there, he became the operations director at the Anbar Operations Command. In 2012, he assumed command of 7th Division's 27th Brigade, and one year later he was nearly killed in an ambush. An exploding improvised explosive device (IED) mangled his right hand, embedded shrapnel in one of his eye sockets, and wounded him in the hip so severely that he walked with a permanent limp that made his gait look like a waddle. Four years after the ambush, he was still receiving regular medical treatment for his eye injuries and his destroyed hand, which frequently succumbed to vicious infections.

In one regard, Numan fit the male Arab stereotype: he had four wives. Qassim and the other Iraqi officers ribbed him mercilessly. In previous years, Numan had shaved his thinning locks, but the other senior officers proclaimed he now kept his hair long, dyed, and styled to please his demanding young wives. The Iraqis also joked that he had resorted to eating endless servings of virility-inducing dates to keep his libido supercharged. Like Qassim, Numan was a committed chain-smoker, although in recent months he had attempted to quit after pressure from his wives. He regularly popped pieces of Nicorette gum from foil blister-packs and chewed them manically, a measure I was pretty sure wouldn't last. Between his partnership with Qassim and the stresses of his job, it would only be a matter of time before he resumed his habit with gusto.

Once he warmed up to us, Qassim conveyed his frustration with Staff Lieutenant General Abdul Amir Rashid Yarallah, the deputy commander of Iraq's

Combined Operations Command. The Iraqi government had designated Abdul Amir as the overall commander for operations in western Iraq, and he had been the senior commander for the Mosul operation the previous year. He maintained a direct line to the prime minister, and he generally had the final word on all operational plans. Qassim wasn't exactly the president of Abdul Amir's fan club. As we discussed the coming operation, he declared his preference for the JaOC forces to clear Rayhanah, Anah, and Rawah in quick succession. In Qassim's mind, the clearance of all three urban centers would be part of one single operation. However, Abdul Amir had been direct with Qassim, telling him to take only Rayhanah and Anah and then hold there before moving on to Rawah.

There was something my new partner hadn't told me that I later learned from the Coalition leaders in Baghdad: Abdul Amir privately worried Qassim would make it through Rawah, declare victory, and then refuse to continue onward. A heavily populated peninsula town on the northern bank of the Euphrates River halfway between Haditha and the Syrian border, Rawah was the proposed site of Qassim's future headquarters. Securing it early would enable him to plant roots and make the rest of the clearance someone else's problem. As far as he was concerned, 7th Division's area of operations and, by extension, the JaOC's, would stop at Rawah. There was more to it, though, than just Qassim wanting a new headquarters. Seventh Division's brigades had reached their limit in checkpoints and battle positions along Route Bronze. As Fridriksson had explained months earlier, the JaOC couldn't clear all the way to Al Qa'im without at least one more infantry division, but Abdul Amir consistently refused Qassim's requests to assign forces from 8th Division to him. Qassim was certain the Shi'a militia groups had something to do with it.

During our first KLEs together, Qassim was remarkably open about his paranoia surrounding the SMGs. He believed Abdul Amir was susceptible to pressure from both the SMGs and Staff Major General Mahmoud al-Falahi, the commander of the Anbar Operations Command who, Qassim insisted, worked directly with and through the Shi'a militia groups. As our meetings grew more frequent and his trust in our team took root, he routinely asked Kelly and me about SMG activity. He only spoke about the militia groups when he was with Leibfried, Awtry, Kelly, and me—and no one else from the Coalition was in the room. Similarly, the only Iraqi officers with whom Qassim would discuss the SMGs were Numan, Brigadier General Kiffa, and Colonel Ahmed. Together, the quartet had earned the nickname "the Fantastic Four" from Fridriksson's team. They were rarely seen apart from one another, and they made most of the decisions in the JaOC.

Kiffa, Qassim's chief fire support officer, oversaw all the corps' artillery and rocket battalions. He was a serious officer, at least until you got to know him and had earned his trust. Only then would he open up and unleash his sense of humor. Like Qassim, he was an unabashed chain-smoker, and he affixed a deeply stained filter to the slim Iraqi Marlboros he smoked incessantly. Also like his boss, he carried a massive gut, which he hid behind a perfectly pressed, albeit untucked, uniform blouse. With his salt and pepper hair buzzed down to the scalp and his habit of periodically shaving his finely groomed mustache, Kiffa appeared to have internalized at least *some* aspects of western militaries. But that wouldn't help his career progression. As a simple brigadier general—not a *staff* brigadier general—he would never be a contender for one of the top jobs in the organization. I appreciated his sense of humor the most. Once he got going with the jokes, he would smile broadly before bursting into gales of deep, belly-shaking laughter. He typically led the charge in ribbing Numan about his wives, his heroic sex drive, and his improbable, slicked-back hairdo.

If there was an enigma among the Fantastic Four, it was Colonel Ahmed. Pear-shaped, with an enviable coif of swept-back silver and black hair, Ahmed was the great observer. With his sad, green eyes moving slowly about the room and a cigarette always burning between his fingers, he scrutinized everyone and everything each time we sat down for a KLE. Throughout the deployment, no matter how close we got with him and no matter how many resources we leveraged, we never truly learned what his actual job was. Although the JaOC already had an intelligence officer—a Shi'a assigned from Baghdad whom Qassim wouldn't trust any farther than he could lob him—Ahmed essentially served in that capacity, and he developed a close relationship with Major Kelly. He had a deceptively keen sense of humor, and despite their seniority he and Kiffa were routinely seen together cutting up, laughing, and giggling as they lit each other's smokes. Everyone has a battle buddy, someone whose mere presence transports them back to the fourth grade. It was no different for Kiffa and Ahmed; that shit transcends cultures and nationalities.

Kiffa and Ahmed were Qassim's closest advisors, the only two officers who could talk him down when he got spun up. Over time, they would become our "inside men." Whenever things grew tense with Qassim, or if I needed an unfiltered message relayed to him, or if we wanted to plant a seed in his mind, Kelly and I would pull Kiffa and Ahmed aside in a private "come to Jesus" session and tell them what we needed. Both Iraqi officers would prove to be two of our most valuable assets in developing what turned out to be an often-strained relationship between Qassim and me.

8

SPEED = AUSTERITY + RISK

IN DECEMBER 2016, just months before our team formed, the senior Coalition commander for Operation Inherent Resolve issued Tactical Directive #1, paving the way for units such as ours to clear and approve their own fire support. It was a significant breakthrough in the way the Coalition was fighting the campaign. In the conflict's initial days, before it even had a name, President Barack Obama himself had been the sole target engagement authority (TEA) for strikes against the Islamic State fighters. He eventually delegated the authority to the CENTCOM commander, but that concession wasn't good enough given the fluid nature of the operation. One day in the summer of 2014, just weeks into the campaign, I received a phone call on my secure line in the Pentagon basement.

"Is this the same guy who graduated from Virginia in 1994?" a voice asked.

"Yeah," I replied. "Who the hell is this?"

He told me his name and then said, "We were in NROTC [Naval Reserve Officers Training Corps] together. I'm the commander for the crisis response element in Baghdad right now. I found your name on the bottom of the deployment order that sent my team out here. I need your help; I don't know what else to do."

He explained how his SEAL team had deployed to help secure the American diplomatic security compound in Baghdad. His unit was regularly observing ISIS forces, which were closing in on Iraq's capital.

"We can literally see these assholes on our feeds, laying IEDs, dropping mortars, and firing rockets," he said. "And we can't do anything about it." The twinge of near desperation in his voice was alarming. The guy I knew in college had been the picture of calm.

"TEA is all the way up at the CENTCOM level," he continued. "By the time we get strike approval, it's too late . . . the shitheads have moved on."

"Can't guarantee anything, but I'll see what we can do," I replied, knowing my reassurances were likely hollow ones. There wasn't a word in the dictionary that described how badly the president did not want to send troops back to Iraq. Accordingly, there was no appetite in the White House to give commanders on the ground the necessary authorities to strike targets without National Security Council approval or oversight.

In the following weeks, the JOD-CENT team engaged the lawyers on the Joint Staff and in the secretary of defense's office to determine a way to get on-scene commanders the requisite permissions to strike legitimate ISIS targets. One savvy Army lawyer, a human tank of an officer known for his ability to "get to yes" on just about any issue with the SecDef's entrenched lawyers, helped us craft the appropriate language. After several weeks, we were successful, and the new set of authorities delegated TEA to the level of the overall Coalition commander. It felt like a tiny coup on our part, but it wasn't until many months later that I truly understood the impact our JOD-CENT team had made on the campaign. Walking through a parking garage in Crystal City one afternoon, I heard someone yell my name. It was my college classmate—the SEAL commander from Baghdad. He ran over to shake my hand and clap me on the back. The change in authorities we had championed became the turning point for his team in Baghdad, and the delegation of target engagement authority had drastically sped up the process to strike enemy targets.

With the December tactical directive further delegating TEA, commanders at my level were no longer beholden to decision-makers far away in Baghdad or Kuwait when it came to kinetic strike approval for self-defense, of either Coalition or Iraqi forces. Additionally, we now had the authority to approve dynamic strikes in support of the Iraqi army if the strike met a certain collateral damage threshold. I would only need to coordinate with Qassim and receive Iraqi MoD approval before I could authorize a bomb dropping from a plane, a missile launching from a drone, or a rocket firing from a HIMARS launcher. It was an incredible responsibility, and it required much training to ensure teams like mine were prepared to make the hard calls associated with delivering Coalition ordnance on a battlefield crowded with civilians.

The man to whom I would entrust that responsibility was Maj Chris Julian, the task force's fires and effects coordinator. A loud, almost boisterous artillery officer from coastal San Juan Capistrano, California, he occupied the most space in the room no matter who was present. A California State University–San Marcos graduate, he was a remarkable blend of liberal southern California surfer dude and conservative-minded hardliner. With features vaguely resembling the actor Chris Pine, he was an avid weightlifter who believed Arnold Schwarzenegger was a national treasure and *Pumping Iron* was one of the greatest films ever produced. Although his voice had a deep, grating drawl to it, he could do a very passable Schwarzenegger impression. He was in continuous pursuit of what he referred to only as "gains"—layers of heavy-duty muscle forged from dedicated gym time.

I never really understood Julian's true political leanings, but he seemed to have a strange fascination with Donald Trump. He often provided a running commentary during our staff meetings, mimicking the president's over-the-top banter by punctuating others' comments with Tourette's-like outbursts of "*FACT!*" or "*SAD!*" If our higher headquarters or an adjacent unit was not performing to his almost unattainable standards, they were, he would announce to everyone, "failing." Or he would describe the situation as "disgusting." He was an intense, almost in-your-face officer, and he alternated between being a highly respected team builder and divisive antagonist—almost a bully in some regards. Near the deployment's end, when the new team arrived to relieve us, his first interaction with their high-strung logistics officer was classic Chris Julian.

"You gonna get it done?" he asked.

"Get what done?" the officer replied.

"*It*," he said, leaning in. "Are you gonna get *IT* done?"

We all hated the Islamic State and everything they stood for, but Julian *really* hated them. He never referred to the terror group as ISIS. Instead, he opted to use the term *Da'esh*—possibly because that word was supposedly offensive to devout members of the organization. But he took it one step further by pronouncing it with such flat contempt that it came out sounding like *desh*. You could almost hear the lower case "d" in his voice. Everything on our ISR feeds that looked suspicious to him automatically belonged to the enemy. There were *desh* motorcycles, *desh* cars, *desh* bongo trucks, *desh* buildings . . . the inventory was endless. If suspected enemy fighters were standing around in the open, Julian would describe them as "just *desh* assholes doing *desh* things."

Julian had valid reasons for his adrenaline-fueled, aggressive dark side. He knew we were involved in serious business—business that demanded strong minds, strong bodies, and strong wills to win. His experience had taught him that, and he refused to tolerate weakness or mediocrity. I could accept his rowdiness because he was so damned good at his job. The country had been at war for his entire career, and like many of his peers he had deployed to "The Show" several times. As a second lieutenant in 2003, he had been an artillery forward observer for one of the Marine infantry battalions advancing on Baghdad. He returned to Iraq the following year and then later served a tour in Afghanistan. Now, as a major, he was a subject matter expert at planning, coordinating, and executing fire support, and he led a team of targeteers and JTACs within our fires and effects coordination center (FECC). Once we assumed control from the outbound team and were executing missions in support of the Iraqis, Julian and his fires chief would become the conductors of the COC orchestra.

Two days before the transfer of authority, I attended a video teleconference with Julian's Marines and several other key staff members to complete required training for ground force commanders and on-scene commanders. Back in

Camp Pendleton we had discussed the same topics, so the subject matter was familiar. Once the session was complete, I gave the team my guidance.

"Remember, the ISF is our customer," I said. "We will leverage our fires in support of the *Iraqis*; we're not doing it for ourselves.

"We must exercise tactical patience and find the right target with the right munition," I continued. "When it comes to targeting, we will not rush to failure. We will not chase guys on motorcycles around the battlespace unless we think they'll lead us to something bigger. And it's not just a matter of overkill or proportionality; there is also a PGM shortage in theater. A Hellfire for one dude on a motorcycle is an expensive way to get rid of ISIS.

"When it comes to fires approval, I am the sole approval authority within the team. In my absence, fires approval succession is the deputy, the OpsO, and then the fires officer. It's that way because I own all the risk. The FECC team is paid for its proficiency, not to make calls to drop ordnance.

"One last thing," I said, looking each Marine in the eyes. "When it comes to targeting, we must be professional killers, not professional murderers. Does everyone in here know the difference?" Heads nodded.

"Remember what the guys in Baghdad said: our procedures must be so good that they will withstand scrutiny two hours or two *years* after we execute a strike. Because you can be absolutely certain of one thing," I emphasized. "If we screw it up just once, they'll be out here in a heartbeat, crawling up our asses with microscopes."

The transfer of authority between the two teams came and went on August 13. As it always seemed during the turnover between two units, the departing team was eager to get away from the grind and back home to their families. We were just as ready to get our nine-month-long show on the road. There were many decisions facing us, decisions Fred knew I would have to make but could not until he and his team got the hell out of the way. The first revolved around Tactical Assembly Area (TAA) Sagrah and the role it would play in the clearance operation.

The new and improved name for a forward operating base, TAA was now part of the approved lexicon in theater. I wondered if the term had taken hold because of the negative connotations "FOB" had earned over the years. It was indeed now a dirty word, the doctrinal equivalent of persona non grata, and one of the worst slurs anyone could suffer was being called a "fobbit." The decision whether to build TAA Sagrah had consumed a lot of the task force's bandwidth in the previous months. Originally envisioned as a mere launch pad to support the Iraqis for the opening stages of the MERV clearance, it had grown into an outpost that was equal parts artillery base, medical evacuation (MEDEVAC) station, supply staging point, and forward command post. The planners wanted to position it as far forward as possible to maximize the range of the cannon artillery templated to deploy there. That meant building it along 7th Division's forward line of troops, just south of the small town of Sagrah.

As Baghdad's interest shifted from Mosul to Al Anbar, there was a corresponding focus on TAA Sagrah. However, there had been no corresponding uplift in resources or support to build the outpost, and so the project sat dormant until our arrival. With the problem now in our laps and the clearance operation set to begin in three weeks, we were under the gun to determine if the outpost was really a requirement. None of the smaller operations Qassim's forces had conducted in previous months required the construction of forward positions. Instead, all Coalition surface fire support had come from the M109 Paladin tracked artillery systems and HIMARS launchers aboard Al Asad. And while Sagrah was many miles outside of the Paladins' range fans, it was still within HIMARS range. But HIMARS could not be the only precision surface fire support asset. The GPS-guided rockets were just too expensive, and there were not enough of them to go around.

As the mission came into focus, it became clearer that the outpost was indeed necessary to support the operation. But how prepared was the Coalition to source the manpower, equipment, and materials to build it? For all its capability aboard Al Asad, the task force had remarkably little capacity to do much outside the wire. With their national caveats firmly in place, the Brits and Danes were off the table when it came to securing and guarding expeditionary outposts. The Coalition had dedicated its high-demand engineering assets, which were necessary to build berms, fill Hesco baskets, and lay gravel, to base expansion efforts aboard Al Asad. There was a simultaneous demand for their skills elsewhere in theater, especially Syria.

One thing we *did* possess was enough rolling stock. Over the years, the task force had amassed an impressive fleet of tactical vehicles. It was a patchwork of legacy Marine Corps vehicles SPMAGTF had left aboard the base after establishing the task force, along with Army vehicles that had trickled in over the years. There were MATVs, 7-ton medium tactical vehicle replacement (MTVR) trucks, light medium tactical vehicle cargo trucks, and new MaxxPro MRAPs (mine-resistant ambush-protected vehicles). What we *didn't* have was the company of dedicated drivers, vehicle commanders, and gunners necessary to crew the vehicles properly. The task force was also short on critical expeditionary communications gear and the technicians to run and maintain it.

I learned all this from Maj Greg Duesterhaus during our team's first future operations (FOPs) update. Over the course of the deployment, the FOPs updates in my office became as much a family affair among the staff as anything else we did. The updates would morph into weekly "skull sessions" where we identified and sought solutions to the various problems facing us. All were invited, and everyone's thoughts and ideas carried equal weight. Many staff members looked forward to the updates, and it didn't take long for them to become standing-room-only affairs where attendees staked out territory well in advance of kickoff time. I would often be doing work at my desk when one or two Marines would slip in, plop down on the couch, and pull out a book to pass the time until the meeting started. There were times when the gatherings were so packed with Marines drinking Rip Its, chewing tobacco, eating candy, or sipping coffee that it seemed the updates had turned into purely social episodes. But the sessions were invaluable, and they regularly produced decisions from me, and workable plans to execute those decisions. I had no idea how the weekly updates evolved into such coffeehouse, think-tank get-togethers, but I'm sure Duesterhaus had a lot to do with it.

Serving double duty as the team's assistant operations officer *and* future operations officer ("FOPsO"), Duesterhaus was a supply officer who had come from 3rd Marine Aircraft Wing. I had nearly gagged when I heard the person slated to fill the role as my chief planner was a box-kicker. It was a natural bias I brought to the table, and I should have known better. There was no rule decreeing that planners must be combat arms officers. One superb planner who had worked for me the previous year was a logistics officer. And Major Kelly, who was a bona fide School of Advanced Warfighting graduate, was originally a supply officer before he became an intelligence officer. But Duesterhaus was not a SAW graduate, and that worried me in our first weeks as we framed the problems. My reservations vanished once he immersed himself in the myriad planning dilemmas facing us.

Duesterhaus redefined the stereotype of the skivvy-stacking, bean-counting supply officer. As a lieutenant in 2006, he had dual-hatted as his unit's supply officer *and* as the leader of his commander's personal security detail in Iraq—no minor feat given the geographic distances the Marines governed back then. The fact that he was back in Al Anbar twelve years later, grappling with a new set of planning problems centered on those same geographic distances, was not lost on either of us. Despite his periodic aloofness, he was a serious-minded officer who possessed the interpersonal skills necessary to communicate with and understand people with many different points of view. He was also an engaging public speaker. Before we even departed the United States, I assigned him the role as the team's lead briefer for the onslaught of VIPs who would flood Al Asad during our tenure there.

As our operational tempo accelerated, his planning sessions increased in frequency and length. I would often wander into his workspace in search of a cup of coffee, only to find the team's staff officers gathered around the room in various stages of dress, doing the same things they did during the weekly updates: consuming caffeine, sugar, and nicotine at alarmingly unhealthy rates. The room would buzz with conversation as the crowd of Marines either stood, sat unsteadily in wobbly chairs, or sprawled out on a peeling, slowly melting couch that looked straight out of a landfill. He would stand next to a dry-erase board, diligently capturing facts, assumptions, limitations, decision points, and all the other data necessary to develop the courses of action for approval. The team's staff officers were a talented, creative bunch, but sometimes their planning sessions yielded little more than additional questions and requests for information. The Sagrah outpost issue was one of those episodes.

"This is a bigger problem than we anticipated back in CONUS when we first talked about going outside the wire with the Iraqis," he explained. "They need the assembly area built before 10 September, but the timeline doesn't support it. There isn't a true appreciation for the piece of land that was selected for the outpost. EOD [explosive ordnance disposal] hasn't cleared it yet, and we don't have the organic resources necessary to build it to the original specs."

"All the paperwork for the life support contract is in place," Major Math-wick added. "But it will take several weeks to get approved and put in place."

"What's the contract include?" I asked.

"Shower trailers, Port-A-Jons, gravel, billeting tents, laundry service," she replied. "And the local contractors to build it and operate it."

"Well, Jesus," I said. "We don't need all that *shit*."

"The op will probably be over before it all gets put in place," Major Awtry said. "We need to get this thing done fast."

"If we can't get it built in time and get the cannons in place," Major Julian said. "We'll need priority for HIMARS, and fixed-wing CAS [close air support] stacked up."

"And armed ISR," added Major Kelly. "They should darken the skies with it."

"Agree with all," I said.

"I think we can look at Sagrah this way," Duesterhaus said, pointing to a formula underlined on one of the slides: *Speed = Austerity + Risk*.

"Yeah, I got it," I said, recalling a lesson I had learned in the Pentagon. "Good, fast, and cheap . . . you can only have two of the three."

With the short timeline staring us down, we agreed to take a phased approach to the assembly area's construction. It would begin first as a firebase, and then gradually expand with the arrival of each new enabling capability. However, the resourcing issue was the key problem we still hadn't solved. And now that our team was squarely in the driver's seat, *we* owned the problem. So the question dogging us now was: Could we solve it?

9

LION MARCH

ON AUGUST 19, less than a week after the swap with Fridriksson's team, we executed our first "Lion March"—the designation for expeditionary advise and assist missions to the JaOC headquarters that Paul Nugent had pioneered the previous year. Lion March iterations had grown more frequent under Fridriksson's watch, in part because tensions over conventional troops going outside the wire had relaxed. There was a growing acceptance in theater that Coalition advisors would be effectively useless to the Iraqis if they couldn't accompany their partners into the contested battlespace. It was hard to believe this was even an issue. In 2008, the only way teams like mine could succeed was because we had the latitude to chase our partners around the battlespace at a moment's notice. Back then, there hadn't been a requirement to submit intricate plans for approval.

The tolerance at higher headquarters for vanilla units such as ours to move around outside the wire was not nearly as high as it was for the special operations units. In their community, those in charge expected such road trips for the operators to accomplish their partnering mission. No one outside of the SOF world seemed to care that bearded dudes were racing all over Mesopotamia, but God forbid one of the great unwashed, general-purpose force units dare to ask to accompany the Iraqis. Fortunately for us, that mindset faded over time. However, and despite repeated assurances to the contrary by our higher headquarters, there was no room for error, be it a vehicle mishap, a negligent weapon discharge, or stumbling into an enemy ambush as we ventured into the battlespace.

With each Iraqi battlefield victory, the region's Islamic State fighters acted like their backs were up against the wall. Some in the Coalition believed the enemy would attack conventional American forces if the opportunity presented itself. Others insisted ISIS would not risk incurring the wrath of the United States with such a misstep. Such an attack, the thinking went, would free U.S. forces from the leash that had held them back during the conflict's first three years. I wasn't willing to take that bet. Nor was I willing to bet the malign Shi'a militia groups roaming around the country with impunity would never turn their guns on the Americans. We prepared accordingly, and I was confident in the Marines' abilities. They were well trained, and they carried so much firepower every time we exited the wire that they almost *welcomed* an enemy attack. Still, I had a growing sense that a successful attack against one of our Lion March outings would resurrect the risk-averse culture that had previously permeated the theater. At the very least, it could spell the end for the missions outside the wire that Nugent and Fridriksson had worked so hard to perfect.

I would have preferred for our first Lion March to be a simple tactical movement to ease us into the water, but the accelerating situation in Al Anbar demanded otherwise. The mission was twofold: conduct a site survey of the area templated for TAA Sagrah, and meet with Qassim at his Haditha headquarters. As Major Duesterhaus had underscored during our first FOPs update, the draft blueprint for Sagrah placed it along the forward line of Iraqi troops. On paper, the outpost was in a tactically important position to support the ISF assault. Nevertheless, our combat engineers and EOD team still needed to conduct an actual site survey before we could continue planning.

That morning, our vehicle patrol rolled out of the green zone's Camp Havoc to link up with a 7th Division escort team before heading north. Another significant change from 2008 was the absolute requirement for Coalition units to have Iraqi military escorts when traveling outside the wire. Although there was a force protection component to it, more important was the message to the Iraqi people who watched the vehicle columns roll up and down their roads. Gone were the days of American service members and private security contractors driving around at will, muscling civilian traffic off the roads, and hurling frozen water bottles at the windshields of Iraqi drivers who had made the mistake of getting too close. Escorts now meant Coalition forces went where the Iraqi military wanted them to go, *when* it wanted them to go. "No unpartnered movements" was a common refrain during the weekly Coalition video teleconferences. The policy was understandable. We were the Iraqis' guests, and it only made sense that they would insist on escorting us. However, the Iraqi soldiers would eventually become unreliable, and they were often late to the designated link-up points. I could tolerate the tardiness. But I was adamant that, if circumstances compelled me to launch our quick reaction force (QRF) to get Coalition forces out of a jam, I would not wait for a chaperone.

Our escort met us at the northernmost gate of Al Asad's perimeter. Beyond was a barren stretch of land that led to Baghdadi, a small garrison town along the palm-tree-lined banks of the Euphrates River. Al Asad's final barricaded checkpoint, alternately known as either "Hammer Gate" or "Hummer Gate," was the typical link-up point for the Iraqis and Coalition teams departing the base. Joining our escort, Numan met us with an armada of high-mobility multipurpose wheeled vehicles (HMMWV, or simply "Humvee") bristling with soldiers and weapons. It was a peculiar sensation, rolling out of the wire with our heavily armed and armored MATVs and MaxxPros sandwiched between the thin-skinned Iraqi Humvees—proof that, despite visible differences in lethality and survivability, this was the Iraqis' show now.

In subsequent months, as our movements outside the wire increased in frequency and distance, the escorts became more and more anemic. They eventually consisted of one or two pickup trucks that might or might not have heavy weapons. But that was never the case when our escort included either Numan or Qassim. Any time one of their VIPs traveled, the Iraqis broke out their best Humvees, and the *jundis* who formed the security detail were thoroughly disciplined—even if they weren't completely outfitted with the gear they needed to do the job.

Among the Iraqi soldiers, looking good seemed at least as important as being appropriately equipped to fight. Like the generals who led them, the *jundis*, especially those tasked with high-visibility jobs like the personal security detail or headquarters sentry duty, were always impeccably dressed. They wore crisply pressed uniforms tailored to their slender frames, and they tightly folded their shirt sleeves high up their spindly arms the same way Marines did in garrison back home. Most *jundis* sported plate carriers, which rarely included armored plates. Because supply chain problems limited them to only one or two magazines of rifle ammunition, they filled the empty pouches on their gear with black foam blocks. It was bizarre. For nearly two decades, I had railed against a system that continued to heap more and more weight on the backs of Marines. Our body armor had gotten heavier, not lighter. We had begun carrying more ammunition and equipment, not less. Our mobility and, by extension, lethality, had diminished. It was the rare Marine who returned from a combat deployment without an accompanying inventory of aching, degenerating joints from shouldering such heavy physical burdens. Yet here were the Iraqi soldiers, creating the illusion of carrying more gear simply because they had seen the Americans do it for years.

A fascination with tactical clothing also existed among Iraqi soldiers and many of our interpreters. The most popular brand was 5.11 Tactical, which had become synonymous with American private security contractors during the previous fifteen years. Iraqi soldiers proudly wore chest rigs and other equipment styled after 5.11, with its ubiquitous Velcro attachments and Fastex clips. As the months grew colder, many *jundis* draped themselves in jackets and fleeces that, upon closer examination, were almost never actual 5.11 gear at all. The high-end clothing line was beyond their meager salaries—when they got paid, that is. Their natural response was to wear garments from several knockoffs that had appeared in Iraq's bazaars over the years. Most popular were obscure brands like S.11 and A.5.1.1., whose style and logos so closely mirrored the hellishly expensive 5.11 products in both appearance and function that no one seemed to care they weren't the genuine articles. I didn't know what bothered me more. Was it the *jundis* compensating for the lack of ammunition by filling their pouches with weightless ballast, or was it their appropriation of a fashion made popular by private security contractors? I guess the ballast issue was understandable. After all, there were appearances to maintain. But I took issue with the Iraqi soldiers modeling their wardrobes after private security contractors—the same mercenaries who arguably had done just as much damage to the American reputation in Iraq as the U.S. military had with all its unrestrained might in the years between 2003 and 2011.

A slab of dun-colored, undulating ground, the site selected for TAA Sagrah was more than "along the Iraqi forward line of troops" as the planners in Baghdad had described. The real estate set aside for the outpost was *on* the forward line itself, with a berm reinforced by Iraqi fighting positions serving as the western boundary. Months earlier, the attacking Iraqi forces had nearly leveled Sagrah to liberate it from the Islamic State defenders, and rubbled buildings lined the cracked and pock-marked asphalt. Powerlines drooped across the streets. In some areas, the grimy silhouettes of unexploded house-borne IEDs, exposed during the fighting, were visible.

Sagrah was the most recent ISIS-held urban center to fall to the Iraqi advance across Al Anbar. Anticipating an eventual assault, the defenders had ringed the town with obstacles, including a minefield so enormous that its outline was visible on commercial Google Earth imagery. With the entire town surrounded by concealed IEDs baked into the soil by the scorching desert sun, our intel analysts cautioned us to consider everywhere off the pavement an active minefield. The coppery glint of command wires strewn along the road shoulders twinkled in the afternoon's white-hot rays. As

Marines dismounted vehicles to relieve their swollen bladders, they found themselves pissing on the same wires ISIS fighters had used to detonate IEDs against attacking Iraqi forces months earlier.

Despite the incredible sums of money the U.S. military had pumped into the counter-IED effort, the evolution of the devices continued unabated. We now faced the latest generation of a weapon that had accounted for more casualties in the Long War than anything else on the battlefield. Between 2003 and 2011, IEDs in Iraq were most frequently pieces of unexploded ordnance (UXO) left in the wake of the Coalition's rapid 2003 advance across the country. Once the insurgency got ahold of the material and booby-trapped it, that same speed came back to bite us in the ass. The insurgents soon mastered the art of concealing their IEDs, and in the United States an entire industry sprouted to teach deploying service members how to detect and defeat the powerful, hidden roadside bombs. What the devices my Marines had encountered in Afghanistan lacked in explosive power, they more than made up for in ingenuity and camouflage. Without the same bottomless reservoir of UXO to draw from, the Taliban fighters had relied on bombs crafted from fertilizer, encased in plastic cooking oil jugs, and triggered by low-metallic pressure switches. Baked into the hard scrabble trails and dirt alleyways, they were nearly impossible to spot. Although their explosive yield was considerably less than Iraq's roadside bombs, they were more than powerful enough to dismember and kill their intended target: infantrymen patrolling on foot.

In the years since it seized control of Al Anbar, the Islamic State had gone industrial in the IED manufacturing realm. With the retreating Iraqi army no longer a credible threat to the invaders, ISIS reinforced its defensive positions across the province. They worked overtime to mass-produce IEDs of all shapes and sizes, and the results were impressive. The devices typically had milled casings filled with various grades of homemade explosive, and their triggers were long, waterproofed metal pressure strips. When you examined the strips, you could see the manufacturer's inspector seal stamped into them. There was no concern on the part of the ISIS engineers for the high metal content, nor was there much concern for camouflaging the minefields. They knew that, employed in mass, the IEDs would create obstacles large enough to compel any advancing force to address them one way or another. And, the enemy commanders knew, any approaching Iraqi force that slowed down long enough to breach an obstacle belt opened itself to attacks by suicide vehicle-borne IEDs (SVBIEDs) packed to the gills with explosives and piloted by fanatical ISIS fighters. Few enemy tactics ground an Iraqi advance to a halt faster than the detonation of a speeding, up-armored SVBIED. The explosive-laden juggernauts terrified the *jundis* almost as much as the Islamic State's remotely piloted, grenade-armed quadcopters silently hovering above, seeking concentrations of troops upon which to deliver their explosive payloads.

As our column came to a halt along the paved access road that branched north from Route Bronze toward Sagrah, the EOD and engineer teams dismounted. They swept the ground with their compact metal detectors while our vehicles idled nearby with their electronic countermeasures operating silently. With bushy mustaches, shirt sleeves cuffed to their elbows, and long hair poking out from beneath their rail-mounted Kevlar helmets, the two task force EOD technicians were easily distinguishable from the combat engineers working alongside them. If there were two Marines who played the role of the original counterculture buddy pair, it was SSgt. Austin Brian and Sgt. Tyler Rioux. Brian, a Saint George, Utah, native, had joined the Marine Corps in 2007 as a landing support specialist, and he made his first deployment to Iraq a year later. After transitioning to the EOD community, he deployed with SPMAGTF in 2015 to Kuwait, and he supported the newly established task forces at Al Asad and Al Taqaddum. Rioux, who had grown up in Saint Paul, Minnesota, and enlisted three years after Brian, similarly entered the service with what some would call a cushy, rear-echelon assignment. As a supply warehouse clerk, he had deployed to Afghanistan in 2011 to support an EOD unit. Enamored by the techs he supported, he reported to the schoolhouse several years later.

Although they never said as much, I got the impression both men had determined early in their enlistments that safe, administrative jobs in the rear was not how they had envisioned serving in the Marines. Like many techs across the Corps, they yearned for the responsibility—and probably the surging adrenaline rush—of working with live ordnance. In the early years of the Long War, techs across all branches of the military were busy with back-to-back deployments, regularly rendering as safe, explosively reducing, or exploiting IEDs for evidence in both theaters of operation. My Marines in 3/7 were the beneficiaries of this backbreaking operational tempo in Afghanistan, where the EOD team supporting our battalion dealt with nearly a thousand IEDs in just seven months. Now, with major combat operations declared over in both Iraq and Afghanistan, there were fewer and fewer opportunities for techs across the Marine Corps to ply their trade in "real world" deployments.

Brian and Rioux were an odd couple. While no one on the team, with the possible exception of the Marines in Major Julian's fires shop, was particularly rowdy or boisterous, both techs were quieter than most team members. They also pushed the limits when it came to grooming standards. That particular shortcoming riled Sergeant Major Leibfried, who was regularly on Brian's ass about his thick mustache, full head of auburn hair, and perceptible air of contempt for authority. When they weren't doing routine disposal work aboard Al Asad, the two men kept to themselves in their own quarters, sequestered far away from most of the team members in CHU City-1. Their tasks ranged from the mundane, such as collecting UXO on the base's live-fire range, to hairier situations. In one case, months later, they dealt with the aftermath of a Hellfire-armed MQ-1C Gray Eagle drone that inexplicably went haywire and collided with a Hesco barrier while taxiing on the airfield.

The survey team continued its work, and there was little for me to do but wring my hands as the Marines crept around the minefield. Then, almost as if he sensed my fidgeting, Numan invited me into town for chai at the headquarters of 1st Battalion, 28th Brigade (1/28), the 7th Division "hold force" garrisoned there. As my vehicle peeled away, I watched Brian and Rioux creep methodically across the ground in short, measured steps, studying the landscape for the telltale signs of IEDs. Their deliberate movement pattern was familiar. Despite the air-conditioning blowing in the cab of my truck, I was sweating bullets over the danger in which they were placing themselves. It was probably unnecessary for me to be so uneasy about Brian and Rioux doing the job for which they had trained exhaustively. But I had plenty of emotional scar tissue when it came to EOD techs working for me. During the mission briefing the previous evening, I had insisted the two Marines talk me through their actions on the objective.

"Look, I got it," I said as they protested my demand for details. "You're big boys, and I trust you. But don't fuck with me on this. I lost four techs in Sangin, including one KIA [killed in action]. So you'll understand why this has my attention."

In short order, Brian and Rioux confirmed the location of the IED belt in the northern third of the TAA, and with the broiling sun beating down on them they patiently marked each device. They stopped counting after twenty-five. Although Numan told me his soldiers had previously cleared the area, the EOD team and engineers confirmed our suspicions: before construction could begin, we would have to re-clear the ground with counter-IED equipment, surface graders, and human beings on foot. The clock was ticking.

As we returned from Sagrah and prepared to head to the JaOC headquarters, my vehicle paused to pick up Major Kelly, who had remained behind in one of the trucks guarding the survey teams. The security vehicles had parked along the berm on the far side of the site, and someone passed word to Kelly to head to the road for us to pick him up. When I heard this on the radio, it dawned on me what was about to happen. I looked out my window just in time to see him walking along a path across the open assembly area. It was bad enough that Marines were wandering around for photo opportunities on the berm in direct view of enemy fighters to the west. But seeing Kelly ambling through an uncleared minefield sent me over the edge. Before I could holler into the radio, one of the guard vehicles put it in gear, picked him up, and delivered him safely to us on the access road.

Although no one on the team ever spoke about it, everyone knew Kelly's younger brother had been killed by an exploding IED in Sangin in 2010. John rarely mentioned his brother. I was working in the Pentagon when news of Robert Kelly's death hit the wire, and after the attention the tragedy had created, I could understand why John preferred to remain silent. At various austere locations he would periodically pull out a black t-shirt emblazoned with a picture of his brother and the words "Team Kelly," take a quick photo with it, and return it to the faded, ratty backpack he schlepped around with him. But he never talked about his brother's death. And who could blame him? Had the same thing happened to my own brother, it would have wrecked me emotionally. And yet, even though I understood the circumstances, when I saw Kelly later that evening I jumped in his shit.

"Hey man, what the fuck," I said. "You know better than that."

He protested, and I cut him off.

"Look, don't do that again. You know what I'm talking about."

In other words, *Don't put me in a position where I have to explain why General Kelly's second son was also killed by an IED.*

The day after our first Lion March, as we reviewed notes from our meeting with Qassim and analyzed data collected in Sagrah, Major General White approved a course of action (COA) for the opening phase of Operation Desert Lion—the operation to clear Islamic State forces from the Middle Euphrates River Valley. Nugent's and Fridriksson's teams had designed a plan to support the Iraqi advance along one main axis from Sagrah to clear and secure the urban centers of Rayhanah and Anah, but resources to support it were scarce. Although the kinetics in Mosul had wound down, that part of the theater was still consuming energy in the form of manpower, equipment, and ordnance. Moreover, the next step in the greater campaign in Iraq—the battle for the northern city of Tal Afar—was under way. Although the Coalition headquarters still considered Al Anbar the deep fight, we would be wrestling for table scraps as we moved forward. Among my staff and the Coalition planners, we agreed Desert Lion would likely be an incremental operation, with pauses of varying lengths between phases. Wary of historical analogies and comparisons to World War II, I nevertheless began referring to Al Anbar as the "Pacific Theater of Inherent Resolve." Together with our undermanned and under-equipped partners, we would, in effect, be conducting a gradual island-hopping campaign toward Al Qa'im while most of the Coalition and Iraqi resources and attention—both military *and* political—focused on the real prize: the country's north.

The evening after White's decision, a swarm of CJFLCC planners descended upon Al Asad. They set up shop in the command post, eager to assist our team in the detailed planning for TAA Sagrah and the MERV clearance.

"They're offering to help," I told my incredulous staff. "So, make them feel welcome, and listen to what they have to say."

Before long, the planners and the task force staff were rolling up their collective sleeves and sorting out details of the operation's opening phase. In the process, we discovered that, despite all the hard work the previous teams had put into planning Desert Lion, there was still a lot we didn't know . . . and a lot we *didn't know* about what we didn't know.

And the clock continued to tick.

10

HARD TO SWALLOW

ON THE EVENING OF AUGUST 21, the watch officer knocked on my door and told me the local police had delivered a seven-year-old Iraqi boy with a gunshot wound to our trauma unit. I walked to the medical bay, where a team of American, Danish, and Norwegian physicians was working to stabilize the child. A round had entered his chest and passed through his abdomen, eventually coming to rest in his bowels. He was as calm as could be, almost serene, until the doctors stabilized him and the shock of his injuries wore off. Then the wailing started. The sound transported me back in time to my battalion's medical tent in Afghanistan and all the young children the shock trauma platoon had treated during our tour of duty. For whatever reason, the physical destruction of adult human beings no longer seemed to faze me, but the sight of a young child meeting the business end of a rifle or dismembered by explosives still brought me to the verge of tears. Our Coalition surgical team worked on the boy throughout the night, and early the next morning they evacuated him to a local hospital. After that, there would be no telling what happened to him, no way to track his recovery and rehabilitation.

Watching our multinational team work together through the common language of medicine to patch up a local kid was the kind of thing that could make you feel good about yourself and what the United States was doing in Iraq. The whole scene briefed well. It made you think that, after everything we had screwed up between 2003 and 2011, we were finally doing things correctly. However, when it came to the policy governing medical treatment for the Iraqis, not much had changed. We weren't obligated to treat wounded Iraqi civilians or military personnel; the only real obligation we incurred was if it was a *proven* case of U.S.-caused civilian casualties (CIVCAS). Otherwise, each time someone brought a wounded or injured person to us for treatment, it became a judgment call by me or, in my absence, the deputy commander. The safe call would always be to refuse treatment; opening the door for one might lead to a flood of civilians lining up outside the gates. Treating Iraqis in our two-bed facility meant committing finite resources that we might need if a real emergency resulting in Coalition casualties occurred. And, from the advisor perspective, there was the overarching requirement to compel our partners to make their own system work for them. Yet, regardless of the considerations involved, we treated wounded, ill, and injured Iraqi military personnel all the time. Both Qassim and Numan, with their poor health and lingering battlefield injuries, were regular visitors to the medical bay. We frequently treated injured civilians too, especially those wounded by IEDs left behind by retreating Islamic State forces. And, truth be told, the medical personnel aboard Al Asad were hungry for patients to treat. The arrival of each casualty presented an opportunity for the doctors, nurses, corpsmen, and medics to apply and refine their perishable skills. To my knowledge, we never turned away any wounded Iraqis. The standard caveat was that, once our medical team stabilized the casualties, we would insist the Iraqi army or local authorities transport them to higher levels of medical care—if such a thing even existed in Iraq.

Even though it seemed like we were on the right track with medical treatment, we were doing other things that were hard to swallow. As Al Asad expanded, there was an accompanying increase in demand for billeting spaces—a demand that centered on individual housing units, not on the high-occupancy transient tents scattered around the camp. Part of the expansion plan included refurbishing CHUs, a process that frustrated me to no end and symbolized the rampant waste and corruption that had characterized much of the war in Iraq. The "repurposing" process included negotiating with the Iraqis to purchase the ancient housing units scattered along the Boulevard of Broken Dreams, where the U.S. military had handed them over prior to the American exodus in 2011. It didn't take long to put two and two together: we were buying back the same containers we had purchased years earlier—and the Iraqis were happy to oblige. They knew a good deal when they saw it; they also knew a sucker when one appeared. P. T. Barnum would have been proud.

The Coalition's build partner capacity effort, and the way it issued equipment to the Iraqi soldiers, was also perplexing. When a new class of recruits reported for training, the Danish team issued each Iraqi soldier a full complement of tactical equipment, including Kevlar helmet, body armor, and rifle. The soldiers did not receive canteens, as they were nowhere to be found—a revelation that truly confounded me. How was it that we could provide semiautomatic rifles and body armor sets by the thousands, but we couldn't figure out how to get the soldiers ordinary, Vietnam-era plastic canteens in a country where summer temperatures regularly soared well north of 100° Fahrenheit?

Learning more about the program's equipping procedures left me shaking my head. Once each *jundi* received his gear issue, the Iraqi battalion commander would sign for it all, technically assuming responsibility for the entire lot. It was common for upward of three hundred recruits to report on the first training day to receive their equipment, but then less than half would actually show up for the course's remaining six weeks. The previous year, C. J. Chivers had written a *New York Times* article detailing the numerous instances of U.S.-supplied weapons landing in the hands of ISIS fighters. The process Lieutenant Colonel Momme described sounded a lot like Chivers' *Times* piece.

"This is crazy," I said, studying the numbers of recruits we were training each month. "Where's the accountability? I mean, we're potentially arming the opposition."

Momme explained that the Coalition headquarters, which was responsible for the campaign's overall "Train and Equip" program, accepted the existing procedures. The program managers in Baghdad believed the weapons were accounted for because the Iraqi commanders were signing for them. I asked him to consider accounting for weapons the same way the Danish SOF team did. In their partnership effort with the A'ali Al Furat tribal force, Danish special operations forces (DANSOF) would issue and recover weapons on each day of training to compel the tribesmen to at least *show up* for the entire course. He humored me, promising to investigate it, but I doubted my request would bear any fruit. He eventually delivered the same news as he had at the outset: the Coalition leaders were content with the existing process, and there would be no changes. Equipping the Iraqi army was the primary method to entice them to commit to training, and there was no appetite in Baghdad to upset the apple cart. At our level, we could do little more than shrug our shoulders. If our higher headquarters running the Train and Equip program didn't care, why should we? But I often wondered if photos of M-16s issued by Momme's training teams would eventually end up on C. J. Chivers' Twitter feed.

On August 21, one of our counter-UAS systems detected the signal feed from an unidentified platform flying several kilometers from Camp Havoc. We initiated our battle drills, which included deconflicting the airspace around Al Asad and contacting all units aboard the base to ensure there were no friendly systems operating nearby. One of our countermeasure systems jammed the signal twice, and the feed subsequently disappeared from our screen. We had no idea what happened to it, and our inability to recover it and exploit its data frustrated us. A similar incident the following week led me to direct the creation of a daily UAS flight plan by all base units to avoid wasting time confirming who had platforms in the air at any given time. That way, when we received another unidentified signal, we could match it against existing flight plans. If the signal was not on the schedule, we would jam it. But we still had no actual *proof* that enemy drones were overflying our base. That wasn't the case with our sister task force at Al Taqaddum. They were observing regular overflights, and their counter-UAS efforts were similarly unsuccessful.

The enemy small drone threat was no laughing matter. Before our arrival, armed quadcopters and winged drones had killed several Coalition service members across the country, and the new tactic terrified the Iraqi soldiers. We had all seen cringeworthy videos of quadcopters keyholing grenades into open Iraqi tank hatches, and we would later view footage of a drone dropping munitions into an ordnance-packed soccer stadium that had been converted into an ammunition dump. The resulting inferno was a fiery hell on earth. Al Asad's miles of Hesco, T-walls, and concertina wire were no defense against a small quadcopter carrying a 40-mm grenade. It was only a matter of time, many believed, until a drone hovering over Al Asad's apron dropped a grenade on a fully armed and fueled AC-130J Ghostrider gunship. The ensuing shitstorm would be epic.

Although there was indeed a valid concern about the UAS threat, the propaganda videos tended to create a sort of mass hysteria, and the reports became the new UFO sightings of the twenty-first century. Bored and exhausted Marines and soldiers standing guard in perimeter towers were the greatest offenders. In time, many so-called "visual sightings" would turn out to be circling aircraft, or even orbiting satellites that were visible in the desert's crisp nighttime sky. Then there were the half-baked attempts across the theater to shoot down suspected drones with rifles and machine guns—acts so reckless, dangerous, and ultimately futile that I couldn't believe anyone would authorize them.

After several high-profile attacks early in the campaign, the Department of Defense program to counter enemy UAS activity accelerated much like the counter-IED effort had in the war's early years. Experimental systems regularly appeared at our doorstep, and the pattern was always the same: a civilian field service representative (FSR) would deliver the new system, brief its capabilities, and provide rudimentary training to the people assigned to operate it. The FSR would then disappear, never to be seen again, leaving us with another expensive piece of gear that required dedicated person-nel—personnel we didn't have to spare and who really weren't even qualified to operate the damned thing.

Whenever we confronted a suspected enemy UAS with our systems, we were never sure if the countermeasure worked or not because we could never recover the vehicle itself. Iraqi soldiers periodically retrieved drones that had crashed after running out of juice or outranging their operators, and we begged them to turn in the vehicles for exploitation. The *jundis* were reluctant to hand over anything that might have value, so we rarely got our hands on downed enemy systems. Later in the deployment, though, after the soldiers presented us with a handcrafted, winged UAS that had gone down outside the city of Anah, the forensic data we extracted from it led to a successful strike on an enemy position. Explaining the outcome of episodes like that to our Iraqi partners, plus the promise to return any captured devices after exploitation, paid dividends. The *jundis* would eventually turn in all sorts of captured enemy war material, including ordnance, weapons, IEDs, and explosive switches.

When our team first arrived at Al Asad, we received precise guidance from the Coalition leaders in Baghdad and Kuwait regarding how we should advise, assist, and enable the Iraqis. We must make them do the fighting; we must not do it for them. Perhaps more important, as advisors, we must not become the main effort. In other words, our higher headquarters warned us against any action we might take that could result in direct contact or engagement with Islamic State fighters. Particularly frowned upon were actions that could lead to friendly forces sustaining casualties or requiring extrication through the application of Coalition firepower and air support. Becoming the main effort, the reasoning went, would divert attention and precious support resources away from the Iraqis. That could then set the conditions for a return to the bad old days, when U.S. forces were the ones doing most of the fighting.

When it came to "becoming the main effort," the most precarious scenario was the touchy subject of "accompanying" operations with the Iraqis. Coalition forces sustaining casualties in such a situation would likely mean a tightening of the authorities that had enabled us to go outside the wire, which would represent a significant step backward in the campaign. The task force now retained the authority to accompany the Iraqis at the corps and division levels, which meant if Qassim and Numan wanted to maneuver around on the battlefield, then I could move with them outside the wire. The different

SOF teams, with their more permissive authorities, had the flexibility to accompany the Iraqi army and tribal militia units at the battalion and brigade levels. Moreover, almost from the moment we first met, Lieutenant Colonel Bruøygard insisted his Viking team had a national mandate to accompany 28th Brigade all the way across the province to the Syrian border.

Bruøygard's persistence about his mandate could be annoying, but I understood where he was coming from. Like me, he had operated with a permissive set of authorities in Afghanistan, and the constraints under which everyone labored in Iraq exasperated him. He bristled at the notion that his team was under my tactical control, and it frustrated him to no end that he had to submit a concept of operations (CONOP) for my approval before he could venture outside the wire for expeditionary advise and assist missions with 28th Brigade. He insisted that, if his team ran into trouble, he had all the necessary tools at his disposal to get them out of a jam: satellite communications, JTACs, heavy weapons, you name it. He had a point. One look at the inventory of top-shelf equipment the Norwegian government had provided his team convinced me he wasn't hurting in the firepower department. But then again, neither were the task force Marines. The problem was not whether Bruøygard's men and women would survive an ambush, but rather what the consequences would be for our overall mission if his team stumbled into becoming the main effort. It was like trying to make an overly gung-ho reconnaissance team understand that, if the enemy discovers them and a firefight ensues, they have effectively failed their mission.

As tenacious as he was, Bruøygard was correct about his need to get outside the wire with his partners, and I was sensitive about being perceived as the higher headquarters' overly restrictive commander. I had dealt with such intrusive bullshit enough myself, and like the child of an overbearing parent, I didn't want to pass that particular trait on to the next generation. August would soon end, and the Norwegian team needed another opportunity to meet and plan with Staff Brigadier General Qutaiba, 28th Brigade's commander, before Desert Lion kicked off. After reviewing a CONOP Bruøygard put together, I approved an overnight mission for his team on August 23. They would travel to Sagrah with their DANSOF counterparts, who also planned to meet with their A'ali Al Furat tribal partners inside the rubbled town.

Cultural rivalries aside, a natural partnership had developed between the two Scandinavian units. And, since the DANSOF team frequently drove to Sagrah to meet with A'ali Al Furat's commander, I saw no issue with their offer to ferry Bruøygard's team. After all, his vehicles and equipment were still further from full operating capability (FOC) than he cared to admit. On the morning of August 24, as the Norwegians and Danes sat with their partners for breakfast, they heard the deep rumble of approaching jet aircraft. A pair of low-flying SU-25 fighters screamed overhead, and moments later bombs exploded just three hundred meters from the dining soldiers. Two minutes later, another pair impacted one hundred meters closer. As the Scandinavians scrambled for cover, Qutaiba called his higher headquarters and confirmed the attack had come from an Iraqi Air Force sortie. He laughed at the pilots' incompetence, and as the rattled Danes and Norwegians returned to the dining room, he continued shoveling down his breakfast as if nothing had happened.

We would later learn the fighter pilots, who were attempting to hit targets in Rayhanah fifteen kilometers away, had misread their GPS displays. We never heard of any repercussions, and for the Iraqis it was just another day at the office. The accidental "green-on-blue" incident was a reminder for everyone that the Iraqi pilots did not yet possess the skill and precision necessary to deliver ordnance on the battlefield. The episode made it easier to understand why the Iraqis always wanted Coalition aircraft to drop bombs. To be sure, it was a way to preserve their own expensive munitions, but the Iraqi leaders also knew the Coalition pilots were more likely to hit enemy forces than friendly forces. They couldn't say the same about their own pilots yet.

11.

THE DECISION-MAKER

NOT LONG BEFORE our site survey in April, Fred Fridriksson warned me about a disagreement brewing between SPMAGTF and the task force. The conversation continued into the turnover once we arrived in theater, and the closer our team got to assuming responsibility for the mission, the more we got roped into the issue. The friction centered on what role SPMAGTF would play in western Al Anbar, and whether it should assume control of the task forces at Al Asad and Al Taqaddum. Several entities outside of Iraq had championed the idea for months, and there were strong opinions on both sides. Before long, I was neck-deep in the debate, and my position was not a popular one.

For months, the outbound SPMAGTF commander had recommended moving his headquarters from Kuwait to Al Asad. On the way to our site survey in April, we paused at Al Jaber, where the commander briefed me on his vision of SPMAGTF's role supporting the upcoming MERV operation and the overall campaign in Iraq. That vision included adjusting the command relationships so that the two Marine task forces would report to him. The new SPMAGTF commander, who arrived in theater at the same time I did, had also begun his own influence campaign to get his team to Al Asad.

It seemed the issue might die quietly in June, when the J-3 (Director of Operations) in Baghdad sent a curt email to a long list of field grade officers inside *and* outside of Iraq. His message was clear: cease and desist with the unannounced drive-bys and cold calls inundating him with good ideas about getting SPMAGTF involved in western Al Anbar. There were already plans in the can, he told everyone. If the Coalition needed SPMAGTF's help, it would ask for it. Besides, he added, the Iraqis still couldn't agree on a final plan *or* timeline, so offers to introduce new forces into the fight were premature. Regardless, he concluded, whatever role the Marine Corps' Kuwait-based crisis response unit might play would be a decision for the CENTCOM and MARCENT commanders—*not* the colonels and lieutenant colonels populating the "To" line.

For my part, I thought SPMAGTF was showing up to the party late. The time for the Marine Corps to go all in with its crisis response crown jewel had been 2014, when SPMAGTF first secured Al Asad and established the initial advise and assist mission there. Instead, the command element had returned to Kuwait and spent the following years providing forces for a never-ending stream of CENTCOM-approved theater coordinated assistance (TCA) requests. Designed for CENTCOM to preserve political capital with the Joint Staff and the Secretary of Defense, TCAs were short-duration missions executed by units already in theater. It was an in-house sourcing solution that kept the combatant commander from requesting even more forces than the secretary had previously allocated to him. As a result, since 2014, nearly every SPMAGTF commander had returned home aggravated that his unit had been little more than a spare parts bin for CENTCOM. And so, as the campaign in Iraq gradually shifted from Mosul to Al Anbar, the proposals by successive SPMAGTF commanders to take the helm gained steam.

I had known the current commander, Col Chris Gideons, since late 2001. We had been close friends ever since, and initially I looked forward to being in theater with him during the same deployment cycle. That feeling started to change when, during a joint pre-deployment planning session, he informed the audience that he considered Al Anbar Province SPMAGTF's area of operations. I kept quiet at the time, preferring not to ignite the debate in front of my Marines, and I regretted my silence the moment we set foot in theater. Gideons' team had already drafted a proposal to provide multiple advise and assist teams, as well as other enabling capabilities, for the approaching operation.

When the lines of communication opened between Gideons and me just days into the job, SPMAGTF's future role in Iraq was one of the first things he wanted to discuss. As far as he was concerned, Gideons told me, his outfit should take the lead during Desert Lion. Task Force Al Asad was a cobbled-together unit—a "B-team" lacking both capability and capacity to accomplish the mission. His command element, with the high-demand assets and staff depth necessary to get the job done, should become the battlespace owner and provide command and control for the entire operation. And, he added, it would free up my team to focus on its advising mission with Qassim. He noted that, in such a construct, the task force should work for him to ensure unity of command.

Gideons' implication was clear: my task force was the junior varsity team. He had the studs wearing the letterman jackets, and he intended to tell everyone who would listen that they belonged in Iraq, leading the coming fight. I disagreed, and our conversation ended with the matter unresolved. I was unconcerned, as I had not received a change of mission from Major General White. And, as Ashley had taught me many years earlier, I wasn't going to cry until I was hurt. Several nights later, Gideons raised the subject again, but this time it wasn't during a private session between the two of us. Instead, he made his pitch during a teleconference chaired by Task Force 51/5—the combined Navy and Marine Corps command in Bahrain that merged 5th Fleet's Task Force 51 and 5th Marine Expeditionary Brigade. To reinforce his commitment to the proposal, Gideons reiterated his plan during a subsequent teleconference between the leaders of SPMAGTF and both task forces. I could understand his desire to get his team into the fight—everyone wants to go to "The Show"—but I could not accept the way he was going about it. It was beginning to look like our long friendship might have to take a back seat.

The funny thing was, I didn't completely disagree with the idea of SPMAGTF relocating to Al Asad. Gideons' command element *did* possess more depth than my core team of eighty-five pipe-hitters. He also controlled unique capabilities, such as a squadron of tiltrotor MV-22 Ospreys, that would be useful once the Coalition greenlit the operation. But time was running out. Desert Lion was gaining momentum, and it was too late to inject another unit into the mix and expect it to have any real chance of succeeding. It would be better to introduce SPMAGTF the following May. By then, Desert Lion would likely be nearing completion, if not over.

Gideons wasn't the only one eager to see the Marine Corps take the lead in Al Anbar Province. There was a growing cabal of senior Marine leaders who seemed to feel the same way, among them the generals commanding Task Force 51/5 and I MEF, as well as the Commandant of the Marine Corps himself. The Marine Air-Ground Task Force concept had been the Marine Corps' bread and butter for decades. Its legacy and primacy were inviolable, and there were those in the institution who believed it was the panacea to any tactical, operational, *or* strategic problem. Some of us didn't see it that way, but we were the minority. It was heresy even to *suggest* the crisis response MAGTF might not be the correct force to apply to the problem set facing us. The overarching service mindset was simple: as Marines, Al Anbar Province was in our DNA. Ergo, if Marines were going to lead the operation in Al Anbar, then SPMAGTF was the only possible solution.

The narrative was spinning out of control, and soon it was on the lips of seemingly everyone outside of the team: *Task Force Al Asad is unable to command and control the operation; only SPMAGTF can save the day.* It was difficult not to be offended. For years, no one in the Marine Corps had paid attention to the task force. However, now that it was on its way to becoming the Coalition's main effort in Iraq, people were coming out of the woodwork saying it was "just an advisor team" that was incapable of doing anything else. That was a crock of shit, and everyone in our crew knew it. At the urging of both Nugent and Fridriksson, we had trained together as a battle staff. Since Day One we had planned for the eventuality of the clearance operation, and we had trained for a very specific mission set: enabling operations in support of a foreign partner force. We were better suited for the mission than the

SPMAGTF staff, which hadn't trained to partner with *or* support the Iraqis to the degree we had. Desert Lion was not intended to be a sweeping advance of American troops duking it out against Islamic State fighters in the desert and the cities. The Iraqi soldiers would be the ones doing the fighting; the task force would just backstop them as they maneuvered west.

Each time Gideons proposed that the task force fall under his tactical control, I politely declined, telling him I didn't support his plan. Never mind that I had no desire to take direction from another colonel, close friend or not. Such an arrangement would never fly with my partner. Qassim was certain Abdul Amir would tap him as the operation's overall Iraqi military commander. It would make no sense for me to "focus on advising him" if I wasn't also in charge of the Coalition effort supporting the operation. I didn't know my partner very well, but my conversations with Fridriksson had made me understand one thing for sure: Qassim would only collaborate with "The Decision-Maker," which to him meant the man controlling the fire support and intelligence platforms. If the SPMAGTF commander was in charge—if he was the Decision-Maker—Qassim would have nothing to do with me as the middleman. He would cut out our team because he wouldn't need us, and our mission supporting the Iraqis would be an empty effort. We might as well go home. My argument to Gideons was always the same: *Be careful what you ask for. If you want to bring your crew into Iraq, you won't get to pick and choose your missions. You will work directly for the Coalition headquarters, and they'll tell you what to do with all the support you're offering, including all your aviation assets. They will pick you apart. And as far as Desert Lion goes, you'll own the whole enchilada—including the advise and assist mission with Qassim and his staff—and it will consume you.*

As Desert Lion approached, it became more apparent: Gideons expected me to advocate on his behalf. And before long, a series of ambiguous emails and phone calls from the generals commanding I MEF and 51/5 made me suspect that they too believed I should go to White and suggest—if not flat-out declare—that I was incapable of handling the mission that had landed in my lap. I should, they implied, recommend that the Coalition headquarters call forward SPMAGTF to get the job done. And, their communications further suggested, I should offer my task force to work for Gideons to make the command relationships easier on everyone. The entire situation was preposterous. The Marine Corps' senior leaders appeared stuck on the idea of getting SPMAGTF into the mix. It seemed like no one had ever stopped to consider if it was actually the right force to apply to the problem in the first place. The politics of it all represented service parochialism at its worst, and it made me sick to my stomach.

"By, with, and through," was the vehicle through which the Coalition was conducting the counter-ISIS campaign: *by* local forces, *with* U.S. and Coalition support, and *through* appropriate permissions and authorities. Operating that way levied unique requirements for logistics and command and control, something of which our team had become acutely aware. Even though SPMAGTF possessed the capability and capacity necessary to lead Desert Lion, doing so would increase the risk to its "no-fail" crisis response mission. But the queue of SPMAGTF advocates continued to grow, and the latest convert was CJOC-Baghdad's director, a brigadier general who was also the senior Marine in Iraq.

The only senior Marine leader whose viewpoint mirrored mine was Lieutenant General Beydler. "A lot of people think we should send in the 'mighty-mighty MAGTF' to do the job in Anbar," he told me. "But I'm not so sure." He was proud of the crisis response capability that SPMAGTF provided to the theater commander. However, he was hesitant to commit the unit's command element or large chunks of its subordinate elements to a mission for which teams like mine had been expressly designed, manned, trained, and equipped. Regardless, and despite the moral support he threw my way, I figured it was just a matter of time until the loudest voices in the room—the other Marine generals outside of Iraq—eventually told me to get on board and take one for the team.

Changing horses in midstream was a bad idea for nearly everyone, including Qassim and his staff. Although he had expressed his trust in me and my team, I wasn't so naïve that I couldn't see what was really going on: he was *only* working with me because I was the Decision-Maker. He knew I reported directly to White, who could *really* make things happen if I asked. As it turned out, it was an issue of loyalty. But, as Fridriksson had reminded me, in these circumstances loyalty in Iraq meant "mutually beneficial to both parties." The entire situation was, Fred remarked, like *Game of Thrones* on steroids. Qassim would not be interested in what I had to offer if I wasn't the guy who could say "yes." It was as Ashley had told me repeatedly: *Don't take "no" from someone who isn't authorized to say "yes."*

I faced a decision: give up and bow to the pressure to sideline my team or move out with the mission. I chose the latter. For whatever reason, someone had selected me to lead the task force. Perhaps I was the most expendable colonel. Or perhaps I *was* the most qualified person to lead the team. In truth, I would never know. I would also never know if the powers that be had any idea that I would eventually land in a position to lead the Coalition effort in Al Anbar. In the end, none of that mattered. I was the commander, and my team had trained precisely for this mission. No matter how anyone felt, we were in the middle of it now; there would be no turning back. I remembered Beydler's parting words in Tampa: *You are the main effort. Act like it.* And so I made my choice: I was the Decision-Maker, and I aimed to keep it that way.

PART 2
TASK FORCE LION

August 2017—October 2017

The fact of being an underdog changes people in ways that we often fail to appreciate. It opens doors and creates opportunities and enlightens and permits things that might otherwise have seemed unthinkable.

—Malcolm Gladwell

Maybe they are right. They sent me to this pile of shit because they think I belong here. I want to find out if they're right. There's a whole machine that works because everybody does what they're supposed to. And I found out I was supposed to be something I didn't like. That's what's in the program. That's my rotten little part in the rotten machine. I don't like it.
So I'm going to find out if they're right.

—Marshall William O'Niel, *Outland*

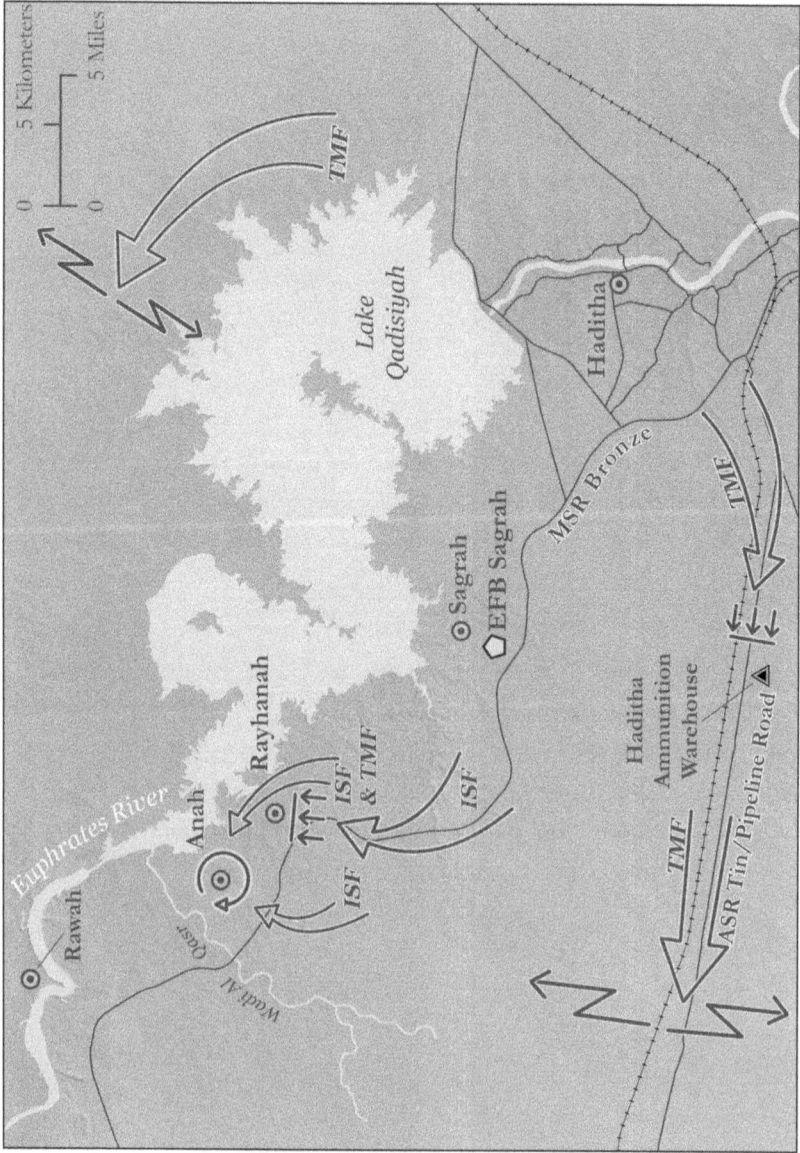

Map 2. OPERATION DESERT LION—PHASE I

12

DRUNK DIALING

KEY LEADER ENGAGEMENTS with Qassim and the rest of the Fantastic Four were exhausting and often frustrating affairs. They were not short, either. A typical meeting could last two hours or more if the conversation went down rabbit holes. Planning and coordinating our movement across base for events at 7th Division's Camp Majid added hours to each event. The time commitment increased dramatically when we executed Lion March movements to Qassim's Haditha Dam headquarters.

During his tenure, it didn't take long for Fred Fridriksson to figure out that Qassim and Numan always wanted to have engagements at their offices because there was no appropriate meeting place within the task force's barren command post. Both generals had plush setups that included overstuffed couches, coffee tables, carpets and tapestries, glass-topped desks, framed photographs and certificates, ashtrays, televisions, and banks of telephones and intercom systems. Everything adorning their offices was ornate and gilded—even their mobile phones were gold—whereas everything in our command post was bland and dirty. Common, even. It was, as Lieutenant Colonel Merritt often quipped, undignified—at least for the Iraqis.

Fridriksson's solution to entice our partners to more meetings at the command post was to build upon what Paul Nugent had previously begun: allocating money to transform a vacant office into what became known as the "greeting room." With its padded couches, carpeting, laminated maps, and framed, outsized photographs of Qassim and Numan striking dramatic poses, it resembled an Iraqi office in every way but one: our guests were forbidden from smoking inside the building. It was a singularly American prohibition that was a constant source of silent irritation for the chain-smoking Iraqi officers. To ameliorate the friction, Nugent had allocated a CHU for the Iraqis right outside the command post entrance. Although in time I would refer to the greeting room as "the green room," in truth it was the designated can that served that purpose. The CHU was a private location where, whenever they felt like it, the Iraqis could relax, drink chai, and smoke their asses off without feeling judged by the Americans.

Engagements with Qassim and his team were drawn-out affairs for another reason. They were all-hands events that included the members of my own Fantastic Four: myself, Leibfried, Awtry, and Kelly. Saif, the interpreter I inherited from Fridriksson, attended each session as well, as did senior leaders of the SOF teams from the other side of the base. I would eventually extend the invitation to other key members of the task force, including the leaders of DANCON, NOR TU, and the French artillery battalion from Task Force Wagram that eventually joined our team. With each new addition to the invite list, the time commitment expanded, and it grew more challenging to maintain a disciplined schedule. After a period of fighting it, I eventually accepted that the sessions might have an official start time, but they certainly had no hard stop time unless it was Qassim who decreed it.

In many ways, we were at Qassim's beck and call. Although we attempted to inject some degree of order and predictability into the process by recommending Tuesdays and Saturdays as standard "KLE days," Saif would often pop in my office and announce that Qassim was on his way to our command post for an unannounced meeting. And then there were the phone calls. Had Qassim been a drinker, we might have considered him a compulsive drunk-dialer. Fridriksson had hinted at this earlier, and Saif later confirmed that Qassim was notorious for calling the commander in the middle of the night to fret about the topic du jour that had energized him that day—or that particular hour in the middle of the night. Although it was my job to support my partner in whatever way possible, I drew the line there. After a couple of pointless midnight calls early in our relationship, I told Saif I would no longer put up with the nocturnal interruptions.

"If he insists on waking me up in the middle of the night," I warned, "there better be a good goddamned reason why. Otherwise, it can wait."

The midnight drunk dials dried up, but Qassim still got what he wanted. As much as I tried to keep a sustainable schedule, which included waking and hitting the rack at reasonable hours, I eventually fell into a personal battle rhythm that kept me in my office late each evening. There was always some urgent email I needed to answer from someone in Baghdad or Kuwait who either couldn't or wouldn't sleep. I despised the ubiquitous Type-A officers who thought it was both cool *and* part of their job description to work past midnight every evening while they were deployed. The worst were those who also expected *everyone else* to burn the midnight oil. There were also the phone calls that rang in my office at all hours, often from people in the United States who were oblivious to the time zone difference. Just as I would accept that key leader engagements had no real stop time, so too would I eventually accept that remaining in the office late each evening was part of the job.

To ease the sting, I settled into a routine. When my work was finished each night, I would plop down in front of the television mounted on my office wall and stare at movies streaming from a hard drive, packed with pirated media, that one of the Marines had let me borrow. Qassim eventually discovered my night owl routine. Once he figured out I was usually in the office until at least an hour before midnight, the calls resumed—bizarre, three-way conversations between Qassim, an interpreter, and me over a mobile phone with questionable cell reception. Most of the time, he just needed someone to make him feel better. Whether it was me listening to him yell, or me heaping praise on him, he usually left the conversation satisfied. But we couldn't accomplish everything by phone, and so in-person meetings remained a necessity.

On the afternoon of August 25, we drove to Camp Majid to link up with the Coalition's senior SOF leaders, who had requested a meeting with Qassim to discuss tribal militia matters. Everyone filed into Numan's office, where we shared thick, scalding coffee from the same tiny ceramic cup and drank hot chai so infused with sugar that the little stirring spoons practically stood on end in their glasses. We talked for nearly an hour before moving into an adjacent room for lunch around a table piled high with platters of vegetables, bread, and steaming rice, lamb, and chicken. After wolfing down our meal, we followed Qassim and his deputies back into the office, where the meeting continued.

Once the SOF contingent departed, my own Fantastic Four was left to talk with Qassim alone. We stayed for close to two hours, but the situation, which had seemed somewhat strained before lunch, didn't improve after the operators left. At first, I thought it was because Trident had requested the meeting for Friday, which was traditionally the day the Iraqis rested. For them, doing business on a Friday was roughly the equivalent of some clueless son of a bitch scheduling a meeting on a Sunday for a bunch of devout Christians. Then I remembered that Qassim, while at least *somewhat* devout, didn't really adhere to that tradition. He was a professional military officer; he knew that when there was work to be done, it had to get done no matter what day it was. I shrugged, figuring he was giving us the cold shoulder because he didn't particularly trust the SEAL commander.

Once we returned to Camp Havoc, I pulled Saif aside to ask him what the hell had happened. His answer surprised me. Qassim hadn't been irritated with the operators; he was aggravated with me and my officers.

"He misses Colonel Fred's team," Saif said.

"Go on," I replied. I had seen this movie before and was surprised it had taken so long for the conversation to occur this time around.

"Qassim thinks Major Awtry and you don't talk enough," he continued. "He doesn't think you are giving enough information about what is going on around the country."

"Jesus, Saif," I replied. "I tell Qassim what I know and what is important for him to hear. It's not my job to give him a rundown of current events every time we meet."

"He doesn't get much information from his bosses in Baghdad, and he needs a lot of reassuring from you."

"Okay, got it," I said, nodding. "What else? Let me have it."

"General Qassim thinks you should act more like a commander."

"What?"

"He thinks you should act more like a senior Iraqi commander," he continued. "You should speak the most, you should control the meeting, and you shouldn't let your staff talk as much."

"You know that's not gonna happen," I replied. "I didn't get here by acting like an Iraqi officer. Qassim may do all the talking for his team, but I don't roll like that. Part of my job here is to show him what it's like on the other side—to give him a window into how *we* do things. You know, things like delegating authority to your subordinates. That means during our meetings he's gonna get the ops shit from Awtry, he's gonna get the intel shit from Kelly, he's gonna get the devil's advocate shit from the sergeant major, and he's gonna get the commander shit from me."

"But that's not how Colonel Fred did it with the old team," Saif said. "He did most of the talking during the meetings."

"Listen, I appreciate your honesty," I said. "But I really don't give a rat's ass how the old team did it. They're gone, and Qassim is stuck with the new team."

Saif walked out of the office, rolling his eyes. No doubt he'd had similar conversations with the previous commanders. For him, it was like watching a revolving door of headstrong Marine officers, each with his own ideas of how to run things. I could understand his frustration, just as I could understand Qassim's, and I should have caught on early when I noticed Qassim never had anyone with him in the KLEs other than his Fantastic Four. I should have noticed when, during one of our first meetings, he unrolled a map in front of us and drew tactical graphics for Desert Lion himself.

There had to be some give on my part, and I realized after my conversation with Saif that I might have to change my personal style if Qassim and I were to get along. I had no intention of dominating the meetings as Saif suggested. But I *would* have to be more direct and forceful with Qassim. My first order of business would be to convince him to command Desert Lion from Sagrah instead of Al Asad.

When it came to how Qassim commanded his forces, the assessments from both Fridriksson and Major General White were accurate. Qassim was indeed addicted to watching the high-resolution video feeds—also known as "Predator porn" or "ISR crack"—that filled the flat-screen televisions in our theater-like COC. During previous operations in the urban centers along Route Bronze, as well as similar actions in the Jazeera Desert west of Al Asad, Qassim had been happy to command the battle from the comfort of Al Asad. Sitting atop the COC's elevated platform, he would coordinate with his battlefield commanders either by mobile phone or via the Iraqi digital mobile radio (DMR) system his soldiers had piped into the building. He would even arrange for extravagant meals to share with the task force members at the command post during lulls in the fighting.

The problem wasn't Qassim commanding from the coziness of the rear; we had come to expect that in the Iraqi culture. Still, many believed—me included—that he should lead his men from the front as we had all learned from the beginning of our education as officers. But the real issue was Qassim's refusal to employ drones in the same manner we did. He preferred to use our tactical systems to supervise and direct his own troops, rather than tasking the drones to search for enemy targets deeper on the battlefield. During operations, he insisted we keep the drones above his troops as he yelled position corrections to commanders who weren't where they were supposed to be. Major Awtry was particularly sensitive to this. Many years earlier in Husaybah, a senior U.S. officer miles away watching an ISR feed had directed the movement of Awtry's unit block by block through the city. He even ordered Awtry to make corrections on individual Marines' movement and security posture along the way. For those imbued with common sense, someone trying to micromanage the fight from so far away was an offense of the highest order.

During our tense meeting on August 25, I had broached the subject of Qassim positioning himself forward on the battlefield during Desert Lion. He drew a line in the sand: unless we could replicate the same ISR capability, he intended to command the operation from his air-conditioned perch in our Camp Havoc command post. "Why should I move all the way out there when I have everything I need here at Al Asad?" he asked. My gentle pleas for him to lead from the front fell on deaf ears. Even shaming didn't work; Qassim was above shame.

Throughout our team's pre-deployment training, we had experimented with ways to crew and operate a mobile command post in addition to our regular watch teams. The challenge the team faced now was that we couldn't agree among ourselves on the actual requirement, much less how to solve the problem. The staff pushed back against the idea almost from the moment I announced my intent, and the inability of everyone to get on the same sheet of music aggravated me. I initially believed they were simply reluctant to abandon Al Asad's creature comforts. It wasn't just the climate-controlled housing, the dining facility, and the gym we would abandon if we went forward. We would also leave behind reliable, uninterrupted power, as well as hard-wired communications, computing equipment, and other enabling capabilities that were less than expeditionary in nature yet altogether more important to the operation's overall success. To be sure, the staff's resistance was based almost entirely on our meager resources and *not* a hesitancy to move outside the wire. *Everyone* wanted to get into the fight in some degree or another. Sitting inside the relative safety of Camp Havoc was not what most Marines signed up to do.

Earlier in the deployment, I had asked Major Mathwick to evaluate our team's vehicle and equipment inventory to determine whether the entire command element—the eighty-five core members plus additional strap-hangers—had the means to mobilize and self-move across the battlespace if necessary. She and her team crunched the numbers and briefed me what it would take to move the team. It wasn't pretty, but we could do it with what we had on hand if the order came. Still, even though we would be able to move and briefly sustain ourselves, our minimally crewed command element was, as the saying goes, a mile wide and an inch deep. That lack of depth hadn't been an issue for the previous task force rotations. Rather, it had been their can-do attitude and back-to-back successes that compelled the Coalition leaders in Baghdad and Kuwait to assign them increasing levels of responsibility. The difference was that the previous teams hadn't been called upon to displace from Al Asad.

Simply put, our bench was not deep because the team was never designed to be expeditionary. With the political prohibitions on U.S. ground force movement outside the wire so firmly in place in 2014, no one had envisioned a day when the advise and assist teams might actually need to accompany their Iraqi partners across a battlespace as vast as Al Anbar Province. Fred believed the task force could operate either as a battlespace owner or as an accompanying advisor team, but not both. Quite a few others in positions of authority or influence had latched on to that perceived vulnerability and wanted to use it to their advantage. Senior Marine leaders across the globe were quick to point out our "ad hoc nature" as one more reason why SPMAGTF should take over the operation. And to be fair, we had yet to do the stubby pencil drills necessary to determine if we even *could* do it.

Further complicating the matter, we were not yet in a position where we could drop our base oversight responsibilities like a hot potato. During the previous year, the MARCENT staff had worked behind the scenes to relieve the task force of the base support requirement. As a result, the same week we landed at Al Asad, a U.S. Army colonel and his BOS-I team arrived to assume the base commander responsibilities. The colonel was an eager, willing partner, and I jumped at the prospect of divesting our team from that particularly onerous role. Fridriksson had been correct: we would soon be too busy to worry about administrative minutiae like gray water disposal, medical waste incinerators, and supervising billeting assignments. However, even though the newly arrived Army team was quickly getting the hang of running base operations, we weren't quite ready to take our hands off the steering wheel.

It was only after a couple of closed-door conversations with Leibfried and Awtry that I realized I had not properly framed the matter for the team. The staff didn't understand what I needed, and so I sat down and wrote out the issue for myself before handing it over to them to work through. After some thought, I drafted a problem statement: "Given the resource-constrained operating environment—and the requirement to command from a forward area and maximize the JaOC commander's situational awareness—how can the task force generate and operate a command-and-control architecture that includes a Main, Tactical, and Jump command post without assuming unacceptable risk or sacrificing efficacy across the warfighting functions?"

The process led to me sifting through military publications to review the doctrinal functions of a command post, and I confirmed those that the Main at Camp Havoc performed. It controlled and assessed the overall progress of operations; received, analyzed, and processed reports from subordinate units; and processed and submitted information for our higher headquarters. It was also a secure, fixed location for us to synchronize and execute the targeting process, as well as plan future operations and integrate intelligence into them. As the task force's central hub for plans, analysis, sustainment coordination, and assessment, the Main included representatives from each staff section and a complete array of communications and computing systems to plan, prepare, execute, and assess operations.

It was painfully obvious that we didn't have enough people *or* equipment to man a true Forward command post, which by definition replicated many of the main command post functions. My focus instead turned to determining the capabilities we would require for a tactical command post (TAC) at TAA Sagrah. Its primary role would be to provide situational awareness for Qassim, but it would also be a forward location for issuing orders, providing input to targeting and future operations planning, and controlling decisive or shaping actions in conjunction with Qassim and his deputies. It would also be a place to conduct short-range planning with the Iraqi leaders; it would rely on the Main for more detailed planning, analysis, and coordination. It would only include the bare minimum in terms of personnel and equipment, yet it had to be capable of maintaining continuous communication with the Main, our subordinates, our higher headquarters, and adjacent units. There was also the question of how we would protect it, which was to say it would rely on whatever SecFor we could find to guard the outpost.

The easiest nut to crack was the Jump. Its focus would be accompanying operations with Qassim—primarily battlefield circulation—and it would serve as my mobile command post. By design, the Jump would have a small footprint to enable our communications with the entire force, but it had to be capable enough to move to critical locations so I could personally assess situations, make decisions, and influence Iraqi operations. Ideally, it would include team members who could affect current operations through functions such as maneuver, fires, and intelligence, but the mission would dictate its composition. The challenge, everyone agreed, was that the Jump would pull its protection requirements from whatever small SecFor element that was protecting the outpost. The people and equipment that composed the Jump would come from the TAC as well. In other words, to establish a mobile command post capability, we would have to rob from the TAC Peter to pay the Jump Paul. The same could be said for establishing both a TAC and a Main simultaneously.

I handed my work over to Major Duesterhaus and his FOPs team, asking them to develop several options for review. I also asked for a thumbnail sketch of the basic table of organization and equipment for each option. Remembering what the MARCENT commander had said about the team starting at Al Asad but possibly not finishing there, I added one last task for good measure: be prepared to identify resources and capabilities necessary to displace the *entire* Main to another location for future operational phases.

It wasn't long before Duesterhaus called me into his planning space to review the team's work on their filled dry-erase board. A fully resourced option was entirely aspirational, as it would rely on generous personnel and equipment augmentation from the Coalition and SPMAGTF—augmentation we were certain not to get. That went double for SPMAGTF, who would likely counter with *If you're going to nickel and dime us for all these extra people and equipment, we should be the ones doing the operation ourselves.*

"We've run the numbers," Duesterhaus said. "We think, with what we have on hand, that we can support COA 3: a Main, a TAC, and a Jump."

"All three?" I asked. "Without augmentation?"

"Yes," he replied. "Here's the caveat: as we already knew, if you fully employ the Jump, you will be pulling from the TAC, significantly reducing its capability. But a completely fleshed-out Jump would have the satellite comms suite with it and the people to man it to ensure you had the necessary situational awareness."

"Okay . . ." I said, nodding.

"You can also keep the TAC in place and go mobile with a light Jump," Duesterhaus added. "We can get everything you need in four to six MATVs; two for you and your PSD team, and the rest for security. In that configuration you would have, at a minimum, VHF, SATCOM [satellite communications], Blue Force Tracker, and Iridium to reach back to the TAC or the Main. The only capability you wouldn't have is data."

I considered what the crew had put in front of me, and I turned to Awtry.

"Regardless of how we do this," he said, "it's gonna be light. We're really going to stretch the team, especially if the first phase goes longer than a couple of weeks."

"We've decided we should call this 'Operation Shoestring,'" Duesterhaus added.

"Hmph," I muttered. "Yeah, I get it: Guadalcanal. What else?"

Major Julian, who had remained uncharacteristically silent throughout the brief, piped up.

"We can't do fires and intel from the TAC," he said. "Those functions *have* to stay here at the Main."

His comment didn't surprise me. Earlier, he had privately conveyed his irritation about my insistence on approving strikes rather than delegating that authority to him. My response didn't help the situation. Although he believed it was his responsibility to plan and approve fires on my behalf, the current operating environment no longer supported that model. I would own the risk for every strike, so I had to be the approval authority.

"Chris, I never said we needed to do fires and intel from the TAC," I replied. "Trust me, you and John have made it agonizingly clear we can't do that."

"Then how will we do strikes from the Main if you're not there to approve them?"

"That's what the deputy is for," I replied, nodding toward Lieutenant Colonel Merritt. "And if what Greg and you guys are briefing is accurate, we should all be looking at the same ISR picture . . . so I'll know what you are targeting while I'm forward. We're just gonna have to work through it."

My answer didn't please Julian, but we had some time to figure it out. The Iraqi military leaders still couldn't make up their minds about the overall plan for Desert Lion, and the Coalition staff in Baghdad seemed afflicted with a similar paralysis. And, while it was important for our team to continue planning—"plan early, plan often" was the saying—there was a limit to what we could do without making certain assumptions and without understanding exactly what the Iraqis wanted to do. Everyone knew what the gringos wanted. But that didn't matter. The Iraqis were our clients, and they couldn't seem to get out of their own way.

13

CLEARING THE AIR

ON THE EVENING OF AUGUST 27, Qassim visited me after his trip to Baghdad. Although Desert Lion's first phase would have to address the Islamic State fighters dug into Rayhanah and Anah, he continued his fixation on Rawah. He still wanted to include it in the operation's initial phase, but he was the only one.

"Abdul Amir wants to attack Rawah from the north with FedPol [Federal Police] and the PMF," he growled as he plopped down on the couch. "Then he wants to attack Al Qa'im with 9th Division and CTS [Counterterrorism Service]. This isn't what we should be doing."

Rather than consider ways he could work within Abdul Amir's plan, Qassim rehashed the plan he had advocated for all along. There could be no other solution to the problem, he insisted. Seventh Division should clear Rayhanah and Anah, and then 8th Division would clear Rawah from the north. He also had a plan to integrate the tribal militias. His scheme called for the DANSOF-supported A'ali Al Furat Brigade to hold Sagrah, serve as a QRF, and then conduct disruption operations west of Anah. The Jughayfi tribe would partner with the SEALs, and together they would clear along ASR Tin's Pipeline Road to the Haditha ammunition warehouse and the T-1 train station. Throughout all this, the Nimur tribe would screen to the west of Lake Qadisiyah to prevent enemy reinforcements from attacking 8th Division from the rear.

"The operation must begin as soon as possible," he said. "The ISF must get to Al Qa'im quickly; we must get there before the Syrians and the Russians. And the SMGs."

"It's a good plan, *Sayidi*," I said. But there was one hang-up: his proposal hinged on employing units that didn't belong to him.

"How will you get 8th Division for the operation?" I asked.

"No problem," he said, smiling.

I wasn't so sure. Eighth Division was one of the Anbar Operations Command's subordinate army divisions, and Qassim didn't get along with the AOC's commander, Mahmoud—which was to say the two men pretty much hated each other's guts. I later described Qassim's plan by phone to Col Damian Spooner, the Task Force Al Taqaddum commander partnered with the AOC's leaders. He confirmed my suspicions: Mahmoud had no intention whatsoever of handing over 8th Division to Qassim, and any unit getting assigned to the Jazeera Operations Command would be a decision for Abdul Amir. Until that time came, I would just have to humor Qassim as he continued to set his heart on taking control of 8th Division.

———

As August neared its end, the friction between Colonel Gideons and me became obvious not only to the two of us, but also to our mutual staffs. On August 28, Gideons and several members of his command element visited Al Asad for a routine visit with the SPMAGTF Marines supporting the UK SecFor contingent and the base's airfield. Shortly after touching down on the airfield, Gideons and his crew sat down with me and my staff. The tension in the conference room was palpable. As the meeting wrapped up, Gideons directed everyone to give the two of us the room. I braced for what was sure to be a touchy conversation. Once the space was ours, he turned to me.

"Look, man," he said. "I want to clear the air about this rift that seems to be brewing."

"Okay," I said.

"You and I have too much water under the bridge together over the past fifteen years to get cross-threaded about whether or not SPMAGTF comes here."

"Yep," I said. "We've been friends for a long time."

"Well, look, let's cut to the chase. I think it makes the most sense for my team to C2 this operation. It will enable you to focus on advising."

"I hear you, man," I replied. "And, in general, I don't disagree with what you're saying. The SPMAGTF command element probably *is* the best choice to run the show out here . . . *eventually*. But not now; not at the eleventh hour. This train is already moving."

"I just don't see why we would leave something this important to—no offense, man—an *ad hoc* headquarters," he said.

"Yeah, and this is just what my team was designed for," I said. "Look, I would support the change beginning with the next deployment rotation in April. That would give us the space we need to transition the mission properly rather than rushing to failure."

"Alright, man," he said. "I just want you know, though . . . I'm gonna continue to push for SPMAGTF to come here and lead the operation."

"Roger that," I replied. "And I'm gonna continue to advocate for the status quo."

It was an unpleasant tête-à-tête, but a necessary one. By agreeing to disagree, we had drawn our battle lines, and I left the meeting fairly certain I could no longer count on any additional SPMAGTF support for Desert Lion. Moreover, as I considered what it potentially meant for the coming operation, I wasn't altogether sure our long, close friendship would survive the deployment.

No one becomes a Marine officer to make friends. As a candidate in Quantico, you quickly learn that you are competing against your peers in everything you do. As the saying goes at OCS (Officer Candidates School), *if only two candidates made it through to commissioning, each of them would think the other is a shithead.* The quiet rivalry with your peers continues throughout your career. As people fall by the wayside, that sense of competition sharpens, making it more and more difficult to trust anyone when advancement is at stake. And, when you do make friends along the way, you often wonder what will eventually drive a wedge between the two of you. My relationship with Gideons had spanned the entirety of the Long War, and I respected him as an accomplished leader and commander. The potential loss of his friendship over such a trivial matter bothered me. At the same time, I knew that if I caved and handed him control of the operation, I would never be able to look myself in the face . . . nor would I be able to look my team members in the eyes. They had worked their asses off to get to this point. Handing over the operation, as difficult as it was shaping up to be, would be telling them they were indeed the B-team. They were anything but, so I held my ground.

Convincing Qassim to command from a forward position on the battlefield was a struggle, but a glimmer of hope presented itself. As I reiterated the concept of a smaller command post at Sagrah for us to monitor the battle together, his eyes suddenly lit up.

"I can provide a CHU for the operation," he said.

The temperatures were still soaring into the triple digits daily, and there was no sign of a cooldown before the operation commenced. Qassim didn't just want the emotional satisfaction of viewing the battlefield through our ISR feeds; he also wanted the luxury of an air-conditioned, dust-free space. The notion of sweltering in a filthy tent wasn't his idea of how to go to the field. By the third time he made the offer, I knew there would be no turning it down. At his insistence, we traveled to his Haditha headquarters on August 31 to get a look at it. The thing was huge. Assembled as kits, CHUs normally had dividers installed to create individual rooms. But Qassim's men had removed the room dividers, and the result was a super-CHU nearly the size of my grandparents' double-wide trailer.

"Man," I said, wiping my sweating brow. "I sure hope he brings A/C for this thing. It's hotter than two squirrels fucking in a wool sock."

"This is a lot bigger than what we need," Major Awtry said. "I'd rather just have a regular 305 tent and be done with it."

"Well, we have to make it work," I replied. "Qassim really wants to help, and this is his way of showing it."

Along with our inspection of the super-CHU, we needed to take one final look at the TAA Sagrah ground before moving people and heavy equipment to clear and build the outpost. Although it was supposed to be a site survey only, Staff Sergeant Brian and Sergeant Rioux were itching to reduce the obstacle belt embedded in the featureless area. I hesitated. Detonating a stack of explosives would surely tip our hand to the enemy forces west of Sagrah. But then I looked at the convoy of armored vehicles and the collection of Coalition personnel milling about on the road. With the visual signature we had created, the local ISIS network probably knew something was brewing the moment our convoy crossed the threshold of Hammer Gate. Not long after I gave Brian the thumbs-up, the thundering *crr-aaack* of five exploding IEDs echoed up the Euphrates River Valley.

Something was brewing, alright. We just had no idea what it was.

We returned to Camp Havoc late in the afternoon, exhausted from the heat and the long drive, but ready to get started at Sagrah in two days. As I wound down in my office for the evening, the inevitable phone call came.

"With Mosul and Tal Afar wrapping up, Abadi has decided to clear Hawija and Al Shirqat first and execute the Anbar campaign later," the J-3 in Baghdad told me. "It could be as much as a three-month delay before Desert Lion kicks off."

It was hard to conceal my disappointment. But the bad news came with a silver lining: the delay afforded more time to refine our plans, which were shaky at best. It also gave us additional time to coordinate delivery of the critical assets needed to support the operation. When I broke the news to the staff, they didn't try to hide their disappointment. Who could blame them? They had been racing to meet the timeline, and the delay was a terrible letdown.

"We're not gonna let this crisis go to waste," I said. "Consider the delay a blessing. It will give us time to do the things we couldn't do before."

"Good to go," grunted Major Julian. "More time for gains."

"I could use the sleep," Major Mathwick added.

"We all know Perfect Lindsay isn't going to rest," countered Major Kelly.

"Alright, alright," I said, the tension in the room broken. "Listen, this isn't an end to our planning. It's just a pause; it's just a preview of things to come. We need to review the work we've done so far with the OPT. I want a consolidation of all planning materials. We need to refine and validate our current requirements, and we need to identify and scope what we think the future requirements list will be. We also need to analyze any perceived gaps in our initial planning efforts and establish a realistic timeline." The staff groaned.

"Look, everyone has done great work so far. You are all operating at the brigade-level, and it shows. Don't be disheartened; pace yourselves accordingly, and surge when necessary.

"I want to be clear about something: This is still ours to win or lose. If we want to be the main effort—if we want to stay in the game—then we've gotta prove our worth and capability in the weeks and months to come. Because the minute we say we can't do something, you know there will be someone right behind us saying *they* can."

Despite my attempt at a pep talk, the prime minister's decision to delay the operation frustrated the team. Everyone felt deflated, and in the following days there was a good deal of moping around camp. By the third day in September, once the team had gotten all the rest it needed, I directed them to get back to work. The earlier campaign in Tal Afar had gone faster than most planners in Baghdad and Kuwait predicted, and I wondered if the Hawija fight would be over just as quickly. I also wondered if Abadi, who was notorious for changing his mind at the last minute depending on who was in the room, might go ahead and give the order to launch the MERV operation anyway. The moment we made ourselves comfortable would surely be the moment we got caught flat-footed. So our planning resumed.

14

A BILL OF GOODS

BY THE BEGINNING OF SEPTEMBER, I had grudgingly accepted the new operational reality of Inherent Resolve: the fire support and strike approval process did not match the Coalition commander's Tactical Directive #1 from the previous December. The directive remained unchanged. However, by the time we arrived in theater, someone levels above us had decided that delegating target engagement authority down to the task force commander level was really *not* what the Coalition commander had meant. Instead, CJOC-Baghdad and its strike cell would retain target engagement authority for all kinetic strikes that were not in *immediate* self-defense of Coalition and Iraqi troops. In other words, only if Coalition or Iraqi forces were pinned down would the authority to approve fire support reside with me. The whole thing felt like someone had sold us a bill of goods.

If, for example, we discovered a team of armed fighters piling into a Toyota Hilux, I would not have the authority to strike them, even if there was no chance of collateral damage. In such cases of so-called "dynamic" strikes—targets of opportunity on the battlefield—Major Julian's fires team had to request approval from the Baghdad strike cell. Further complicating the process was the fact that the only firepower assets under my immediate tactical control were a pair of U.S. Army Paladins. The gun crews had originally deployed to Al Asad for base defense, and they could reach out and touch someone up to thirty or forty kilometers away. However, we were routinely spotting enemy personnel many dozens of miles away, and the only fire support system aboard Al Asad capable of reaching that far—the HIMARS rocket artillery launchers—was operationally controlled by the Coalition headquarters. In other words, since I didn't "own" the HIMARS systems, I had to ask permission to use them no matter the circumstances.

Ultimately, the determining factor for whether I retained target engagement authority for self-defense was if it was a case of clear and present danger. If Coalition or Iraqi personnel were in immediate, visible danger, no one would question me approving fires as the ground force commander. However, pretty much anything beyond that meant the Baghdad strike cell and whoever was the designated TEA that day would insert themselves into the process and approve or deny strikes at the time of their choosing.

There was a professional disagreement between the two Marine task force commanders and the strike cell about what exactly constituted "clear and present danger." To those far away in Baghdad, a clear and present danger was an Islamic State fighter shooting a machine gun or a rocket-propelled grenade (RPG) at Iraqi soldiers. In our eyes, a stationary suicide vehicle packed with explosives, which could close many miles of distance between itself and a formation of Iraqi soldiers in minutes, was a clear and present danger. The time saved bypassing the strike cell's additional layer of approval could mean the difference between a Hellfire missile stopping a fast-moving SVBIED and the explosive-laden vehicle vaporizing the unsuspecting Iraqis. But the strike cell and its daily revolving door of senior officers with target engagement authority did not see it that way.

It was difficult to understand just what the hell was going on. For the first couple of weeks, as Major Julian's FECC team prosecuted strikes against enemy fighters and battle positions, I had mistakenly assumed *I* was the one approving fires. After all, six years earlier in Afghanistan, I had routinely approved strikes with the same types of precision-guided ordnance we were now employing in Iraq. It had been a regular battle drill in Afghanistan, one my team and I never took for granted or phoned in because of the potential for civilian casualties on the crowded counterinsurgency battlefield of Sangin. Further complicating the issue in Iraq was the airspace above us, which at any given time was crowded with a fleet of manned and unmanned aircraft. There were also the varying degrees of skill among the Coalition pilots flying in support of the campaign. And, to make matters worse, I wasn't certain the people working in the Baghdad strike cell were very good at their jobs—something we noticed within weeks of our arrival.

Each week I met with Julian and his crew to review deliberate targeting packages built from the intelligence that Major Kelly's S-2 Marines had collected, analyzed, and refined. The authority to approve deliberate strike packages rested with Major General White in Baghdad or, in cases of high collateral damage estimates (CDEs), the overall Coalition commander himself in Kuwait. My previous experiences in Afghanistan with such nomination packages told me our higher headquarters in Iraq would judge us by the quality of our submissions. Sloppy packages meant bad headwork by the targeteers; bad headwork meant needless death and destruction in the form of civilian casualties and wrecked property. Therefore, I insisted—and Julian rigidly enforced—that the target packages must be absolutely bombproof. The expectation, then, was that after I had pored over the packages, returned the ones that needed work, and approved the balance, the analysts at Baghdad's J-38 fires shop would similarly endorse and forward the nominations for final approval. To their credit, most of the time they did. Throughout the deployment, White approved many more of our nominations than he denied. The actual execution of the strikes, however, often left a lot to be desired.

One of the reasons we could locate and track multiple enemy targets simultaneously was because the task force tactically controlled several drone systems capable of looking deep into the battlespace. One, an RQ-7B Shadow with the call sign "Airwolf," was operated by U.S. Army soldiers assigned to our team. The other two systems, a ScanEagle known as "Backslap" and a second Shadow referred to as "Strugglebus," were owned and operated by contractors. None of the tactical systems was armed, but their optics suites gave us the eyes we needed to identify potential targets for strikes by other, armed platforms. Backslap's optics were superior to those on Airwolf and Strugglebus, and it was a more reliable platform. Eventually, a series of maintenance problems that routinely degraded its mission readiness would lead us to believe that "Strugglebus" was indeed an appropriate name.

On September 3, the Coalition approved a target package for a house in Anah that we had determined was a known meeting point for local Islamic State commanders and a bed-down location for transient fighters. "Slayer," the call sign for an orbiting Gray Eagle, was loitering far above the target. The heavily armed brother of the MQ-1B Predator drones we had employed so frequently in Afghanistan, the Gray Eagle sported surveillance capabilities far beyond our own tactical drones. As we lined up the strike, three adult figures walked down the street and entered the house. Slayer's controller, who was likely sitting in an air-conditioned control station thousands of miles away, typed in the chat window monitored by one of Julian's Marines.

"Slayer says one of the individuals is a child," the Marine said.

"What?" replied Julian. "That's not a fucking kid."

"They're aborting the strike."

"Huh?" I said from my seat in the COC's front row. "That's not their call to make; it's mine, and we have PID [positive identification]."

But the deed was done. Even though there was no child present at the target site, Slayer's report convinced the Baghdad cell to call off the strike. The next day, we made another attempt to strike the same target, but the process was fouled again—this time by the strike cell insisting we reevaluate our initial collateral damage estimate.

"You know what?" I said in frustration. "Fuck it . . . just abort the god-damned thing. Someone is letting the air out of us, slowly."

As I stood to leave, the last thing I heard was Julian growling on the phone at his counterpart in Baghdad.

"No, bullshit. We already did the CDE [collateral damage estimate] work, and our boss approved it. You want it recertified? *You* fucking do it!"

⬛⬛⬛⬛⬛

Early in the evening of September 5, Julian knocked on my office door.

"We've got five armed *desh* assholes in a car in Anah," he said. "They just pulled up to a house, and three more dudes just showed up."

"Alright, let's go," I said, following him back to the watch floor.

He gave a quick roll-up of his team's observations, and we submitted an immediate strike request to Baghdad. The strike cell's target engagement authority quickly approved the request, allocating Al Asad's HIMARS launchers for the mission. But, as one of our JTACs deconflicted the crowded airspace, he couldn't contact the controller of a Predator loitering in the target's vicinity. Thirty minutes later, the controller came up on the net and responded to our urgent requests to get his aircraft the hell out of the way. As the Predator shifted its orbit, three rockets soared out of the air base. Two and a half minutes, the time it took the rockets to fly across the desert from Al Asad to Anah, was a long time to wait. As we watched the ISR screens in white-knuckled anticipation, people filed out of the target house. We were too late.

"Come on, come on, *come on*," Julian said as the house emptied.

"We're gonna miss them," I said, shaking my head.

Before the warheads could connect, six men had left. Two mounted a motorcycle and sped off, and another four climbed into a sedan and drove away in the opposite direction.

"Keep one bird on the house and stay on the car with the other," Julian directed.

The JTAC called out, "Splash!" indicating the rockets' imminent impact, and the house imploded in a towering column of smoke, debris, and billowing dust. The carload of fighters, which was cruising through Anah's twisting streets, skidded to an abrupt halt. All four of the sedan's doors sprang open, and the men inside shot out in every direction. The strike killed the two remaining fighters inside the house, but those on the motorcycle and in the sedan escaped—the luckiest men in Iraq on that day.

Our procedural frustrations continued on September 7. Studying video footage beamed back to us by Backslap, we zeroed in on five armed fighters in a truck heading west toward Shirwaniyah, a dorsal fin-shaped peninsula on the southern bank of the Euphrates River known as the "shark fin." By the time I arrived on the watch floor, Julian's team had submitted a fire support request and received strike cell approval.

"What do we have on tap?" I asked.

"Australian F/A-18 with GBU-54s," Julian replied. "We're talking him onto the target now."

Minutes later, he rattled off a series of commands that had become a familiar script on the watch floor:

"Stay on the truck; pan out. Scan right; scan left. Transient scans are green."

"Aircraft inbound," the JTAC said.

"Cleared-hot."

"Copy, cleared-hot," the JTAC replied. "Time of flight: thirty seconds."

Then the wait. The inevitable explosion. And a miss. As was the case two days earlier, all five men sprang from the vehicle and ran for the hills.

"Mother*fucker*! Stay on them!" Julian shouted, but the fighters melted into the desert before our eyes.

"Keep hunting," I said, shaking my head in exasperation as I stood to leave.

An hour later, the fires team spotted four more enemy soldiers climbing into a truck near Rawah. Not long after we dropped a strike request, a French Rafale jet checked in on-station. But the pilot had difficulty understanding our JTAC's talk-on to the target, and after thirty minutes and several aborted attempts he made his final attack run. The Rafale's laser-guided bomb missed its target—so far, in fact, that we couldn't even find its impact location.

"Disgusting," Julian huffed as he briefed the episode to the staff later that evening. "Failing French Air Force." He was so angry that I thought he would have a stroke.

The friction between our team and the Baghdad strike cell got even worse once Julian explained to me what else was going on. In the targeting process, we spoke in terms of "find, fix, and finish," meaning we would *find* the target through a variety of means, *fix* it by maintaining continuous surveillance and positive identification, and *finish* it through whatever ordnance was available and—equally important—appropriate for the mission. The fires team's collective aggravation centered on the fact that our team was doing all the hard work of the "find" and the "fix." In most cases, once the strike cell and whoever happened to be the target engagement authority on duty had approved the targeting request, they would take terminal control for the "finish."

From my perspective, if colonels and brigadier generals in Baghdad were insisting on taking control for the finish, that meant one of two things: either they wanted the morbid satisfaction of "pushing the button," or the CJOC director did not trust the task force commanders to make the right call. Either way, it represented something rotten about how we were now doing business in Iraq. I didn't know which was worse: people in the strike cell potentially wanting credit for the kills, or general officers not trusting subordinate commanders. When, on separate occasions, my counterpart at Al Taqaddum and I confronted the leaders in Baghdad about the issue, they resoundingly disagreed with our argument. Retaining strike authority in Baghdad was not a matter of trust, they insisted, but rather one of situational awareness. They never budged, either. Throughout our time in Iraq, the targeteers and senior Coalition officers in Baghdad insisted they had a better picture of the battlefield than we did, even though we all had access to the same ISR feeds. It was, quite frankly, absurd.

In some respects, I could understand the CJOC-Baghdad director's reluctance to delegate target engagement authority. Several months before our arrival, there had been a disastrous strike in the country's north that accidentally killed a number of civilians. And, despite the strict organizational controls that were in place, it continued to happen in both Iraq and Syria. After the stress and strain of working to prevent it day and night for seven long months in Afghanistan, I certainly understood the potential consequences of accidental civilian casualties on the battlefield. But the targeting and approval constraints under which we now operated brought about a painful revelation: I had more authority as a lieutenant colonel in

Afghanistan in 2011 than I did as a full colonel in Iraq in 2017. The more I thought about it, the more I realized just how backward the situation was. In my capacity as the task force commander, I had all the responsibility associated with the job but almost none of the authority. And no one who was in a position to do anything about it cared. To them, the issue was, as the saying goes, no big whoop.

Aerial view of Al Asad Air Base in western Al Anbar Province (Author's collection)

Key leader engagement in the Task Force Lion command post's "Greeting Room." *Left to right*: Staff Major General Qassim, MG Pat White, Colonel Folsom, Maj Aaron Awtry. (Official photo by SP4 Torrance Saunders, USA)

The destroyed hulk of an ISIS armored suicide vehicle-borne improvised explosive device along Main Supply Route Bronze leading to Sagrah, Rayhanah, and Anah. (Author's collection)

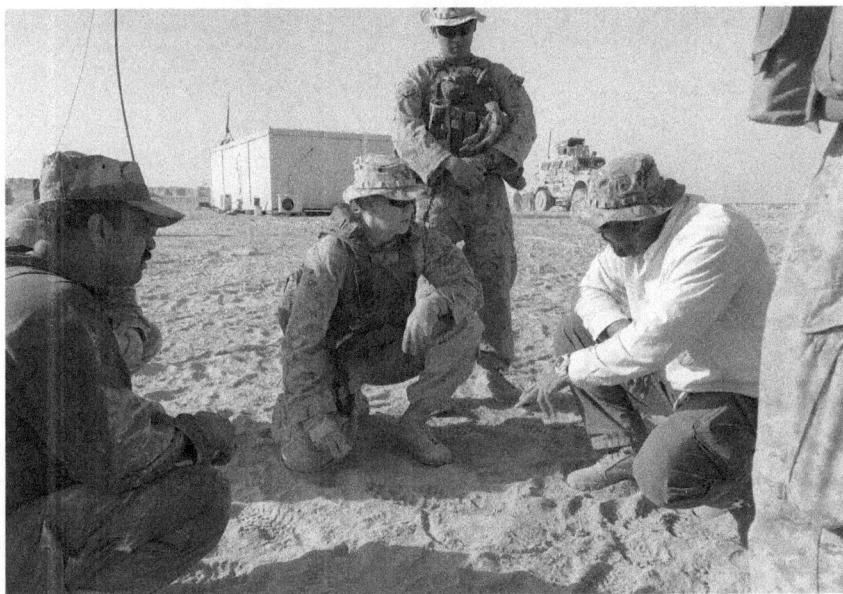

Maj Lindsay Mathwick plans the next round of logistics and sustainment operations at Expeditionary Firebase Sagrah. Staff Major General Qassim's "super-CHU," which served as the task force's tactical command post, is visible in the background. (Photo by Capt Robert Jankowski, USMC)

Capt Robert Jankowski (*top row, middle*) and Task Force Lion logistics team members pose with one of the U.S. Army M109 Paladins that provided fire support for the Iraqis from the outposts during Operation Desert Lion. (Photo from the collection of Capt Robert Jankowski, USMC)

The Task Force Lion Jump team moves through the shattered town of Rayhanah on its way to the city of Anah during Operation Desert Lion's first phase. (Author's collection)

Iraqi soldiers pause at "Qassim's Strongpoint" after liberating the city of Anah during Operation Desert Lion's first phase. (Author's collection)

Iraqi commanders from the Jazeera Operations Command and Task Force Lion advisors gather in Anah after the government of Iraq declared the city liberated, ending Operation Desert Lion's first phase. (Author's collection)

Task Force Lion conducts its rehearsal of concept drill aboard Al Asad Air Base prior to Operation Desert Lion's third phase. (Photo by Maj Lindsay Mathwick, USMC)

Maj Aaron Awtry briefs Task Force Lion's site survey team at Tactical Assembly Area Fuhaymi as a three-day dust storm builds. (Author's collection)

The smashed rail yard—also known as "the train station"—that Task Force Lion transformed into Tactical Assembly Area Al Qa'im to support the Iraqi Security Forces assault on the Al Qa'im District during Operation Desert Lion's third phase (Author's collection)

Special Purpose Marine Air-Ground Task Force Marines provide security for Tactical Assembly Area Al Qa'im, while Task Force Wagram's French Caesar artillery pieces in the background support the Iraqi Security Forces with indirect fire during Operation Desert Lion's third phase. (Author's collection)

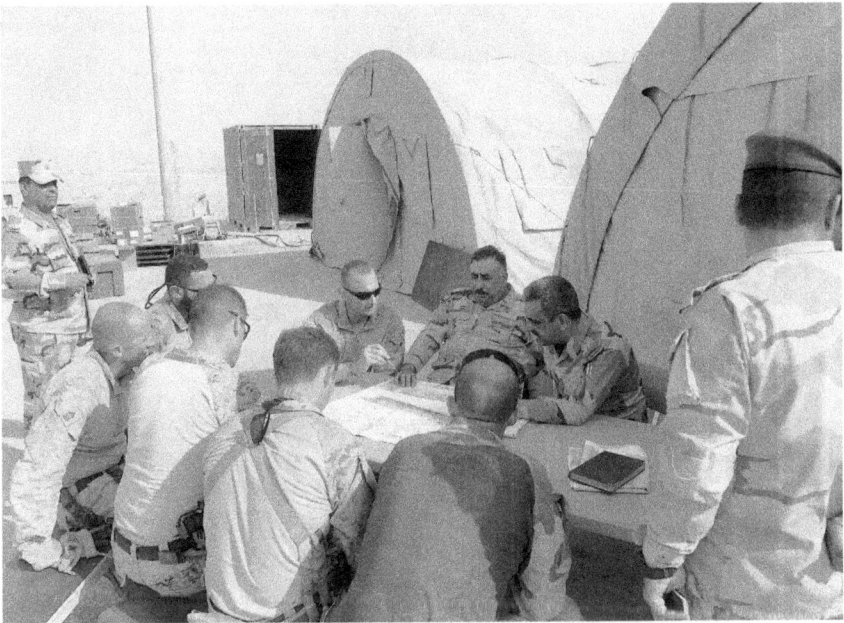

Staff Major General Qassim and Task Force Lion advisors coordinate final details at Tactical Assembly Area Al Qa'im in preparation for the Iraqi Security Forces' clearance of the Al Qa'im District during Operation Desert Lion's third phase. (Photo by Capt Robert Jankowski, USMC)

U.S. Army soldiers from Task Force Thunder fire their M777 howitzer in support of the Iraqi Security Forces during Operation Desert Lion's third phase. (Official photo by SP4 William Gibson, USA)

Jughayfi tribal militia fighters celebrate at the Tactical Assembly Area Al Qa'im train station after the Al Qa'im District's liberation by the Iraqi Security Forces during Operation Desert Lion's third phase. (Author's collection)

An Iraqi Counterterrorism Service soldier raises the national flag in the Al Qa'im district center on November 5, 2018—the day Prime Minister Abadi declared the district liberated. (Author's collection)

Task Force Lion's forward command team poses with the Jazeera Operations Command leaders in Al Qa'im after the district's liberation by the Iraqi Security Forces during Operation Desert Lion's third phase. *Left to right*: SgtMaj Alex Leibfried, Maj Aaron Awtry, Staff Major General Numan, Staff Major General Qassim, Colonel Folsom, Colonel Ahmed. (Author's collection)

Iraqi rockets fire from Anah in support of the Iraqi Security Forces attack on Rawah during Operation Desert Lion's third phase. (Official photo by SP4 Torrance Saunders, USA)

Task Force Lion's staff at Al Asad Air Base. *Sitting left to right:* Col Seth Folsom, Maj John Kelly, Maj Aaron Awtry, Maj Chris Julian, SgtMaj Alex Leibfried, MSgt Nicholas Slicker. *Standing left to right:* Maj Roberto Falcon, Maj Lindsay Mathwick, Maj Greg Duesterhaus, 1stLt Ben Miles. (Photo from the collection of Maj John Kelly, USMC)

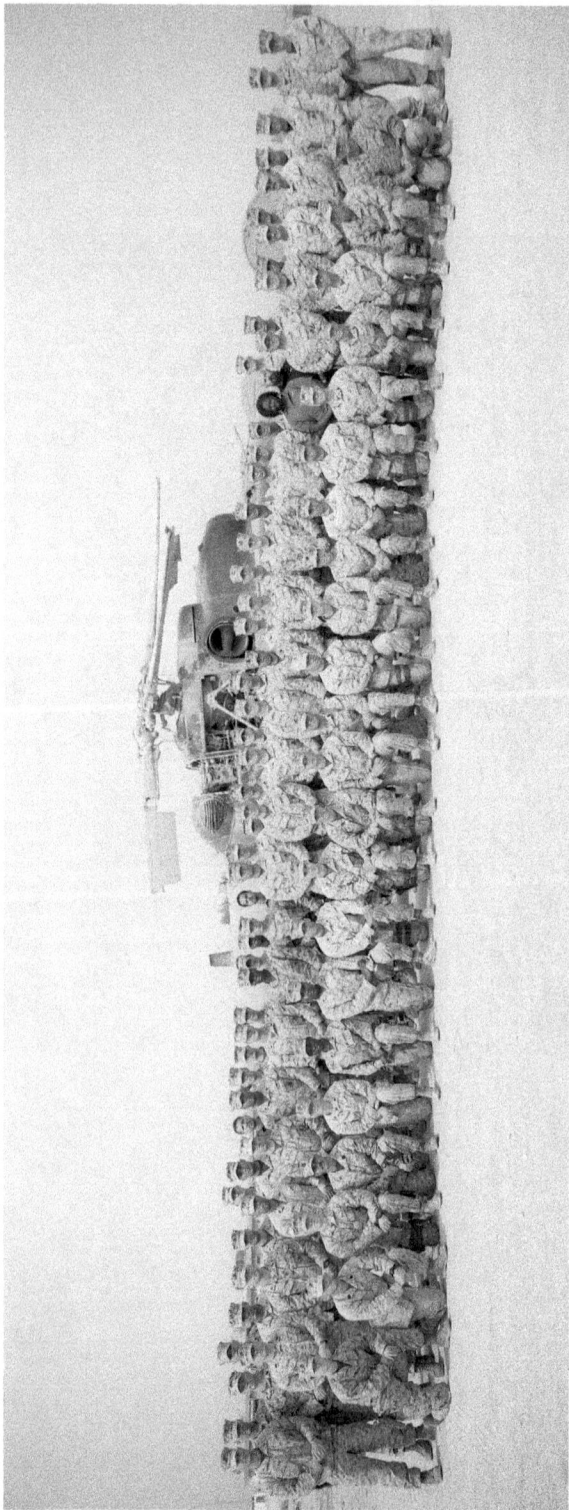

Task Force Lion team photo aboard Al Asad Air Base prior to redeploying in April 2018 (Official photo by SP4 Zakia Gray, USA)

15

EFB SAGRAH

AS THE WEEKS PASSED and Desert Lion inched closer, Qassim spent more time in Baghdad with Abdul Amir and the Iraqi planners. As far as Qassim was concerned, Al Anbar Province—at least the large patch of territory that included the Middle Euphrates River Valley—belonged to him. Well, maybe *belonged* was too strong a word, but he sure as hell believed the coming operation was rightfully his to command. However, he couldn't seem to convince his masters in Baghdad to listen to him or act on *his* personal timeline. In addition to more control over the plan, he argued for more time and resources. It was hard to blame him; by most accounts, the Iraqi commanders in the north had gotten just about everything they could possibly want from the Coalition to conduct the Mosul offensive.

In the afternoon of September 6, Muhammad Amador appeared in my office to announce Qassim was returning and wanted to meet with me and the newly arrived Trident commander. Preferring us to call him by his last name, Amador had taken over as the interpreter after Saif jumped ship for a higher-profile job in Baghdad. Although the two men were Iraqi-born Americans, the similarity ended there. Saif was a squat, pudgy chain-smoker; Amador was lean, fit, and a regular gym patron. Gregarious and outspoken, Saif had succumbed to the temptation of the interpreter: because of the critical role he played as the linguistic intermediary between the task force commanders and the Iraqi generals, he tended to overstep his bounds and insert himself in the process where he had no business. Amador, on the other hand, was quiet, introspective, and respectful almost to a fault. He knew I couldn't interact with Qassim without him, but he also knew the difference between interpreting conversations to help us understand each other, and unilaterally deciding what he should or should not articulate in the conversation. Despite their different personalities, one trait both Saif and Amador shared was a mutual desire to give back. The money as an interpreter was good, but both men had also volunteered because they wanted to play a role in the survival of their birth country.

As I got to know Amador in our first weeks together, I learned about his amazing backstory. Born in Baghdad, he spent the first six months of his life in jail. His father was a journalist who had run afoul of Saddam Hussein, and the Iraqi dictator retaliated by imprisoning the entire family. They fled the country in the mid-1980s, but Amador eventually returned to attend the University of Baghdad in the late 1990s. He left for good in 2002, not long before the American invasion. In 2005, Shi'a militants kidnapped and murdered his mother when she returned to Iraq to visit her family amid the sectarian violence splitting the country at the seams. Despite that tragedy, Amador went on to earn a master's degree from Northeastern University. He also joined the Air National Guard. Now, years after his mother's murder, he had returned.

He told me all this during one of our many trips to Haditha, and over time we would grow close after spending countless hours together, many in the same truck. As he dispassionately recalled the tragedies that had befallen his family, I thought of all the ways the war had affected so many people. And yet, despite everything terrible that had happened in Iraq since 2003, had it not been for the war I never would have met this remarkable young man.

The blacked-out SUV carrying Qassim and Numan rolled to a stop at the command post's entrance, where we waited patiently. The two generals debarked and strolled toward us, and Qassim hugged me a little harder than usual. I ushered him into the greeting room.

"I am very happy," he said in uncharacteristically perfect English. Everyone knew he understood more than he let on, but this was the first time he had blurted out anything like that. He grinned and told me Abdul Amir had just approved a new timeline. The PMF would begin clearing Akashat on September 12, and a week later Qassim's forces would move out to clear Rayhanah and Anah. His sequencing didn't match what we were hearing; by all accounts, the Hawija operation was the priority and was supposed to go first. But he was on a roll, and I didn't want to kill his buzz. His next question caught me off guard.

"Now, when will the Sagrah base be ready?"

"*Sayidi*," I said, glancing over at Major Awtry, who pursed his lips and subtly shook his head. "Sagrah won't be ready by the nineteenth."

"Why?" he demanded.

"With the changes Prime Minister Abadi made this week, my team no longer has the support assets we need to build and man the outpost. Everything is going toward operations in the north."

"No, no," he said, shaking his head. "You said Sagrah would be ready in eight days."

Everything was coming into focus. Late the previous evening, Qassim had called the Iraqi liaison officer and convinced him to wake up Awtry. Once he had the OpsO on the phone, he peppered him with questions about the construction timeline. Despite Qassim's pleas, Awtry had resisted the demands to wake me.

"*Sayidi*," I replied, "that timeline went out the window last week when the operation was put on hold. It could be as long as three months before we're back at it."

My answer agitated the two generals, and they rapid-fired questions at me. They implied I was a liar—a coward, even. I was usually pretty good about getting dressed down without losing my cool, but Qassim was now railing on me in front of my subordinates. It was something I would never do to him, so I fired back.

"Look," I said. "You're asking me questions I have no answer to. I'm sorry you misunderstood the timeline. You'll just have to wait until I can talk with General White."

"Yes!" he exclaimed. "Please, *please* talk with General White. Ask him for support so I can tell Abdul Amir."

Then it clicked: he was embarrassed. He had portrayed an incorrect timeline to his own boss, and now he was looking to me to get the top cover he needed from White. Although he had cooled down as he prepared to leave, he hugged me a little less vigorously. It was a physical confirmation of what I already suspected: we had just achieved the milestone of our first fight.

The next morning, Major General White sent me a brief note.

"Lion-6, need you to have Sagrah at IOC [initial operating capability] by 1 Oct and FOC by 15 Oct."

Plenty of time, I thought, heaving a sigh of relief. *Five weeks is practically forever.*

The challenges associated with building the outpost had subsided somewhat after Major Duesterhaus's planning team refined the list of necessary capabilities. To get everyone to understand the outpost's bare-bones design and temporary nature, we had dropped the term "TAA" and began referring to the future outpost as Expeditionary Firebase (EFB) Sagrah. We didn't expect it to be in place very long; if we had anything to say about it, Qassim and his soldiers would move west beyond Anah as soon as possible. After acknowledging they had nothing to contribute in the way of tangible supporting assets for the outpost, the Coalition planners relented. We were free to plan the base the way we wanted.

The operation's delay gave Major Mathwick a bit more breathing room to navigate the muddled Iraqi contracting process and coordinate the civilian vehicles and personnel necessary to support the construction. The process, which included routing all support requests to the Prime Minister's

National Operations Center (PMNOC) for final approval, was notoriously slow and prone to the whims of the prime minster. It typically required weeks to process the requests and receive approval before contract execution. Moreover, even when the Iraqi contractors eventually appeared with their vehicles, you never really knew what you would get. Sometimes the trucks didn't work; sometimes the drivers were drunk or high. But we were stuck with the process. Gone were the days when American forces could choke the highways with endless columns of supply convoys. The force management level restrictions in Iraq did not support the bloated logistical tail the Americans had grown accustomed to earlier in the war. Just as important, the Iraqi government wanted to control movement inside its own borders and provide its citizens a way to contribute to the war effort and get paid for it in the process. I didn't disagree with the policy, but the process was just not responsive enough to support us on the narrow timelines the Iraqis insisted we adhere to.

On top of it all, there was still the bizarre fact that the Coalition planners had templated the firebase in the middle of a minefield. Moving the earth would be the easy part, as we had the personnel and equipment from the U.S. Army's 2120th Engineer Company to support us. An Oklahoma Army National Guard unit, the 2120th had deployed to Al Asad to provide vertical and horizontal engineering support for the base's expansion efforts. They were all combat engineers, but they didn't have a counter-IED mission. And, we had quickly confirmed, the ground needed a dedicated clearing effort by EOD technicians and additional combat engineers to ensure no one would get blown up during the construction and occupation. Our team had exactly two EOD techs—Staff Sergeant Brian and Sergeant Rioux—and one combat engineer officer dedicated to our counter-IED program. We also had access to a pair of SPMAGTF EOD techs and several Norwegian engineers who could assist in the sweeping effort, but that was it. Other than a temperamental 7-ton truck with a semi-functional mine roller, we had no heavy equipment designed to locate and clear buried ordnance from large plots of land. Our only choice would be to clear the firebase on foot with handheld metal detectors. For something that was intended to be a small, inconspicuous outpost, it still measured about 300 meters by 400 meters—roughly three football fields wide and four deep. The clearance team would have their work cut out for them.

New problems popped up daily, but White's directive underscored one thing: Desert Lion was back on. As we expected, the Hawija operation would continue to be the main effort, and Desert Lion's first phase would be a supporting effort. The Coalition had asked for a list of requirements needed to accomplish the mission, but we could read between the lines: no one outside our team had much to offer apart from emotional support. The timeline was too tight, and the available manpower and equipment pool in Iraq wasn't what it needed to be to assist us. Once initiated in mid-October, Phase One of Desert Lion would likely be us—and only us.

As we struggled to convince Qassim we were still on board with his vision, everyone in our Marine Corps chain of command in the United States seemed more concerned about the task force's name. On September 4, the Coalition headquarters in Baghdad had officially redesignated our team as "Task Force Lion." And, as many team members had predicted, the name change brought an unwanted level of scrutiny. The drama had been several weeks in the making. Once White announced his intent for us to expand our command and control role for the upcoming operation, we immediately started shedding our base support responsibilities. The arrival of the Army regional support group several weeks earlier had supercharged the transition, and the task force was free to focus almost entirely on Desert Lion.

The Coalition orders outlining the name change confirmed we would still have tactical control of those units aboard Al Asad, which would enable us to succeed during the operation's initial phase. Our higher headquarters in Baghdad would assign additional forces to us as necessary in later phases of the operation. And, as if another reason was needed, the name change conformed to the Coalition's existing unit naming convention: 2-82 Brigade Combat Team, the U.S. Army brigade in the north, was Task Force Falcon; their replacement, 3-10 Mountain, was Task Force Patriot. "Task Force Al Asad" implied the team was geographically tied to the base. "Task Force Lion," on the other hand, eliminated that distinction, and the name stuck. I guess it made sense. After all, White never referred to me by my first name. Instead, he always addressed me as "Lion-6." The name of the task force at Al Taqaddum similarly changed to Task Force Spartan, and there would be hell to pay for *both* of our teams once the news made its way back to home station.

Sure enough, when word of the name change reached the commanders and staffs in Bahrain, Tampa, and Camp Pendleton, you would have thought the world was ending. Our email boxes lit up with messages demanding explanations for the change and implying we had unilaterally rebranded the task force ourselves. Despite the pointed questions, the team collectively dug in its heels and embraced the new moniker. If nothing else, it seemed to confirm we would soon move beyond Al Asad's green zone to support Qassim's forces fighting in the red zone.

16

GET IT DONE

BEFORE WE COULD ADJUST to the new timeline, it shifted again. In the early evening of September 8, just twenty-four hours after Major General White told me we had more than a month to build and occupy EFB Sagrah, his J-3 emailed a long, bulletized note to an even longer list of commanders and staff officers across Iraq.

"Desert Lion will execute on September 19 as a supporting effort," the colonel said, outlining a list of expectations and refined guidance from White. The not-so-subtle message for the task force was what we had expected: *Use what you have at Al Asad, and get it done.*

We were back to the original timeline Qassim had described two days earlier. I wondered where the disconnect was. The Coalition and Iraqi planners in Baghdad were supposed to be joined at the hip and speaking with a single voice, but that didn't appear to be the case. Either no one on the Coalition side got the memo, or Qassim had somehow convinced Abdul Amir and Prime Minister Abadi to change their minds and return to the original start date. One phrase that had taken root within the Coalition was "Never make the Iraqis wait on us." The expression, and the mindset it promoted, underscored the Coalition's commitment to supporting the Iraqi Security Forces. But it also created unrealistic expectations. The Iraqi leaders thought we could turn on a dime, which we certainly could not. For Qassim's part, either he didn't understand the timeline and resources necessary to build an outpost like Sagrah, or he didn't care. It was probably a little of both.

The news that the operation was on again would no doubt please Qassim, but it had us jumping through our asses to refine our own timeline to get Sagrah up and running. Five hours after the J-3's email blast, we had what we believed was a workable solution. I sent a note to White, summarizing our plan.

"We can start the build on September 11," I said up front. "It will be IOC by September 14 and FOC by September 18 to support the attack on September 19. TF Lion TAC will be in position at EFB Sagrah with JaOC commander, 2 x Paladins, Q-53 radar, and SecFor; our Main CP [command post] at Al Asad will also be ready to battle-track, collect, process, and distribute intel, and control ISR and fires."

After pressing the "send" button, I knew I had just written an enormous check. There would be no calling it back. I had just committed our tiny, under-resourced headquarters to the operation, and we now had ten days to see if that check would clear or bounce.

<hr>

The final days before setting out to build the Sagrah outpost were a frenzy of last-minute coordination as the staff calculated and recalculated everything needed to establish the firebase. The effort consumed us, and there was little time to consider how we would fulfill our supporting role in the Iraqi attack on Rayhanah and Anah. Simply establishing the firebase had become the mission—the "alligator closest to the boat." As the staff feverishly drafted orders and lined up the assets needed to begin construction, I reconsidered some of my decisions.

Foremost in my mind was risk management. I was far from being a risk-averse leader. And yet, in examining the problem, I knew that executing as planned would incur a significant degree of risk. My decision to move Al Asad's howitzers, counterbattery radar, and mortar tubes would effectively uncover the base, leaving it vulnerable to a rear-area attack. The HIMARS launchers, which were not mine to move, would remain. However, with their trajectory and extended range fans, they were not useful for local force protection.

Because MSR Bronze was the only viable supply route between Al Asad and Sagrah, I would also be risking the safety of the men and women who would build and then operate from the outpost. We would tip our hand once the task force's heavy equipment and resupply convoys rolled out of Hammer Gate, and the highway would become a "burned" route. The chances of our convoys triggering back-laid IEDs, or enemy attacks along the extended route, would increase dramatically. And, because the Marine SecFor platoon would guard the firebase, Al Asad would no longer have a local, ground-based QRF. There would be no Coalition ground forces to pull our asses out of the fire if we became decisively engaged.

It would also be a challenge to deal with any significant casualties along the way. The "golden hour" range, which was the maximum distance a MEDEVAC aircraft could reach and then return to a medical treatment facility within one hour, was at the very edge of Anah. The golden hour had been practically written into the individual service member's Bill of Rights since the 2003 invasion. In most cases, any discussion of moving beyond it was considered heresy. The only on-site medical support available was a shock trauma section from SPMAGTF, but there was no trauma surgeon to accompany it. That was a problem. Although most of the men and women occupying the firebase would not leave its boundaries, the SOF teams and the Norwegians would accompany the Iraqis during the attack. Without a forward-based surgeon to stabilize a critically wounded Coalition member, the chances of it turning into a fatality increased dramatically, especially if weather or maintenance delays grounded the MEDEVAC helicopters.

One risk stood out in my mind the most: the necessity to build and sustain the outpost with only the team's organic personnel. It was a heavy task. On paper, Task Force Lion's personnel strength exceeded 2,300, which implied that we possessed the same battlefield capacity as an Army brigade. But the numbers were deceiving. National caveats continued to prevent most of the task force's non-U.S. Coalition members from venturing outside Al Asad. The UK caveats forbidding 2 Rifles from stepping foot outside the wire—once an annoyance—now outraged and professionally embarrassed Lieutenant Colonel Bellamy. When our planning accelerated, he made it his mission to convince his UK chain of command to expand the restrictive authorities under which he and his battalion operated. He eventually elevated the matter to the British Parliament, and although his government agreed to lessen the restrictions slightly, it was not enough to make a difference in time for Desert Lion's first phase. I harassed Bellamy mercilessly over his inability to get it done, but the jabs ceased when I saw my good-natured ribbing was hurting the situation more than it was helping.

Only the SEALs and the Coalition SOF teams were able to go outside the wire with our Norwegian advise and assist team. But because the operators were not part of the task force, they were not interested in the boring details and significant effort required to build and sustain the outpost. They were happy to simply show up on game day and go forward on the battlefield with the Iraqis. When all was said and done, the responsibility for crewing the construction and resupply convoys, as well as building the firebase itself, would fall squarely on the backs of the Marines, sailors, and soldiers from the task force headquarters and the 2120th Engineers. The long days and weeks ahead of us on the road would increase the likelihood of individual burnout and mishaps, but there was no other way to do it. Once the first convoy rolled outside the wire, the Marines would earn their pay until that phase of the operation was over.

The issue of risk eventually caught the attention of the Marine brigadier general at Task Force 51/5 in Bahrain, and I conveyed my concerns during a phone conversation.

"We're all set to go," I said. "But I gotta tell you, I am accepting a lot of risk here. We've mitigated it as best we can, but it's still there."

"Don't worry," he said. "It's my job to help you elevate that risk to my level."

I appreciated his reassurances, but this wasn't my first rodeo. I knew the rules of the game. Whether it was a rocket attack against Al Asad, an armored suicide vehicle crashing through the barriers of our thinly guarded outpost, or a fatigued driver steering a resupply truck off a bridge—the responsibility for whatever happened would rest on my shoulders. I wasn't trying to shirk my responsibilities; rather, I embraced them. I just wanted to go on record beforehand and register the realities on the ground to ensure everyone in my various chains of command knew what we were facing. Marines take orders with limited guidance and accomplish the mission with a bias for action, and that was exactly what we were doing. However, despite everyone's insistence that they would support the commander's call on the ground, I didn't trust the system to take care of me if things went south. I had to be prepared for what would happen when the music stopped.

Early in the morning of September 11, our first construction convoy rumbled to life in Camp Havoc's staging area. The previous evening, the team had squeezed into the conference room for the operations order. As we prepared to head out the door, I gave my final guidance.

"We have a job to do, and not a lot of time to do it," I said. "But let me be clear: do not sacrifice safety, security, or accountability for the sake of expediency."

Thirty minutes after the team mustered and climbed into our vehicles, we were exiting Hammer Gate with our escorts and heading north along Route Bronze. Al Anbar's punishing summer heat had not yet begun to subside, and as the convoy arrived at Sagrah the temperature climbed above 100° Fahrenheit. As the Marines cordoned the area, Staff Sergeant Brian and Sergeant Rioux moved out with their metal detectors to begin the systematic sweep and clear of the outpost. With the working parts in motion, Capt Bob Jankowski and the communications team set up the satellite system to link them back to the Main.

A Naval Academy graduate with a mechanical engineering degree, Jankowski was a combat engineer officer from Philadelphia who had originally joined the team as the task force's COPsO. His work ethic and precise, almost anal-retentive personality had been the critical component during our pre-deployment workup that kept everyone's disparate training requirements on track. I appreciated his detail-oriented nature, which put me and pretty much everyone else around him to shame. An automobile crash had nearly killed him when he was seventeen years old, and he still sported a relief map of pale white scar tissue that spider-webbed across the side of his head. He had one of the darkest, thickest mustaches I had ever seen. But, when combined with his youthful appearance, it just made him look like a boy-faced serial killer.

Upon our arrival in August, we discovered that a British captain from 2 Rifles had been serving ably as the COPsO. Rather than upset the apple cart, we redesignated Jankowski as the S-3's plans officer, but what he really became was a professional problem solver. Methodical and precise in everything he did, and with a clipped, almost robotic speech pattern, he was a weird blend of Dustin Hoffman's character Raymond from *Rain Man* and Kyle MacLachlan's Agent Dale Cooper from *Twin Peaks*. He had a peculiar, self-effacing sense of humor, but he was one of the team's most reliable members. Each time I asked him to do something, there was no doubt in my mind he would make it happen one way or another with superb results. His quirkiness and laser-focused attention to detail, which led to many pointed questions and tasks, irked many of the team members—Major Julian probably most of all. But it didn't bother me; Bob Jankowski could get it done. As a lieutenant, he had led construction projects in Thailand and the Philippines, thus making him a natural fit to be our foreman at Sagrah. As my section of the convoy split off to visit Qassim at Haditha, I knew the outpost's clearance team would be in good hands.

Any part of me that felt guilty about the spread Qassim put on for my command team at his extravagant headquarters went out the door when I learned he had arranged for lunch delivery to the crew at Sagrah. It was an act he would ensure took place every day during the firebase's construction and, later, throughout the operation itself. The Marines were accustomed to choking down MREs (meal, ready to eat) for days on end, but Qassim would hear nothing of it. Each day his portly chief of staff appeared with a squad of *jundis* carrying plastic cling-wrapped platters of rice, lamb, chicken, flat bread, and vegetables. After each delivery, Marines wandered around the construction site, nibbling on the savory, rubbery Iraqi flat bread, which was a highly coveted treat when you could score some.

Two Marines who didn't appear to be partaking in the Iraqi food fest were Brian and Rioux. Before we returned from Haditha, the two techs had located and blown in place more than forty IEDs they found arrayed along the firebase's northeast boundary. By day's end, the number would climb to more than fifty. When I linked up with them, they were, apart from the sweat, grime, and sun-reddened skin, all smiles.

"Hell of a way to commemorate 9/11!" they both exclaimed.

"Yeah, you said it," I replied, looking at the Marines positioning equipment around the outpost's perimeter. "Hell of a way."

The next day, we started moving earth.

***

As we made the final preparations to get the counterbattery radar and howitzers on the road, Major Mathwick darkened my office doorway.

"I have some . . ." she said, pausing, "*bad* news."

"Okay," I said. "Let's have it."

"None of the contracted trailers are wide enough to carry the Paladins."

"How wide are the Paladins?"

"Ten feet, four inches."

"And the trailers?"

"Not that wide," she said sheepishly.

"Ooookay," I said, taking a deep breath. Major Duesterhaus and his FOPs team had refined the construction timeline almost down to the minute. I could only imagine how this was going to jack up his finely tuned schedule.

"I don't know how this got past me," she said.

"It's done, Linds," I said. "Let's figure out how to fix it."

"We're working a rapid contract request, but I'm not sure it will get approved in time."

"Don't have much choice," I said. "Keep working the contract; I'll weigh in with the J-4 as well. I'll also ask Qassim if he can get us a flat bed. He's got to have one to carry around his tanks."

Mathwick turned on her heels and darted out of the room. She had thought I would kill her when she delivered the bad news. But how could I? *I sure* as hell didn't know how wide an Army Paladin was. Lindsay was a logistics officer who had spent her time in the service learning how to move Marine equipment. The Corps had shed its self-propelled artillery decades earlier; the only howitzers in our inventory were towed variants. It was one of the hidden pitfalls of Joint operations: you had to get out of the comfort zone of your own service culture, procedures, and equipment and learn about everyone else's. It was also a reminder of something I had internalized years earlier: bad things will always happen; it is how you react that makes the difference. I also remembered what my battalion commander once told me when I was a company commander: "Most people don't wake up on Monday morning and say, 'You know what? I think I'll fuck it up this week.'"

The deceptively wide artillery pieces were just one of many problems that surfaced as we transitioned from planning to execution. Early in Sagrah's design phase, as the FOPs team debated what the outpost needed to support the Iraqi soldiers, a comment from one of the officers brought the session to an abrupt halt.

"We won't be able to show the ISR screens to Qassim if we don't get the DVB back online," said Maj Roberto Falcon. All heads turned toward him.

Introverted and subdued, Falcon was the team's pensive, almost down-trodden communications officer. A native of Puerto Rico and a graduate of its university, he had experienced many of the same life-altering events as I had over the years. Like Major Julian and me, he had been with 1st Marine Division during the 2003 Iraq invasion. He had also served as a civil affairs team leader in Afghanistan at the same time I was in Helmand Province with 3/7. He was the most conscientious member of our staff, and there was never any doubt where his heart was. He was no dummy, either, and despite his reserved nature he had a wealth of expertise and operational experience. Together with his small team of Marines in the dusty S-6 (communications) workshop that filled a corner wing of CHU City-1, he would routinely grind himself down trying to fix whatever problem du jour had cropped up in Al Asad's fragile communications network. He regularly sported a perfectly shaved, gleaming pate, and it wasn't long before we could make the connection between a period of his personal, intense optempo and the stubbly growth of hair on his unshaved head.

He had a peculiar way of smiling with only his teeth, and even though he had a gentle soul, that emotionless grin could be unsettling. Some of the team's Brits had nicknamed him "the ghoul" because of how he roamed the passageways late at night, often appearing as a silent, shadowy outline in the doorways of people working late into the evening. It was an unfair dig because Roberto Falcon was anything *but* a ghoul. He had a wickedly dry sense of humor, as well as a deep reservoir of fascinating yet generally useless Hollywood pop culture trivia that rivaled my own. Recognizing my obsession with obscure films, he would sometimes disappear after hearing me talk about a particular movie. Then, after leveraging his extensive contractor network across the base, he would appear at my office door with a thumb drive containing a bootleg copy of the film. It was a gesture I tried several times to stop, but after a while I recognized it for what it was: an attempt to connect with his somewhat distant, often brooding commander.

Most important, Falcon understood far better than any of us the complicated communications systems we employed. So, when he announced out of the blue that our mission to support Qassim was in jeopardy, the conversation screeched to a stop like a record needle scratching across vinyl.

"What's the issue?" I asked.

"We're having equipment issues that are affecting how we get information to the strike cell," he replied.

"It's what the strike cell's been screaming at us about," Major Julian grunted. "They say they won't approve our strikes unless we fix it."

"Wait, what?" I asked, looking at the two of them.

"We need to get ours fixed; it's receiving but not transmitting," Falcon said. "And we need another one to use at Sagrah."

"Great, glorious screens of ISR," snarked Major Kelly.

"Well, okay," I said. "So, what's the problem?"

"There's only one FSR in the entire country authorized to work on it, and he's in Mosul right now," Falcon said. "They're saying it could be two weeks before they can get him here."

"Bullshit," I said. "Nothing takes two weeks."

"He doesn't have airlift priority; he's just a contractor."

Mathwick was in an altogether better place with her artillery dilemma than Falcon was with the router. At least she had the Paladins on hand; for her it was just a matter of sourcing new trucks to haul the howitzers. Falcon faced a greater challenge with the satellite receiver shortfall and the mysterious, absentee contractor who was the reputed digital savior for all things DVB.

Although Mathwick and Falcon may have thought otherwise, I wasn't angry that they had brought their problems to my doorstep. The two officers had worked their respective issues as much as they could, and they finally reached the point where they needed additional guidance and assistance. It was one of the hallmarks of good staff officers. What aggravated me was the inaction by their counterparts in Baghdad when Mathwick and Falcon communicated their issues to our higher headquarters. After several days passed with no movement in a positive direction, I injected myself into the process, which is to say I mentioned the logjam in my weekly update to Major General White. Once he got interested in the problem, his staff got engaged . . . and in turn they got pissed off at me for dropping a dime on them. But I didn't have time to waste being gentle or tap-dancing around the issue. September 19 was right around the corner.

17

DO IT LIVE

AS THE MINUTES TICKED CLOSER to kickoff, pressure built within the team. No one wanted to fail, and that determination was leading to some questionable decisions on the ground. Even though September had reached its midpoint, the heat the Marines and sailors were working in had not relented. My concern climbed when team members returned from the long convoys practically dead on their feet. Our armored vehicles, many of which had been festering at Al Asad since 2014, were in poor shape. Their air conditioners routinely malfunctioned or were nonexistent—a significant health hazard inside a sealed vehicle with windows that didn't roll down. On more than one occasion, Marines completed their convoys with serious cases of heat exhaustion. In one instance, Major Duesterhaus spent all day inside a truck with a broken air conditioner. The temperature inside the cab rose past 100° Fahrenheit, slowly broiling its occupants. By the time he showed up at the command post, he looked like a cadaver, his skin white as a sheet and his eyes sunk deep in their sockets. Other Marines would return similarly wiped out, and they often spent hours recovering in the medical bay with IV bags plugged into their arms.

Meanwhile, the clearance effort at Sagrah was behind schedule, in part because the Norwegian engineer team was moving too slowly. We were happy for their contribution—resources were so scarce that we wouldn't have turned away *anyone*—but they swept at an agonizingly slow pace. It was like watching paint dry. Even Staff Sergeant Brian and Sergeant Roux, whose lives and limbs literally depended on their slow, smooth, and deliberate procedures, fairly groaned at the Norwegian team's glacial progress. And then, without warning, the Norwegians left the site—ostensibly to prepare for the operation with the rest of their Viking counterparts. To make matters worse, the EOD Marines from SPMAGTF supporting our effort also departed prematurely, leaving just Brian and Rioux to sweep 120,000 square meters of earth by themselves. The situation grew more precarious on the night of September 13.

"Sir, are you aware there are a bunch of Marines sweeping for IEDs out at Sagrah?" Sergeant Major Leibfried asked after cornering me in my office.

"What do you mean, 'A *bunch of Marines*'?" I asked, raising an eyebrow.

"Yeah, the SecFor grunts are sweeping. Our own engineer officer is out there swinging a metal detector too."

"*What?*"

"I don't think they should be doing that," he said.

"Geez, you *think?*"

In earlier years, I wouldn't have given such news a second thought. An entire platoon of combat engineers had supported my battalion in Afghanistan, and it *still* wasn't enough Marines to prevent casualties or make a dent in the enemy's efforts. Back then, it was necessary to train ordinary riflemen to take point on patrol *and* operate metal detectors. But 2011 was a different time. The Marines had been engaged in daily combat operations, and everyone readily accepted that casualties occur in combat. They became so commonplace that, whenever one of my Marines was killed or gravely wounded, the only requirement was a serious incident report capturing all the details. A questionable shoot, or the loss of a weapon or other piece of high-value equipment, resulted in a more detailed investigation than the death of a Marine in combat. That wasn't the case now in Iraq. Conventional units like ours going outside the wire and placing themselves in environments of increased danger was still a relatively new phenomenon. Any casualties among our team would result in an uncomfortable level of scrutiny from our higher headquarters—especially our administrative chains of command back in the continental United States.

Muttering to myself, I picked up the phone and called Captain Jankowski at the construction site.

"Hey, man, no one out there should be sweeping except actual combat engineers and the EOD techs," I said. "And tell Kyle to stop sweeping. Combat engineer or not, a captain doesn't need to be looking for landmines. That goes for you too, Bob."

"Yes, sir," Jankowski replied.

"I'll be out there tomorrow to check progress," I said. "We'll talk more then."

My next step was to send a note to Colonel Gideons. If I was going to make a call regarding his Marines' personal safety, I owed it to him to bring him in the loop. In most other circumstances, nothing would require me to consult him before directing the tactical employment of his people assigned to me. But until that point, his Marines at Al Asad had not been involved in operations that carried as much risk. He deserved communication from me, and we didn't need anything else increasing the friction between the two of us. Our earlier agreement to disagree loomed like a black cloud over our friendship, and I hoped he would see my note for how it was meant: an attempt to reach out and bring him into the decision-making process.

"It's your call," he replied. "You're the commander on the ground. But I appreciate you talking to me about it. Good luck."

The next day, Leibfried and I hopped on a convoy delivering the team's ailing mine roller to Sagrah, which was now a bustling construction zone with Marines and soldiers moving around the work site. The SecFor Marines had cordoned the site with their vehicles, and a section of mortar men were attempting to cool themselves in the patchy shade of a camouflaged net draped across their excavated gun pit. Iraqi soldiers also moved back and forth as they delivered components of the super-CHU that, once assembled, would form the outer shell of the tactical command post. The EOD team had marked the cleared areas with strips of white cloth engineer tape, and bulldozers from the 2120th Engineers kicked up choking clouds of dust as they filled Hesco baskets and pushed up perimeter berms. With each pass, the bulldozers pulverized the sand into a chalky powder.

I turned to Sergeant Major Leibfried. "This place is gonna be nasty," I said, wiping away the film of dust that was caking together with the sweat running down my face.

"You sure we're doing the right thing out here?" he asked, surveying the area. "I mean, why do we really need to build this thing *and* occupy it?"

"The Iraqis need our arty [artillery]," I replied. "We've got to support the A3E teams. And we've got to get Qassim out front with his troops. Otherwise, he'll try to do this whole thing from Al Asad."

"And what's wrong with that?"

"A lot. We need to show him what right looks like," I said. "Come on, there's Bob."

I grabbed Jankowski and motioned for the team's other engineer officer and the SecFor platoon commander to join us.

"How's progress?" I asked.

"Slow, sir," Jankowski replied. "We're pretty sure the minefield was confined to the northern edge of the site, but we still need to confirm there's nothing else out here. There's a lot of sweeping to do, but having the mine roller now will help. Once it's up and running, things will speed up."

"Okay, good," I said. "But listen: EOD sweeps; SPMAGTF's engineers sweep. I *don't* want the grunts sweeping."

"That's gonna slow us down," the combat engineer officer said. "We've already trained the grunts to sweep."

"I don't give a shit," I replied. "This isn't Afghanistan. I'm not willing to get dudes blown up when they shouldn't be out here sweeping in the first place. We good?"

"Yes, sir," the three officers replied.

"Then get after it."

The pressure seeped into everything we did. It wasn't until after I returned to Al Asad on the evening of September 14 that I realized the construction project had pulled my attention away from other important aspects of our mission. Despite Leibfried's persistent questions about the outpost's value, the person who made me see I had begun to lose focus was Lieutenant Colonel Bruøygard. In the previous week, he and his Norwegian team had spent what seemed like an inordinate amount of time with the SEALs at their camp. Between that and the friction that had built up between the CJSOTF commander and me, I was beginning to think the special operations community was unduly influencing the Norwegians. The CJSOTF commander, a colonel whose interpersonal modus operandi was to draw in close to try to physically intimidate you, was unhappy about Desert Lion's command relationships diagram. In a loud phone call, he had proclaimed, in no uncertain terms, that the SOF teams participating in Desert Lion would never, under any circumstances, work for me. Even though he knew I was the battlespace owner and the operational commander, he implied that his operators should be allowed to do as they pleased on the battlefield with no oversight or external controls from me and my team.

There was no question about it: we needed the SOF teams to execute the operation's first phase. With only the Norwegian unit to employ as an accompanying team, we didn't have the capacity to partner with all of Qassim's and Numan's battalions that would assault Rayhanah and Anah. The Coalition couldn't spare anyone because of the operation in Hawija, and we were too far along to get any SPMAGTF Marines and their equipment from Kuwait to partner with the Iraqi battalions. In some regards, the utility of the SPMAGTF Marines would have been limited anyway. Only the SOF operators had the authorities necessary to accompany the tribal militia units, who would play an outsized role in the assault. However, because of the SEAL team's secretive nature, we had very little awareness of any pre-operation planning they were doing, or even what they intended to do once they were on the ground with the Iraqi soldiers and the Sunni tribesmen. It was all extremely aggravating.

When Bruøygard detailed his planning and coordination with the SEALs, I told him what was on my mind.

"Hey, listen," I said, conveying my understanding of his plight. "I don't want the SEALs to be an obstacle between you and my staff."

"No, actually it has been just the opposite," he said. "We've gotten everything we need from Trident, not from Task Force Lion."

His words were a cold splash of water to the face, and I was unable to conceal my physical reaction.

"*What?*" I bristled.

"We're getting better support from them than we are from your headquarters."

"And how's that, exactly?"

"They are giving me all the information I need to conduct my planning and preparation," he replied. "And there's been nothing from your staff yet about an orders brief or ROC [rehearsal of concept] drill."

"Sorry, man," I said through clenched teeth. "We've been a little too busy building Sagrah to hold your team's hands. In case you haven't been paying attention to what's going on around here, every single member of my headquarters is working their ass off to get the outpost built."

"I apologize," he said, seeing how much his comments had put me off. "I didn't mean to offend you."

"You didn't offend me," I said. "Just remember whose team you're on."

As he left the office, I shook my head and stewed. Awtry and Kelly walked in several minutes later. Awtry took one look at me and knew something was up.

"What's going on?" he asked.

"Viking-6 thinks we're not supporting his team enough, so he's hanging his hat with the SEALs now."

"What?!" he exclaimed. "All we've *done* is carry them since we got here. We've been helping them get their equipment ready, we've set up ranges for them, we've given them all our planning products . . ."

"We've also consumed a hell of a lot of bandwidth giving them intel support," Kelly added. "They've asked for so many maps that our plotter is running out of ink."

"Colonel Fridriksson warned me about this," I said. "They're just needy. But one thing's for sure."

"What's that?" asked Awtry.

"Viking has gone over to the dark side with the SEALs," I said. "We really are on our own now to get Sagrah built."

After much prodding, Qassim agreed to host the orders brief on September 15 before everyone moved out to their staging points. It was a small victory for us as advisors. He'd had no intention whatsoever to meet with his subordinate commanders, but after we suggested the idea several times he finally replied, "Yes, I was planning to do that." It didn't matter if he had planned to beforehand or not; he had finally committed to doing it, which was the important part.

The normally vacant lot outside Numan's command post was crowded with Humvees, SUVs, and pickup trucks. Rather than the nominal quartet of *jundis* relaxing in the shade of the lot's metal awning, armed Iraqi soldiers stood guard everywhere. It was a good sign. We climbed from our vehicles and shed our body armor, and together with Lieutenant Colonel Bruøygard and the SOF team leaders we filed from the parking lot into Camp Majid's grand meeting hall. The place was packed. Uniformed Iraqi army and tribal militia officers, robed and gilded sheikhs, and local police and civilian leaders sat at the long conference table that was the room's centerpiece. Artificial flowers, bottles of water, cans of soda, and glass ashtrays lined the table, and a hazy, bluish plume of cigarette smoke shrouded the hall. As I moved toward a chair along the wall, Qassim motioned for me to sit next to him and Numan at the head of the table.

I don't know what I had expected to happen. Nine years earlier, I never saw my Iraqi partner give an orders brief. The few operations his battalion had actually conducted were usually done on the fly, and the enemy situation at the time was so minimal that the commander hadn't felt compelled to give an operations order to his subordinates. Times were different now. However, while Qassim had gone through the motions to gather his leaders, the session was less an orders brief than it was one long stream of consciousness rant to everyone present. He focused on low-level issues, and he threatened to penalize his commanders if they didn't comply.

"When the assault echelons are moving," he shouted, shaking a fist, "I don't want anyone getting out of their vehicles. If anyone gets out of their vehicles, I will punish them!"

Oh well, I thought, watching my hopes of a doctrinal orders brief spiral down the drain. *At least he's got everyone in here. Better than nothing.*

After a few more minutes of dressing down everyone, Qassim introduced me to the crowd. I leaned forward in my chair.

"In the name of God, the most Gracious, the most Merciful," I said. "It is an honor to be here today with the commanders and tribal leaders who will lead this operation.

"They have called this the beginning of the Middle Euphrates River Valley operation. I know that's not true; the soldiers of the Jazeera Operations Command and their tribal partners have been waging this fight for three years now. You have already pushed the Islamic State out of places like Hit, Haditha, and Baghdadi. What you will do now in Rayhanah and Anah is the beginning of the end for ISIS in Al Anbar.

"I was with 28th Brigade nine years ago in Al Qa'im. When I left, I knew there was unfinished business for me. Back then, I didn't know what that unfinished business was. Now I do. My unfinished business was to return to 7th Division and help you all destroy the Islamic State and get your country back."

Heads nodded amid grunts of approval, and then Qassim returned to his yelling and finger-pointing. As he outlined details of the plan, which had changed yet again since the last time we talked, I leaned over to Bruøygard.

"Do you understand now why we haven't done our own ROC drill yet?" I asked. He nodded and seemed to have gotten the message: Qassim and the Iraqis were changing the plan so often that we couldn't keep up. Any rehearsals the task force might have done by that point would be irrelevant.

Bruøygard's newfound understanding of our partners aside, he had made an important point: one way or another, the task force needed to conduct a rehearsal. By September 16, between the now-daily changes to the plan and the Sagrah outpost's new initial operating status, we could wait no longer. We had to figure out some way to get everyone on the same sheet of music. That afternoon, close to a hundred men and women from the Coalition filled a warehouse in the corner of Camp Havoc. The variety of uniforms was an indicator of just how multinational and multidisciplinary the mission had become. There were Marines in pixilated desert utilities, Army soldiers in operational camouflage pattern fatigues, SEALs in rumpled Nomex outfits that resembled the Marines' (but looked oh-so-much-comfier), and the Coalition teams from the United Kingdom, Norway, Denmark, and Spain—each with their own exotic pattern and style.

The crowd circled around a rudimentary terrain model on the dusty concrete, and I took the floor to convey my commander's intent to all hands. I was in the initial stage of an upper respiratory infection—the curse of Al Anbar Province to which nearly everyone serving there eventually succumbed—and my voice was hoarse and reedy. The same thing had happened to me on the night my company moved up to the Iraqi border nearly fifteen years earlier. Now that it was happening again at such a crucial moment, I feared it was nothing more than some weird version of the flop sweats. I cleared my throat and stepped forward.

"The purpose of Desert Lion's first phase is twofold," I croaked. "One: to capitalize on recent gains made in Mosul and Tal Afar, and two: to compel Islamic State forces to confront the Iraqi Security Forces along two major axes within AO Patriot and AO Lion. This phase of the operation will enable the Iraqis to establish a foothold in western Al Anbar Province, and it will set conditions for them to execute the remainder of the MERV campaign.

"Key tasks include the clearing, building, and sustainment of Expeditionary Firebase Sagrah; embedding, coordinating, and supporting the Task Force Lion and SOF teams partnering with ISF forces; and coordinating, deconflicting, and employing armed ISR and precision surface and aviation-delivered fires.

"The end state for this phase will be Islamic State forces destroyed in zone, the Iraqi forward line of troops expanded northwest of Anah, and Task Force Lion postured to support Iraqi forces for future phases. There will be three keys to our success for this op: flexibility, patience, and over-communication among everyone on the battlefield."

With the rogue's gallery participating, we were going to need those three keys. To be sure, Phase One would be a task force operation—*not* a SOF operation. But the senior special operations commander had yelled loud enough and long enough to get his way: the operators would *not* work for Task Force Lion. There was no one in Baghdad, including Major General White himself, with enough *wasta* (connections) to affect that change. Going into it, we could only agree that the relationship between the task force and the operators would be "supporting-supported," which was the most confusing of all command relationships in the book. It all boiled down to one question: who was the supporting unit and who was the supported unit? On paper, our task force was the supported unit, but we knew the relationship would shift over time—not just during Phase One, but throughout the entire operation.

Between the lack of resources, a compressed timeline, and wavering signals of willingness and commitment from the Iraqis, the odds were stacked against us. The tension created by different service cultures, personalities, and operational authorities aside, everyone knew we had to make it work somehow. No one was going to swoop in and tell us how to accomplish the mission or how to get along. That was up to us. The ticking clock had run out; it was showtime. We had no other choice but to emulate Bill O'Reilly's infamous televised flip-out. When it came to Desert Lion's first phase, we would have to do it live.

18

HEADING TO A PARTY

THE SUN WAS APPROACHING the horizon on September 18 when the Jump linked up with our escorts at Hammer Gate. We were getting on the road later than planned, but there had been so much to do beforehand that we were now leaving at the last possible minute. The previous evening, I had dialed up Major General White and his staff for a final burst of pre-operation synchronization. Line by line, I read from a list of coordinating instructions depicted on a green, yellow, and red highlighted conditions check slide. When I reached the end, I turned my gaze back to the video camera.

"We're all set, Iron-6," I said. "The Iraqi engineers are cheating forward and clearing up Bronze to give the ISF a head start. Sagrah's Paladins are fire-capped, the DVB contractor is on site and working on getting our video feeds online, and the firebase is fully operational. I'm heading up there tomorrow to link up with Qassim; we'll be ready to go on the nineteenth."

"Alright, Lion-6," White grunted. "I'll try to make my way out to see you in a couple of days. Be careful out there . . . and kick ass."

"Goddamned right, sir," I replied, signing off.

There was one final thing to do before heading outside to the staging lot. Back home, Ashley was almost completely in the dark about what we were doing, so I typed a brief email to let her know I would be off the net for a bit. My words were cryptic, but easily decipherable: *My friends are heading to a party up north a ways, but I won't be going all the way with them; I'll just be hanging out with a bunch of TVs and watching them have fun.*

As we rolled through Sagrah's razor-wired entrance, the convoy lurched to a stop so the Marines could ground-guide us through the darkened camp. We waited in our vehicle cabs, the only illumination coming from the digital readouts of the dashboard consoles. Suddenly, the jet-black night shrouding the outpost flashed electric white, followed immediately by the overpowering *boom* of a Paladin firing. My heart skipped about three beats at the unexpected flash, report, and concussion wave. Then the second howitzer fired, lighting up the sky again. Staff Sergeant Rick, the security detail's gritty enlisted leader and a fellow Sangin Valley veteran, later told me he had made the mistake of opening his vehicle hatch and hopping out just as the first artillery piece fired. For a moment he thought he was dead, thinking the blinding flash and concussion was an IED detonating beneath his feet.

As the Paladins fired in short intervals, prepping targets inside and around Rayhanah farther west, the Marines on foot led our vehicles through the outpost's dusty interior, guided by a glowing breadcrumb trail of green ChemLights. We stopped next to the vague outline of the super-CHU, and I felt my way toward the unbroken rectangular line of white light leaking out from the door. As my eyes adjusted to the darkness, a small forest of antennas poking up from behind the command post appeared. Nearby, a stack of roaring generators drowned out any conversation within twenty feet.

Inside, Captain Jankowski sat behind a computer terminal, a Motorola radio in one hand, curtly directing someone on the other end of the line. The container was no longer recognizable as a CHU. It was now a fully functioning tactical command post with an Iraqi flair. Large, laminated maps lined the walls, and the Marines had pushed together half a dozen folding tables to make two long, parallel rows. Behind them were a separate table and chairs for Qassim and his team to preside over the operation. Computer terminals and phones filled the tabletops, and a bank of radios dominated one end of the front row. A small DMR radio receiver with a handset rested on Qassim's table. At the front of the room, further replicating the Camp Havoc watch floor, the Marines had erected a set of wobbly wooden stands for the flat-screen televisions on which we would view the precious ISR video feeds.

After hounding his counterparts in Baghdad, Major Falcon had finally succeeded in getting Josh—notoriously the only American contractor in Iraq authorized to work on our digital router—to the firebase. Narrow-framed, with a wispy beard and clad in a dark hoodie and faded denim, he looked barely out of his teens. But he knew his job. As he tinkered with the router, one by one the television screens turned from blank slates to moving video footage broadcast by the drone fleet cruising the heavens above us.

"That should do it," Josh said, grabbing his backpack and returning a handful of small tools to one of the pouches. "The images may pop in and out sometimes, but it should work fine now."

"You're a hard man to get ahold of," I said, looking at the silent footage scrolling across the screens. "You're like the most popular dude in Iraq right now."

"Yeah, I get that a lot," he said with an awkward chuckle. He looked around for a moment. "So, when's the next convoy? I need to get back to Mosul."

"Not so fast, dude," I replied. "You're sticking around until we're sure it works. That thing you just installed is pretty much the only reason we're out here in the middle of nowhere. If it shits the bed, we need you around to get it up and running."

"Okay, whatever," he said, shouldering his backpack and heading toward the door. As he wandered off into the night, I got the impression he really didn't give a crap about what we were trying to do. He was just there to do a job and make some money—and probably a ridiculous amount of cash at that. But I was digging in my heels: he would remain with us until I was confident the router worked and, more important, until Qassim was satisfied. Anyone who wanted to redirect Josh before that would have to pry him from my cold, dead hands.

Once Jankowski finished giving us the command post tour, I looked over toward the other half of the room where I had entered. Rice and breadcrumbs, the cold remnants of an Iraqi meal, were scattered all over a folding table along the wall. The platters had been picked clean.

"Qassim's men still delivering food to you guys?" I asked.

"Every day since we got here."

In the far corner was a glass-topped coffee table, a set of brown, wood-framed, overstuffed chairs, and a matching couch. From the looks of it, Qassim had spared no expense to make the CHU like a home for us. But then, plopping down on the couch and feeling the rock-hard foam cushion under me, I saw that 'spared no expense' was probably an exaggeration.

After several hours of pre-operational checks, I looked around one last time and turned to Major Awtry.

"Alright," I said. "What's left? What have we forgotten?"

"Everything's all set," he said. "The Iraqis will move out tomorrow at 0600."

"Then let's get some sleep. It's gonna be a long couple of weeks."

He grabbed his gear and disappeared out the door. A few minutes later, I hoisted my ruck and followed him. The darkness of the firebase turned to daylight as a volley of 122-mm rockets from an Iraqi BM-21 Grad launcher inside the town of Sagrah screamed westward. Between the rockets' hideous shrieks and their bright orange exhaust plumes that illuminated the night sky, it was a terrifying collision of sight and sound. I wondered what it was like being on the receiving end. When the volley ended, I resumed my search for a place to sleep. Between the command post's brightly lit interior and the fiery glow of the Grad volley, my night vision was shot, and I stumbled over tent stakes, guidelines, stacks of MRE boxes, and other random pieces of gear strewn about outside. I turned around, re-entered the command post, and laid out my sleeping bag on the hard couch. The last thing I needed was to trip in the dark and bash my brains in before The Show had even begun.

I awoke early the next morning to the chatter of radios and people talk-ing. True to his word, Qassim strolled through the door with Kiffa and Ahmed at 0600. As they assumed their places at the table overlooking the room, Qassim gave the thumbs-up, and his lead units crossed the line of departure. Within an hour the force was creeping up Route Bronze, which the Iraqi engineers and EOD teams had begun methodically clearing two days before. As a key part of their defensive belt encircling Rayhanah and Anah, the Islamic State defenders had lined the road with IEDs, burrowing the explosives into the highway's dirt shoulders and even sawing into the asphalt itself—what our own techs referred to as "lollipop" IEDs because of the stick-and-square pattern cut into the asphalt. The Iraqi engineers and EOD teams had developed a reputation for advancing against obstacle belts without cover, and their reduction techniques often amounted to little more than severing an IED's power wire and lifting the device out of the ground by hand—if they removed it at all. They were brave sons of bitches—some might even say foolish—but they were getting the job done.

Just before 1000, Qassim's radio came to life. He barked something into his handset, and I turned to Amador.

"The soldiers are on the move," he replied.

The three brigades split into their separate attack axes south of Rayhanah, and the radio filled with rapid-fire chatter. I turned again to Amador, who had positioned himself beside Qassim.

"What's going on?"

"Thirtieth Brigade just hit an IED on the highway," he said, translating the radio traffic. "It killed an officer—a major—and wounded a *jundi*."

"*Sayidi*," I said, turning to Qassim and placing my hand on my heart. "I'm very sorry for your soldiers."

"Eh," he said, brushing off my condolences with a wave of his hand. "They didn't listen to me. I told them to stay on the road."

That was certainly true. Everyone had heard him growl to his command-ers, "Stay in your vehicles, and don't let your soldiers wander off the road." Apparently those two soldiers didn't get the memo. Both had paid the price, and Qassim had no regret.

By the end of the day, and to our surprise, Qassim's brigades had made significant progress along all five attack axes toward Rayhanah. Before nightfall, the JaOC Commandos entered the town from its eastern corner, only to find the place practically empty. Despite the two casualties earlier in the day, all seemed a little too easy. But the Iraqi military had learned a lot from the battle of Mosul. They weren't interested in slogging it out again with entrenched enemy fighters inside an urban area. At Qassim's insistence, the task force had punished Rayhanah with Coalition firepower for months. By the time the Commandos assaulted through the small town, there wasn't much of it left. The residents had long since fled, and everyone assumed the only people remaining there were either devoutly committed to the Islamic State cause or batshit-crazy. Or maybe both. Either way, Qassim had considered Rayhanah an annoyance, one he had to deal with as quickly as possible. The real jewel, in the near term at least, was Anah, and it would be a tougher fight than any of us imagined.

19

ARGUING DRUNKS

AT FIRST, when Qassim stormed out of the command post on September 20, I figured he would return. There might even be a slight shrug of his shoulders to signal his embarrassment at abandoning us just when things were getting exciting. Before long, however, it sank in: he wasn't coming back. Although he would be on the radio continuously, personally directing his subordinate commanders and communicating with me by radio and cell phone via Kiffa and Ahmed, I wouldn't see my partner in person again until after the battle's end. Throughout it all, in between Qassim's communications with his two loyal deputies and me, his voice dominated the radio waves. One person he endlessly called for was Lieutenant Colonel Adnan Ali Mirza, the commander of 1st Battalion, 27th Brigade (1/27). But Adnan would never answer. The few times he *did* respond to Qassim's calls, he refused to report his location out of fear the enemy would target him.

The Islamic State teams defending from the apartment complex in Anah's southeast corner had become a problem for Qassim's advancing forces. Weeks earlier, Major General White had cautioned me that a single enemy fighter with a rifle and a good firing position in an urban setting could stop an entire Iraqi battalion in its tracks. Now, as we watched the ISIS teams bound from building to building, White's words rang true. Although the JaOC Commandos, the 7th Division Commandos, and 1/27's *jundis* had arrayed themselves toward the apartment complex, it had taken only a handful of enemy holdouts to pin them down.

Qassim called me repeatedly from his cell phone, begging for fire support to take out the snipers firing on his soldiers. The subtext was unmistakable: he wanted me to flatten the apartments with an airstrike. It was something I wasn't prepared to do. As White had emphasized several times, it was our responsibility to convince the Iraqis to leverage their own resources first before we resorted to a kinetic solution. The automatic answer couldn't always be the Coalition dropping a building for the advancing *jundis*. As Qassim harangued me, I turned to Amador, who held his cell phone with my partner waiting impatiently on the line.

"*Sayidi*," I said, exasperated, "can your soldiers see the fighters in the buildings?"

"Yes!" he yelled through the phone.

"*Jesus Christ!*" I shouted. "Tell them to shoot back! Tell them to shoot with everything they've got!"

Moments later, the twinkling of muzzle flashes lit up the video feed trained on the apartments. Showers of brick and concrete shards sprayed in all directions as rifle and machine-gun rounds peppered the outer ring of buildings. Then an explosion filled the screen. Once the smoke cleared, we saw a gaping hole in the side of one of the apartments. I turned to Jankowski and Awtry.

"What the hell was *that?*"

"SPANSOF [Spanish SOF] just lit up the building," Jankowski said, looking up from his terminal.

"We've got air inbound too," Awtry said.

"Got it," I said. "But don't drop the entire complex. It needs to get a lot worse before we level the place."

By day's end, the combined effects on the apartments from the Iraqi soldiers, the accompanying SPANSOF team, and our own air support had enabled Qassim's forces to regain their momentum. But it wasn't enough. Three armored suicide vehicles also attempted to ram themselves into the attacking soldiers. In one case, we watched in horror via a high definition ISR feed as the event unfolded. Once a pickup truck, the vehicle was now a blocky, metallic hulk on four wheels. It snuck through Anah's winding alleys, the driver guiding it via the tiny slit of a porthole in the patchwork armored plating. When the juggernaut made it to a long straightaway that pointed toward a formation of attacking Iraqi troops, the driver stepped on the gas. Even as slowly as the vehicle had rolled through the streets, once we spotted it, we could do nothing to stop it.

"Oh shit!" someone on the watch floor shouted in alarm. I can't be certain, but it might have been me.

As the lumbering vehicle gained speed, the cluster of soldiers in its path frantically opened fire. Rifle and machine-gun rounds ricocheted off the armor plates, the impacts making tiny plumes in the dust and debris scattered along the road. Having seen dozens of video clips of similar attacks, I knew what would happen next. Undeterred by the small-arms fire, the vehicle would barrel through the initial line of defending troops. Once it came to rest among the assembled soldiers, it would explode, sending flaming debris and shattered, lifeless body parts in all directions. This time was different, though. At the last moment, the vehicle prematurely detonated in a gigantic fireball—the target of an Iraqi gunner manning the cannon of his BMP-1 fighting vehicle. As a junior officer, years before the American invasion, I had persistently drilled my Marines for the day when they might have to identify and destroy advancing Iraqi armor. Even though the 1991 Gulf War was behind us, we all believed there would be another showdown one day. Back then, a BMP (*boyevaya mashina pyekhoty*, Russian-made infantry fighting vehicle) silhouette meant one thing: an enemy target. Now, nearly two decades later, I was cheering for the Iraqis and their skill with this crude, albeit effective, Cold War relic. *Jesus*, I thought, rolling my eyes. *What kind of irony is that?*

Qassim's forces to the east, southeast, and west of the city continued to receive sporadic small-arms and mortar fire from enemy positions inside

Anah for the remainder of the first day. As the sun dipped out of sight, the swift seizure of Rayhanah faded from everyone's memory. The *jundis* settled in for the night, and the Iraqi radio in our command post went silent. There would be no attempt at nighttime maneuvers; for the Iraqi forces, combat operations were very much a nine-to-five job. For those of us in the Sagrah and Al Asad command posts, however, the evening had just begun.

Apart from a few deskside discussions and the ROC drill itself, our team had not rehearsed how we would operate with my small command team at the TAC and Lieutenant Colonel Merritt leading the rest of the staff back at the Main. We were building the aircraft in flight, and there were fumbles and missteps along the way. I was committed to the notion of commanding from a forward position, and I knew that would mean giving up much—if not most—of my control of the battle. Merritt would be running things back at the rear, while the rest of the staff would be putting their noses to the grindstone.

With Awtry away, Major Duesterhaus had tabled his FOPsO duties and stepped into the operations officer role at the Main. He worked together with Julian and Kelly as they struggled to balance managing the battle *and* our partners at the same time. Just as I was dividing my time between focusing on the kinetics of the operation with Awtry and the advisor teams and coordinating with Qassim, Kiffa, and Ahmed, Julian and Kelly were dealing with the same thing at Al Asad. Julian and his fires chief, a stocky master sergeant named Nicholas Slicker, had set up shop on the watch floor. Working the targeting process through the Baghdad strike cell had devolved into a full-time job—a negotiation, even—where Julian often found himself pleading for clearance of fires with a reluctant target engagement authority on the other end of the phone line. Slicker, an intense personality who was so good at his job as the fires chief that I had asked him to assume the additional duties of the S-3's operations chief, worked the COC like the conductor of an orchestra—a maestro who barked orders at the watch officers and watch chiefs, the JTACs, and the ISR controllers to ensure everyone was on the same sheet of music.

Kelly, meanwhile, was being run ragged as he bounced between the different office spaces housing his analysts and the watch floor, where he relayed real-time intelligence information to the two Iraqi liaison officers. He also spent an inordinate amount of time fielding phone calls from Qassim. When he wasn't begging me for fire support, Qassim was chiding Kelly for not finding more enemy targets and not keeping the ISR assets trained on his own forces full-time. It was an interesting dynamic. Qassim would pester me, he would beg me, but he rarely raised his voice at me; he knew I controlled what fire support and intelligence assets he got. But he didn't have the same restraint with my intelligence officer, and throughout the operation he frequently bellowed so loudly that Kelly had to hold the phone away from his ear.

As Duesterhaus, Julian, and Kelly worked to keep the ship afloat and on course, Major Mathwick continued to juggle the operation's logistical house of cards. Carving the Sagrah outpost out of the barren desert had been just the first step. Now, with the firebase up and running and the assault in full swing, all the different entities operating from the outpost needed to be supplied with food, fuel, ammunition, spare parts, and a laundry list of other items necessary to keep everything moving in the right direction. Throughout it all, Mathwick and her S-4 team simultaneously coordinated external support from the Coalition as well as the sustainment convoys moving from Al Asad to Sagrah. Her advance work with the laborious PMNOC process was bearing fruit, and contracted trucks bulging with ammunition, building supplies, and basic life support materials were stacking up at the air base, waiting for escorts to shepherd them to Sagrah.

The only shortage our team had was the personnel necessary to crew the escort vehicles for the sustainment convoys. But what we lacked in numbers, we made up for in talent. My insistence on well-rounded team members—utility infielders who could fill multiple roles—was about to pay off. *No one-trick ponies* had been my oft-repeated mantra, and during our pre-deployment training my stubborn emphasis on the fundamentals of mounted operations—licensing, tactical vehicle movement, convoy patrol operations—had created a cadre of Marines and sailors who could support Mathwick's plan in addition to their primary responsibilities. As the operation got into full swing and the pace of convoys increased, Mathwick's assistant logistics officer combed the halls and office spaces, soliciting volunteers for each day's requirements.

"We need bodies for the 1300 movement!" he would shout to anyone listening as he called out shortfalls. "Two more drivers, three gunners, and a vehicle commander!" In many cases, Marines fresh off eight-hour watch shifts would volunteer. Others, who had remained awake much of the night supporting the operation, would similarly put their hands in the air to join the long lines of vehicles that crossed through Al Asad's gates multiple times each day. The fatigue was etched into their faces, but no one wanted to see the team fail; no one wanted to be the person who could have done more but chose not to.

As Qassim's brigades closed up shop for the evening, I sat down to compose my nightly sitrep to Major General White and his staff. CJFLCC's insatiable appetite for tactical details never ceased, and so I summarized the Iraqis' progress, the challenges they faced, and what assistance we needed. Most pressing was our struggle to obtain fire support. Even though Abdul Amir and Prime Minister Abadi had designated Qassim as the operation's axis commander—giving him the authority to approve strikes on behalf of the Ministry of Defense—there was still a significant lag between our strike requests and actual ordnance hitting the marks. I was constantly on the phone with Julian, asking what the hell was taking so long to flatten the targets that were clearly visible through our ISR feeds. Each time he would reply with a long string of obscenities.

"They don't know what the hell they're doing," he fumed, his frustration resonating through the telephone line. "Each strike is taking longer than the last, and they're only able to process one at a time."

White had announced a visit to see our team at Sagrah the next day, and I made a mental note to discuss the strike process with him. He was a no-nonsense kind of guy; surely he would agree that something needed to change. If it didn't, we wouldn't be able to give the Iraqis the leverage they needed to pick up the attack's tempo.

Just as we had on our first night at the command post, Awtry and I finished the evening with a conference call with Julian to review and coordinate the next day's fire support scheme. Now, on our third late night in a row, the strain was catching up with us. By the conversation's end, our fatigue had reduced us to a couple of drunks arguing at the bar.

"Chris," I said, "I don't feel like I've got enough situational awareness out here about what you guys're doing on the fires floor."

"Command and control, sir," he slurred. "You said it yourself: you got command out there; we got control back here."

"Yeah-yeah-yeah," I shot back. "But if we left the phone line open and used the speaker, Aaron and I'd be able to tell whatchoo guys're doing, what targets you're processing, then we won't hafta to keep callin' you over and over and over again."

"I told you I don' wanna do that!" he replied, anger rising in his voice. "That's what the strike cell makes us do when the strikes are going down. You gotta trust us, sir."

"Alright-alright-alright," I replied, giving in. Julian was right; keeping the line open was a stupid idea. And he was correct about something else: I had to trust them. There was no reason not to; all the strikes our team had conducted to that point had been by the book. There had been no civilian casualties, no unnecessary collateral damage, no squandering of CENTCOM's precious Hellfire missiles and HIMARS rockets. In short, the team at the Main was doing everything I had asked of them, and it was time for me to focus on commanding—not controlling.

"Okay, look," I said, our late-night drunken call reaching its nadir. "Iron-6 is flying out here for battlefield circ [circulation] tomorrow. I'll talk to him 'bout the strike cell nonsense."

"Oh yeah, *that*," Julian grumbled. "We're losing one of our Apaches for a couple of hours so it can escort the general's helicopter."

"What?!"

"Yeah," he replied. "So much for the main effort."

20.

INTERNAL FRICTION

SLEEPING IN THE COMMAND POST was a bad call. The watch teams rotated through shifts all night, and the ceiling's blazing fluorescent tubes burned holes through my eyelids. The chirp and squawk of radios woke me from my restless slumber each hour, as did the opening and slamming of the door whenever Marines checked on and off shift. I rose each morning, joints stiff and aching from the rock-hard couch. But there was an upside to sleeping inside: it kept me out of the fine, billowing dust surrounding the outpost—a blessing now that the illness I had succumbed to was showing the first signs of backing off. I wasn't alone in my misery; Sergeant Major Leibfried had contracted the same bug. Now, just as I was coming around, he was getting worse. His eyeballs sank into his skull, and between his hacking and wheezing I considered ordering him back to Al Asad. Perhaps my own illness was *not* a case of flop sweats; Al Anbar was out to get us all.

Although technically operational on September 19, the firebase was still under construction as the operation commenced. Capt. Amanda Thornton, the 212oth Engineer company commander, had overseen the implementation of Sagrah's final design, and she continued to refine it after we declared the outpost operational. Before long, she even had her crew build outhouses for the camp. Everyone was particularly thankful for that. Earlier, the Iraqi soldiers had tried to dig their own latrine alongside the command post's entrance before we put the kibosh on it. With the desert heat bearing down on us, the stench of an open outhouse would have sent everyone over the edge.

Thornton was a soldier's soldier. Tough as nails, but with a terrific sense of humor to match, she embraced her team's role with the task force. Originally sent to Al Asad to lead the construction effort for the base's expansion, she leapt at the opportunity to help design and build the firebase. Throughout Sagrah's construction—and with each successive outpost we established—she was always walking back and forth across the barren landscape, painstakingly guiding her soldiers in their engineering effort. The only time anyone ever saw her in a clean uniform was in the office back at the air base. Otherwise, her fatigues and body armor were obscured beneath a thick veneer of ochre moondust, her face equally filthy and blistered from the radiating sun.

Her enthusiasm for her job and the mission was as infectious as her smile. Whenever I found her wandering around the outpost's perimeter and asked how she was doing, she would launch into a detailed brief on her soldiers' progress. Everyone marveled at how she managed to get her engineers in place so quickly and build such efficient bases. Puzzles, she later explained, had always fascinated her. In her mind, designing and building an austere support base was little more than a puzzle—just on a grander scale. In some regards, her outlook mirrored what we were doing in Iraq: it was all one big puzzle. We just had to figure out how to put it together, even if some crucial pieces were still missing.

As I roused myself at sunrise on September 21, Kiffa and Ahmed appeared at the door.

"Chai," Kiffa said, grinning through a set of brown teeth and pointing outside. "And cigarette."

I glanced at my watch, my belly rumbling and turning a somersault. "Alright, *Sayidi*. Whatever you say."

As we stood outside, choking down Iraqi Marlboros and sipping from tiny, steaming glasses, Ahmed handed me a slip of paper scribbled with grid coordinates and descriptions in Arabic.

"There are *Da'esh* fighters at those locations in Anah," he said. "They have machine guns and RPGs."

Our morning ritual complete, we headed back inside. Thirty minutes later, Qassim's soldiers were on the move again, bolstered by his throaty shouting over the radio net. As the battalions reshuffled to their new attack points south of the city, desperate calls for Lieutenant Colonel Adnan once again filled the air waves. There was no answer. I motioned for Amador, and when he was by my side I spoke into the radio's handset.

"Good morning, *Sayidi*," I said. "This is *Aqeed* Folsom."

"*Habibi!* [My dear!]" Qassim bellowed. "*Shlonik?* [How are you doing?]"

"I'm great, *Sayidi*. What's your plan?"

He rattled off a long list of tasks, and I turned to Amador for the *Reader's Digest* version.

"Seventh Division Commandos, 1/27, and 1/28 have repositioned. They are formed for the penetration here," he said, pointing on the map to the main path that bisected Anah—a route we had labelled Hornets.

"Okay, *Sayidi*," I relayed. "Let's do this thing."

But the assault stalled when the defending fighters inside the town unleashed a volley of small-arms fire and mortar rounds into the advancing battalions' attack positions. Within minutes, the Iraqi soldiers triggered a series of IEDs, halting their movement yet again as they evacuated their casualties. It was difficult to watch, and it worsened when a bulldozer accidentally backed over a Humvee, crushing two of its occupants. Each time the Iraqis took casualties, the commander and father in me wanted to step in and direct our Coalition assets to assist. In many ways, the young Iraqi soldiers were no different from my own men and women. The *jundis* too had families and friends who worried about them. They were more likely to fight and risk everything if they were confident their chain of command would not abandon them when they fell on the battlefield. To Qassim's credit, he never dismissed my prodding about his casualty evacuation plan. He genuinely cared about his men. But the Iraqi army's procedures, as much as we attempted to help refine them, were just not as efficient, timely, or reliable as the Coalition's process.

And the defending enemy fighters weren't done yet. As the Iraqi soldiers pressed forward, the explosive-laden suicide vehicles continued to sneak out of the city and vector themselves toward the attackers. When the clock neared 1000, someone on the watch floor shouted in alarm and pointed toward one of the video screens. An armored hulk had emerged from its hiding place in the city, and once it was on the open hardball of Route Bronze the driver put the pedal to the metal. The video footage panned out, revealing the bomber's target: a cluster of 28th Brigade soldiers protecting the attack's flank. The Norwegian team and one of the Trident teams were also nearby, positioned on a low hilltop overlooking the Iraqi blocking position.

"Oh shit," I said, fixated on the speeding, four-wheeled missile.

Fred Fridriksson had been correct about the danger the suicide vehicles posed: once one started moving and had set up its attack run, it was too late to hit it with a Hellfire. The explosive-laden truck careened toward its target, a long contrail of dust billowing behind it. Rounds from a group volley of heavy machine guns bounced off the vehicle's armor plating, and it suddenly detonated in a fiery explosion just short of its intended target. Moments later, an orbiting Gray Eagle put a Hellfire into the side of the smoking wreck, finishing it off. The episode was redolent of the events from the previous day, when the Iraqi BMP gunner had thwarted the suicide vehicle rocketing toward him. There was a collective sigh of relief inside our command post.

Numerous parties—Iraqi, Norwegian, and American alike—would later claim to be the one who had disabled the vehicle. Everyone eventually agreed the killing shot had come from the Norwegian team's senior enlisted soldier, a squat, bespectacled master sergeant who had manned his vehicle's .50-caliber machine gun during the attack. It didn't really matter *who* had destroyed it; the threat had been neutralized, and everyone was safe. But once the Norwegian public affairs officer (PAO) uploaded photos, video, and a narrative to Facebook, the master sergeant's engagement became the official story and cemented his—and Viking's—place in history.

Ridiculous as it was, my irritation that SPMAGTF had denied our team's PAO request for the operation overshadowed my enthusiasm for the Norwegians. I had learned my lesson from Afghanistan, where years earlier I had actively resisted efforts by the press to cover my battalion's exploits. Consequently, few people outside our unit knew about the Marines' many victories and what they had experienced while suffering through the meatgrinder of Sangin. Now, as my men and women in the task force struggled to accomplish a mission where the odds were against them, I wanted their story told *while they were doing it.* But no one seemed to care. Mosul had fallen, so it seemed there were no more stories left to tell in Iraq. And, I suspected, there were more than a few senior leaders in the Marine Corps who were rankled by my refusal to call in SPMAGTF to do the job. Accordingly, I believed few among them were interested in exactly what the hell my team of castoffs was doing. The Norwegian PAO aggressively uploading footage of Viking's exploits was a reminder not only of the way Bruøygard's military had embraced his team's mission, but also of my own failure as a commander to look out for my Marines in Afghanistan—and now again in Iraq. I had to admit to a certain degree of jealousy. It was not my finest hour.

The chaos in our tiny command post was growing by the minute. With enemy fire raining down on them, Qassim's battalions couldn't get the foothold they needed to enter the town. Our attempts to engage with Coalition firepower were similarly friction-filled. Orbiting drones and attack aircraft seemed to choke the skies over Anah. Each time we processed a strike request, the Baghdad cell stepped in to clear the airspace to ensure we didn't shoot a HIMARS rocket or an Excalibur round through a drone or a jet. That was understandable. The unmanned platforms cost untold millions of dollars, and we couldn't risk losing one to our own ordnance. More important, the potential loss of life in a manned system was unimaginable. But the process was unnecessarily slow and cumbersome. More often than not, by the time the strike cell cleared the airspace, our target had either headed for the hills or moved into an area cluttered with civilians. Each time I picked up the phone to call Major Julian, his voice grew angrier and angrier.

"Jesus, man," I said at one point. "What the hell's going on? We're watching shitheads walk around in the open in the bazaar. They've got weapons, radios . . . everything, man. We need to air out their asses like *right now*. I'm getting it at both ends from Qassim and Kiffa out here."

I glanced over my shoulder. As if to punctuate my comments, Kiffa leaned over, said something to Ahmed, and then lifted his hand up in disgust toward a video display trained on a group of black-clad fighters. His body language practically screamed *These gringos have no clue what they're doing.*

"It's the strike cell," Julian shot back. "They're fucking killing us."

"Alright, look," I said. "Iron-6 is on his way out here right now. Like I said last night, I'll talk to him about it."

To be fair, with as much pushback as we were getting from the strike cell, we were generating our own internal friction in our coordination with the SOF teams. The SEALs had developed a habit of frequently declaring "TIC" (troops in contact), a brevity code that automatically diverted all nearby, available aircraft to provide close air support. They were declaring it even when they were not in danger of getting decisively engaged, which was the strict condition under which everyone was supposed to employ the term. In most cases, declaring a TIC also triggered the rules of engagement for self-defense, which in turn dramatically shortened or eliminated the approval chain altogether. I didn't want to second-guess the teams on the ground, but frequent declarations of troops in contact indicated the operators were either stretching the truth to gain control of the fire support assets, or else operating too far forward on the battlefield—in effect, fighting the enemy and becoming the main effort themselves. Neither case was acceptable.

The challenge of battlespace deconfliction hampered us throughout the operation. During our planning, after the special operations commander had dropped the gauntlet and refused to place his teams under my tactical control, the task force had divided the battlespace into a series of control measures that would determine who could request and control fires. As the operators advanced with the Iraqis, they would control fires within their corridor up to a designated phase line. The task force, meanwhile, would concentrate on the deeper fight by controlling fires well beyond the SOF teams' operating areas. But we were having difficulty properly tracking the operators as they zigzagged across the desert. They also had ready access to their own dedicated, armed ISR assets, which further complicated our coordination and deconfliction efforts. And, while we were focused on the deeper fight, it wasn't *that* deep. The enemy was inside the town; our scans of the area beyond Anah yielded only empty desert. In most cases, the Iraqis and their accompanying Coalition teams were keeping the Islamic State fighters occupied with direct and indirect fire support along the city's southern and eastern approaches. But there was still significant enemy activity in both Anah's heart and on its northern boundary.

The friction reached a flash point as one of the Trident teams approached the city from the southwest. Major Awtry called me to the map at the front of the room.

"We've got eyes on enemy fighters here," he said, pointing to a cluster of buildings in a remote corner of the city. "We're ready to hit it with HIMARS, but Trident's troop commander is pushing back. He's saying they're within the ECR [effective casualty radius]."

"Where's the team?" I asked. He pointed to a position farther south, well outside the effects of the rocket's blast. I picked up the phone to Julian. "Hey, you're cleared-hot for that HIMARS mission. It's my call."

Julian's team went to work, inputting the final coordinates for the rocket and calling it in to the strike cell. Moments later, the radio net squawked with the voice of the Trident troop commander.

"Negative; abort!" he said. "Ground force commander override!"

"The fuck?" I said, turning to Awtry, who was grimacing and slowly shaking his head.

Before we could intervene, the strike cell ended the mission. Moments later, the enemy fighters dispersed.

"This is ridiculous," I growled. "Our shit's in the street. We need to clean this up with Trident or we're never gonna get *anything* approved for the rest of the time we're out here."

The chaos peaked at midday, just as the commanding general's ill-timed battlefield circulation visit approached. When a Marine manning the radio called out, "Iron-6's flight is inbound," I grabbed my gear, jumped in a waiting truck, and rolled with several other vehicles to the Sagrah access road. The mammoth, twin-bladed CH-47 Chinook helicopter set down on the pavement one hundred meters south of my vehicle as I stood beside it, sweating inside my body armor. The tail ramp lowered, and a motley column of differently uniformed service members exited. They made a left turn off the asphalt and onto an uncleared patch of desert south of the outpost. *Oh shit*, I thought. *That's all I need: the general and his straphangers getting blown the hell up in the minefield.*

"Hey! *HEY!*" I hollered, the helicopter's deafening rotor wash drowning out my words. I waved my arms to get the group's attention. "You're going the wrong way! Back the hell up, you jackasses!"

When the entourage spotted me jumping up and down like a lunatic, pointing to the ground and mimicking explosions, they reversed course and headed for the safety of the pavement and our waiting vehicles.

"Almost got you guys blown up out there," I told White as he climbed into the truck with me.

"I thought this place was supposed to have a graveled landing zone," he said, dismissing my comment and looking at the swirling dustbowl outside his window.

"Not enough time to do it all," I replied. "Hardball has to be our LZ [landing zone] for this go-around."

The entourage debarked the armored vehicles, and the crowd of curious onlookers packed into our low-rent command post. They included U.S. and Coalition service members—conventional and special operations, officer and enlisted. Some glanced around with varying degrees of veiled disgust, contempt, and—occasionally—amazement at our ramshackle accommodations. Others stared, mouths agape, at the bustling activity on the video screens along the wall. The room rattled and shook from volleys of Paladin fire, and radios blared reports from the battlefield. Qassim's soldiers had gone to ground, still taking enemy fire from within the city, and the friction between the task force, the operators, and the Baghdad strike cell had ground all fire support to a halt. The general and his escorts couldn't have picked a worse time to visit.

"Here you go, Lion-6," White said, tossing me a can of snuff. "I bet you're burning through your stash."

"Thanks, sir," I said, pocketing it. "My great-grandma always said, 'If someone wants to give you something, let them.'"

"Alright," he said, turning to the map mounted on the back wall. Colored bits of tape littered the chart, indicating friendly and enemy battle positions. "So, what's going on? Is Qassim getting it done?"

"Haven't seen him since the second day," I replied. "He wasn't happy with how things were going, so he headed to the front."

"Well, that's what we wanted him to do, isn't it?"

"Yeah, and I don't blame him for leaving . . . it's been pretty hectic in here."

"What's the issue?"

"We're having a lot of challenges with the strike cell," I said. "They're just not responsive, and they're insisting on terminal control. They're making the process more difficult than it needs to be. We're missing a lot of opportunities to hit valid targets—the same targets that are pinning down Qassim's soldiers."

"Well," he replied, slowly shaking his head. "Remember what I said: we can't just drop every building that has a single fighter in it. We did that in Mosul, and we pretty much leveled the entire city. Qassim's got to figure it out for himself; we're just here to give him the extra push he needs."

"Yes sir, agreed. I don't want to wreck any more buildings than I have to, and preventing CIVCAS is my first priority out here," I said. "But, to be blunt, the strike cell is barely getting the basic things right. I'm concerned they won't be responsive enough when someone—either the Iraqis or our A3E teams—really needs immediate steel on target."

"Okay, got it," he said, nodding. "I'll talk with them. And I'll be honest with you, I'm not entirely surprised. The crew in Baghdad is just not as talented as the strike cell in Erbil."

As I continued my brief, the special operations commander appeared at my side.

"Okay," White said, looking at each of us. "So, what's the deal?" The SOF colonel had obviously gotten to White before their arrival, and it caught me unprepared.

"General, we need to lay flat this fire support issue between my Trident team and Folsom's task force guys."

I turned to him and cocked my head. "What's there to sort out?" I asked. "I'm the commander on the ground out here. It's my battlespace, and all fires have to go through the Task Force Lion Main COC."

"No, absolutely not," he spat. "Unacceptable."

"Yeah?" I said. "Well, that's how we rehearsed it with your operators. And no one except you ever said anything to *me* about it."

"Alright, alright," White said, practically stepping in between us. "Listen, I'll go back and talk with CJOC, and they'll circle up with you guys so we can sort it all out. In the meantime, you two need to come to an agreement so we can get this thing over and done with."

The clamor overhead of White's returning helicopter signaled it was time to wrap up the visit. The entourage mounted up for the return trip to the hardball and the waiting Chinook. As our vehicle hissed to a stop, White turned to me before opening the hatch into the desert heat.

"Alright, Lion-6," he said. "Keep up the good work out here, and tell Qassim I said hi."

"Thanks. . . . Sorry for that back there. I'm just a bit frustrated right now."

"Anything I can do for you and the team?"

"Honestly?" I replied, wary of venting my spleen to my boss.

"Yeah, of course."

"Okay, then," I said, taking a deep breath. "I could use some top cover, especially with these SOF dudes. Feels like I'm getting steamrolled out here."

"Don't worry about those guys," he said, grinning his crooked smile. "There's only one commander out here right now, and I'm looking at him."

"Thanks, sir," I replied. "But someone better tell *them* that."

"Look," he said, leaning over with an outstretched hand, "don't bother with any of that bullshit. Just remember this: there are colonels all over the Marine Corps right now who would kill to be doing what you're doing."

"Iron soldiers, sir," I said, gripping his hand. "I appreciate your support. No shit."

"Iron soldiers," he echoed, clapping me on the shoulder before climbing down to the asphalt and boarding his waiting helicopter.

21

NO RALLY PLAN

WITH THE ROAR of the Chinook fading, I dropped my gear into a dusty pile in the corner.

"Man," I said. "Glad *that's* over."

"They couldn't have picked a worse time," Major Awtry mumbled. "We really could have used the Apache that was escorting him, too."

"Yeah, yeah, yeah," I said. "I got it. Let's just focus on what's in front of us."

It was a good thing Major General White and his team left when they did, because the Iraqis were finally gaining traction. The command post's walls shook more frequently from the howitzers belching rounds, and as we fused the information coming at us from the video screens, the radio traffic, and the digital chat rooms, it was clear the fight's tempo was increasing. For all my complaints about the Baghdad strike cell, the pace of strikes *had* picked up since White's departure. The phone rang, and moments later Captain Jankowski called my name.

"Major Julian on the line for you."

I picked up the line. "Tell me something good, Chris."

"Look at the ScanEagle feed," he said. "There's a whole shitload of *desh* assholes staging in the bazaar."

A horde of armed fighters had gathered in the bazaar's center. Even through the grainy video feed, a sense of nervous energy surrounded them, as though they were awaiting instructions from The Man.

"We're working the deconfliction and collateral damage estimate issues with the strike cell," Julian said. "The Judge is on the phone with the SJA [staff judge advocate] in Baghdad right now. They're calling Iron-6 to get his approval; I think we're gonna get it."

Back at Al Asad, everyone was running hot. Once the FECC coordinated the strike on the bazaar, the pace on the watch floor became unsustainable. Working multiple targeting solutions at once, Julian and his Marines barely had time to relieve themselves. They had taken to eating their meals from cardboard trays brought from the DFAC by other team members. At one point, at the height of the commotion, Julian was seen bent sideways at the hip, one hand holding the phone to his ear and shouting at his counterpart in the strike cell. With the other hand, he clutched a half-gnawed steak, taking quick bites in between profanity-laden bursts of dialogue. One team member who saw the spectacle later described it as the most American thing he had ever seen.

The team's staff judge advocate was running hot too. As we formed in Camp Pendleton the previous February, the complexities of the fire support process had spurred me to request an SJA for the team. The primary role of Kurt Sorensen, the Marine captain I would refer to as "The Judge," would be to advise me on the lawfulness of potential strikes in the same way my SJA had done years earlier in Afghanistan. Sorensen was now busy working through the legality of the strikes Julian was coordinating. Nearly every target inside Anah was adjacent to other buildings, and we had to assume they had civilians inside them. Even though the Baghdad SJA would do his own legal review of each strike, the work Sorensen did beforehand ensured Julian's target packages were airtight. Two days earlier, a strike we prosecuted against an antiaircraft system next to a hospital had been so technically risky that The Judge wrote his own legal opinion to explain the circumstances and the legal framework that guided my decision to authorize the strike. It was the closest thing I ever had to a "get out of jail free" card. Now he was working the same process for the bazaar, and once Julian told me they were calling White for final approval, I knew we were in business. Minutes later the phone rang again.

"Iron-6 approved the strike," Julian shouted over the noise in the Main. "We're gonna put some HIMARS into these *desh* assholes right now."

"Roger, good to go," I said, hanging up.

From his battle captain seat, Captain Jankowski turned to Kiffa and Ahmed. "Gentlemen," he said, pointing to the video feed of the fighters milling about in the bazaar. "Watch *this*."

The bazaar disappeared in a brilliant flash. A volcanic geyser of atomized concrete shot skyward and spread through the adjacent streets and alleys in smoky tendrils, blanketing the area for blocks. As the dust and smoke dissipated, we studied the surrounding structures. They barely had a scratch. The same couldn't be said for the men who had assembled there earlier; there was nothing left of them. But then, at the edge of the screen, another enemy soldier rounded the corner and stopped dead in his tracks when he saw what had just happened. He fled in a jittering panic, sprinting erratically through the streets, bringing his radio to his mouth again and again, craning his head back and forth. He was confused, terrified, like a small child who had lost his mother while walking through the big city. I could only imagine what he was saying on his radio, what he was thinking. *What do I do now? What happened to everybody? What's going to happen to me?* With all the ordnance we had dropped inside Anah, I wondered if there was anyone left to answer his frantic pleas for help, or if he was getting nothing but static on the net.

The strike on the bazaar, and the immediate, deleterious effect it had on the morale of the defending fighters, spurred Qassim to give the final order for his forces to penetrate the city. Brigadier General Firas and his 7th Division Commandos pushed in from the southeast and seized a foothold on the city's outskirts. They resumed their advance toward the apartment complex, firing volley after volley of rockets into the area that had caused them so much trouble the previous day. A stack of Coalition aircraft loitered overhead, their pilots patiently waiting to deliver their ordnance. With each strike, the *jundis* moved closer to the city. By midday, the frequency of my radio conversations with Qassim had increased, and when he finally directed 1/27 and 1/28 to push into the city's heart, I found myself playing a cheerleading role for my Iraqi partner.

"This is it, *Sayidi!*" I shouted into the radio handset. "It's fucking go-time!"

Back at Al Asad, Major Kelly was having similar motivational sessions with Qassim via cell phone, at one point howling into the phone, "Tonight we dine in Anah!"

Time raced by in a blur. As the two battalions pushed up Route Hornets, their momentum stalled when another suicide vehicle slammed into the lead elements and detonated, wounding two soldiers. But it wasn't enough to stop the Iraqis, and they split the city in half. To the east, Staff Brigadier General Athir's JaOC Commandos were pouring fire into the apartment complex, suppressing the remaining enemy fighters holed up there. The buildings became the focus of the Iraqis' ire, a symbol of everything that had delayed their advance, and the soldiers took every opportunity to fill the area with lead and high explosives. Shards of glass and shattered chunks of brick and mortar sprayed in all directions. *Man*, I thought, *No one's ever gonna want to live there now.* With the apartments no longer a threat, Athir's men turned their assault west toward their final objective: the soccer stadium at the city's center.

Qassim's forces were now hitting Anah simultaneously from three directions. As sunset approached, the coordinated defense the enemy fighters had employed to stymie the attack for three days collapsed. The shock of the suicide vehicle attack behind them, 1/27 and 1/28 accelerated up Hornets, closing in on the city's center. As the attack's intensity increased, so too did my cheerleading.

"Yaaahhh!" I shouted to Qassim through the handset, clapping both Kiffa and Ahmed on the shoulders. The two officers were grinning from ear to ear, nodding at my encouragement. "Keep pushing! You can do this, *Sayidi!*

Keep the pressure on those *desh* assholes! You're killing them; the cowards are running for their lives! With God as my witness, *Sayidi*, you have cut Anah in half. *The city is yours!*"

And then, as if on cue, Qassim's soldiers broke through the enemy's final defensive line. The breach point along Hornets became a compromised levee, with hundreds of *jundis* streaming into the town like waves of water. They kept going, stopping only when they hit their limit of advance in the city's north. The JaOC Commandos linked up with 1/28, and the units inside the city dug in for the evening. The noise in our command post was almost unbearable. The room had filled with many different colors of uniforms, and everyone chattered excitedly, unable to pull their eyes away from the video screens. The radios were alive with traffic, and the Paladins rattled the walls as they hurled volley after volley into and around Anah. Amid it all, Kiffa stood up, pulled Amador by his side, and spoke to me.

"I know it is not your culture," he said. "But I am going to kiss you now."

He leaned forward, gave me a long embrace—what my family referred to as "the thirty-second hug"—and planted three quick smacks on my scruffy cheek. He then looked me in the eyes and took hold of my hand.

"This was your idea," he said, his eyes softening with tears. "This was your plan that got us into the city."

Kiffa's words and physical gestures touched me in a place deep inside that I didn't know existed. Words escaped me. It really wasn't my idea; it wasn't my plan. I hadn't done *anything*. Paul Nugent, Fred Fridriksson, and their teams had been the architects of the fight for Rayhanah and Anah. There was no way I could take credit and continue to look myself in the mirror. But Kiffa had reached out—had breached the cultural divide—and I couldn't leave him hanging.

"It was a team effort, *Sayidi*," I said, nodding and placing my hand over my heart. "We did it together, but it was *your* soldiers on the ground who broke into Anah."

Watching the penetration of Anah was inspiring, and yet somewhat confounding at the same time. Awtry and I agreed: had *we* been leading the assault, we would have continued the attack to pursue the routed fighters. But now, with daylight gone, Qassim's soldiers were content to call it a day. The old line about the Iraqis punching the clock at sunset apparently included high-intensity combat as well. *Ah, what the hell,* I thought. *I guess they earned it this time. Leave the exploitation to us.*

The battle was indeed unfinished. As afternoon turned into evening, the task force continued to interdict Islamic State soldiers fleeing to the north, targeting the exhausted, confused fighters as they ran in circles trying to get to safety in Rawah. There was no order to their withdrawal. Like the lone, terrified fighter running for his life after we flattened the bazaar, they radiated waves of panic as they ran-walked-ran through the twisting network of goat trails that led to the Euphrates. Major Kelly, observing the disorder from his feed in the Main, shrugged his shoulders and said, "Wow, I guess no one got the rally plan."

I picked up the phone to Julian.

"A lot going on here, Chris," I said, looking from screen to screen. "What do we have on tap?"

"Everything," he said. "We're working up packages to take out the boats they've been using to get the shitheads across the river. We're planning to drop the footbridge that *desh* put across the missing span in the Rawah Bridge. We're also getting ready to put a Hellfire into that bongo."

A squat, white truck, one of the ubiquitous flatbeds rolling around Iraq, was making its way up and down the trail network, picking up exhausted fighters in ones and twos, who would then pile into the flatbed. The process repeated itself again and again, and by the time the armed drone circling overhead lined up its missile shot, more than a dozen fighters had loaded themselves into the truck's bed. It was going to be like shooting fish in a barrel. The missile struck the vehicle's cab, shredding the men inside, and the warhead's detonation blew all the fighters stacked in the flatbed high into the air like a child's collection of rag dolls. Dazed and disoriented, the men righted themselves and rabbited in all directions.

"Jesus wept," I said, slapping my forehead. "You gotta be kidding me."

"Jacked up those guys in the cab, though," Awtry replied.

The boats Julian described were an easier matter. For years, the ISIS leaders had employed a network of shallow-draft wooden boats to avoid the watchful eyes of the Coalition aircraft flying above them. As the enemy defense inside Anah collapsed, many of the retreating fighters made a beeline for the boats moored on the river's western shoreline. It only took one or two artillery lobs to convince the local ferrymen to abandon their boats and to convince the fighters seeking passage to alter their plans. To ensure it stayed that way, we dropped volleys of high-explosive shells around the ferry sites, splintering the moored boats with white-hot shrapnel. Some might say we were destroying the livelihood of the local ferrymen, but it was a trade-off I was willing to make. If it came to it, I would be happy to fork over the cash to reimburse them for their troubles.

Neutralizing the Rawah Bridge, a modern marvel of Iraqi engineering built across the Euphrates, proved to be one of our greatest challenges during the interdiction. Many months earlier, Coalition airpower had dropped the bridge's center span, and almost immediately someone had emplaced a makeshift metal footbridge across the wide chasm. It was not only Islamic State soldiers who used the footbridge; locals from both sides of the river traversed it daily to visit markets and see friends and family. But there were no locals now—only deserting fighters trying to make their way to the Promised Land in Rawah. Julian's targeteers were skilled in plotting mensurated grid coordinates, and they calculated and recalculated the delivery point for our Paladins' Excalibur rounds. But, even with precision-guided munitions, it was like trying to hit a fence post with a pistol at five hundred meters. Every other shot missed its target, and even those that hit home caused minimal damage. The only perverse satisfaction we got from our efforts was one strike that impacted just as a group of withdrawing soldiers attempted to cross. The explosion knocked one fighter onto his back on the narrow span, and moments later he rolled off the ledge, plummeting into oblivion.

To the casual observer, our exploitation of the enemy retreat—and our barely restrained giddiness at our success—might have seemed detached, cold . . . inhumane. I never saw it that way. The fleeing fighters were legitimate military targets, and throughout their reign they had shown no mercy to Al

Anbar's residents. Every time an artillery round detonated amid a group of them, I remembered the gory execution videos I had viewed years earlier. I thought of the sheer terror those victims must have experienced as the masked executioners put the sharpened blades to their throats or doused them in gasoline before setting them ablaze.

Despite our successes, many more escaped that night than were killed by our pursuing fires. Although we would later receive unconfirmed reports of hard-core leaders in Rawah executing those who had abandoned their posts in Anah, the fact remained that the enemy was getting away. On multiple occasions, as Julian's team lined up targeting packages to strike large forma-tions of retreating enemy forces, the Baghdad strike cell obstructed our efforts by forcefully injecting itself into the process and muddying the waters. Each time, they answered our protests with the same, tired refrain: *We have better situational awareness up here than you do.* But they didn't, and for the life of me I couldn't figure out what the hell was going on. I began to wonder if our Coalition masters in Baghdad really wanted to win this war.

22

MAN OF THE PEOPLE

BY EVENING'S END on September 21, Qassim had repositioned his exhausted soldiers into defensive positions along Anah's periphery. The next morning, emboldened by their success, the battalions started back-clearing throughout the city. Despite any previous tensions that may have existed, Iraqi soldiers and tribal fighters now worked together, fanning out across the grid in a methodical, sector-by-sector search of the buildings and their remaining civilian inhabitants.

As the Iraqi forces moved into the urban center, our targeting inside the city ended. There was no longer any way, if there ever had been, to track the friendly soldiers' movements precisely. Throughout the battle, they were either unwilling or unable to properly use their Coalition-supplied digital tracking systems. Meanwhile, the only distinguishing factors the tribal fighters had were their tan Toyota Land Cruiser pickups, and that had nearly led to disaster the previous day. Taking a cue from *Black Hawk Down*, we had instructed the tribal militia units to mark their trucks with large Xs of black duct tape before the operation. Most vehicle crews followed our instructions, but the markers were smaller than we intended and, accordingly, much more difficult to identify through the lenses of our orbiting drones. In one case, an adjacent Coalition unit targeted a tan truck bouncing through an area we thought devoid of friendly forces. Only when our targeteers saw a bright orange Igloo cooler strapped to the truck's bed did we recognize that it was a tribal vehicle and make the call to abort the strike.

As Qassim's forces moved through the city, they found only light resistance and a handful of house-borne IEDs, which the EOD teams from 7th Division neutralized. Numan's techs were busier than ever as they continued clearing and proofing Route Bronze, which was still polluted with explosive devices embedded in the macadam and along the roadsides. Qassim dispatched what was left of his formations to the city's periphery, where they would secure the different routes from Sagrah to Anah and block the area. To support his plan, we shifted our focus to the ingress and egress routes north of the city to target reinforcing or withdrawing enemy forces. But the well was dry; the enemy fighters had learned their lesson. The Iraqi soldiers had walloped them, and they had no plans to return to Anah. For now, Rawah, which was beyond the reach of our organic fire support, was still an Islamic State safe haven. But we could deal with that later. There was much work left to do inside Anah.

Overnight, Qassim transitioned into the role he knew best: public figure and man of the people. As soon as his *jundis* were moving about uncontested, he rolled into the heart of the city, established his command post in a lush, walled-in compound previously occupied by an enemy commander, and immediately met with Al Anbar's provincial governor. The two men engaged Anah's civic leaders to assess the humanitarian situation, and the governor pledged assistance to support the beleaguered residents. Although the governor had declared the city liberated, the Iraqi forces and the government still had a daunting amount of civil-military work ahead of them if they wanted anyone to take them seriously. Before the day was over, Anah's mayor committed to delivering food, cooking oil, and water to support his residents. Qassim likewise promised to provide generator fuel for the locals until the electrical grid was restored. For my part, I committed to working closely with Qassim to help develop the civilian aid situation. Yet there was only so much our team and the Coalition could accomplish. The heavy lifting would be for the Iraqis themselves to do.

By the morning of September 23, there was no longer much to do in our tactical command post. Qassim was busy adjusting to his new role as Anah's proconsul, and the enemy targets around the city had dried up. As I chugged a tall can of Monster Energy that a sympathetic Marine had given me, Awtry plopped down next to me.

"We going to Anah?" he said with a slight hint of adolescent excitement.

I looked around the room. The radios were silent; nothing was moving on the ISR screens. The crud I had been fighting earlier was gone, and even Sergeant Major Leibfried seemed to be on the mend. There was no excuse.

"Oh, screw it," I replied. "Tell the Jump to mount up. We're heading west."

At 0900 our small patrol, with Kiffa's Humvee in the lead, rolled out of Sagrah. As we headed along Route Bronze, the first thing to capture my attention was the shot holes. Massive, blackened craters pockmarked the highway's shoulders along both sides. Square holes, which previously housed lollipop IEDs, marred the pavement. Once we passed the main obstacle belt west of Sagrah, unexploded lollipops remained embedded in the asphalt, their command wires severed by the exhausted Iraqi EOD techs who seemed to have run out of energy along the way.

We turned north and drove first through the heart of Rayhanah. The place was leveled. Rubbled buildings surrounded us on all sides, tangled in a web of twisted power cables drooping from leaning pylons. Every hundred meters or so we traversed craters the size of swimming pools. At one point, we edged by a flattened compound that showcased a huge, unexploded bomb, its twisted guidance fins protruding from the ruins. As we approached Anah, we reached the apartment complex that had been such an incredible thorn in the side of the Iraqi soldiers, I was struck by the brilliant red accents, which our fuzzy ISR feeds had muted into dull shades of gray. Blackened pavement and jagged shards of warped metal marred the access road where the BMP had blasted the suicide vehicle three days earlier. We pushed on, driving straight into the heart of the town until we found the Iraqi field headquarters.

"Qassim's strongpoint," as the *jundis* now called it, was surrounded by armored vehicles, pickup trucks, and rifle-toting soldiers and tribesmen.

They exuded a perceptible air of confidence and greeted us with cheers and enthusiastic thumbs-up as we worked our way through the crowd. We passed through the compound's gate and blossoming garden into a dimly lit room on the first floor. Couches lined the walls, and at the far end of the room Lieutenant Colonel Bruøygard and several Trident operators were jammed together on one. Qassim and Numan sat in overstuffed chairs, sunbeams passing through the windows behind them. The light, which cut through the haze of cigarette smoke clouding the room, cast a golden aura around the heads of the two generals. Qassim hoisted himself from his chair and embraced me in a suffocating bear hug. Like Kiffa two nights earlier, he kissed me repeatedly on the cheek. I returned his embrace and plopped down on a couch next to his chair as an aide handed out steaming glasses of chai.

"Well, *Sayidi*," I said. "You did it, man. I think it's time for a smoke." He bellowed his approval and passed me a cigarette.

I congratulated him on his victory, and after a few minutes of "Thank you," "No, thank *you*," "No, thank *YOU!*" it was time to get down to business.

"So, what's your next move?" I asked.

The man had done his homework. He described how Anah's workers and his soldiers were restoring water service, and his next priority was to reestablish power and get the city's hospital up and running. By his estimate—and despite the Coalition's efforts to convince Anah's residents to flee before the fighting—there were still as many as two hundred families hunkered down within the city. Qassim was as committed to restoring essential services as he was to hardening the city's defenses once his soldiers had cleared it. From there, he would extend his forward battle positions to the south wall of Wadi Al Qasr—a giant, southwest-running gulley that acted like a natural barrier to anyone coming from the north—then expand his defensive line farther southwest until it intersected with ASR Tin's Pipeline Road. He further intended to secure Pipeline Road west from Route Bronze all the way to the Wadi Al Qasr intersection in preparation for continued operations west toward Al Qa'im.

With business out of the way, Qassim's subordinate commanders filed into the room and crammed themselves onto the couch across from me. He introduced the officers one by one, recounting what each had done during the operation, and he told us all repeatedly how he had handpicked each man to serve under him. Qassim was in rare form. He was practically glowing, and not just from the sunbeams passing through the window. His commanders clung to every word, and between his praises and the group's accomplishments, I was certain the team of Iraqi officers sitting across from me would do absolutely anything for Qassim from that day forward.

I noticed Ahmed was not among us, and then I remembered no one had seen him in the last twenty-four hours. He soon appeared in the room, his eyes red and swollen. He walked over and embraced me, and he then handed me a roughly stamped coin etched with Arabic script. Throughout Anah's occupation, the enemy leaders had confiscated all the Iraqi cash they could get their hands on, melted down the coinage, and issued new Islamic State currency. As I stared at the ISIS coin resting in my palm, Ahmed explained how, the previous evening, he had found his brother, mother, and wheelchair-bound father—all of whom he hadn't seen in the three years since the Islamic State took control of the city.

I would later learn that the enemy position reports he had produced during the battle had come from his brother, who moved block by block through Anah's neighborhoods, alternately calling and texting Ahmed each time he spotted concentrations of fighters and weaponry. It had nearly cost him his life. A group of ISIS foot soldiers caught on to what he was doing, detained him, and were preparing to execute him when our supporting fires into the town intensified. With the explosions of Coalition ordnance reverberating all around him, Ahmed's brother managed to escape as the enemy fighters fled for their lives.

"If it weren't for you and your Marines, I wouldn't be with my family today," he said, his eyes brimming with tears. "When you look at this coin, I hope you will remember us and what you did for me."

My throat closed in on itself, and my eyes welled up. I could do nothing but nod my head and smile. It was then, in that smoke-filled room, that I understood the true reason for my return to Iraq after all those years. Before Desert Lion, I told the assembled Iraqi commanders I had returned to help them regain control of their country. And that was true. But listening to a tearful Ahmed recount the reunion with his family made me understand that there was indeed goodness and meaning in our new mission in Iraq. There could never be complete redemption for the sins we had committed by invading and occupying the country. Perhaps what we were doing now was as close as we could get to that redemption before this thing was over. From the beginning, our war in Iraq had been unwinnable. Perhaps what we were doing now was as close as we would get to not losing.

PART 3
THE LIBERATORS

October 2017–November 2017

You gain strength, courage, and confidence by every experience in which you really stop to look fear in the face. You are able to say to yourself, "I have lived through this horror. I can take the next thing that comes along." You must do the thing you think you cannot do.

—Eleanor Roosevelt

Remember, today is the tomorrow you worried about yesterday.

—Dale Carnegie

Fighting for a forgetful nation and spilling our blood for an ungrateful people. May God protect us all . . .

—Unknown

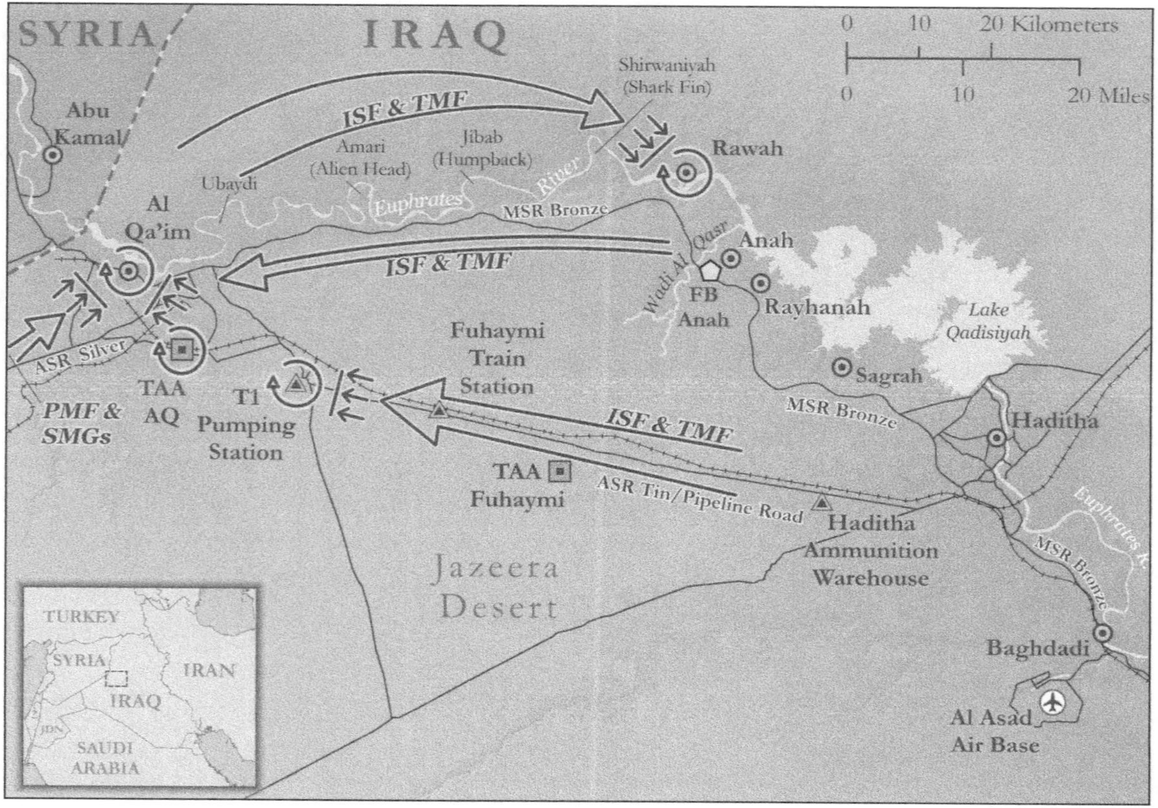

Map 3. OPERATION DESERT LION—PHASE III

23

BY THE BOOK

AS THE JUMP RUMBLED back inside the wire of EFB Sagrah, I grudgingly accepted that there wasn't much left to do at our outpost. Qassim continued to press the flesh with the city elders, his soldiers were stabilizing Anah, and the retreating Islamic State forces had moved beyond the reach of our Paladins *and* the HIMARS at Al Asad. As fast as the situation was progressing, our small piece of Anbar real estate was just as rapidly losing its relevance. Not long after we returned, I pulled Major Awtry and Sergeant Major Leibfried aside.

"We've worked ourselves out of a job here," I said. "It's time to head back."

"What about all this?" Awtry asked, looking over his shoulder at the people manning the radios and computers. It had taken a hell of a lot to get the place up and running, and he seemed reluctant to abandon it so quickly.

"Bob," I said, turning to Captain Jankowski, "can you hold down the fort until we figure out how much longer we need to keep this place going?"

"Yes, sir," he said. "Showers are optional."

"Good," I said, turning back to Awtry and Leibfried. "Because we need to get back. There's a lot of work to do, and we're not doing much good hanging out here while Qassim's doing his thing in Anah."

I emailed my intentions to Major General White. Although the key leaders would retrograde, we would leave enough people and equipment in place to support follow-on actions. The Norwegians and the operators still had partnering work to do with Qassim's forces in the city, so for the time being the outpost still served a purpose. But I needed to get back to Al Asad. There was still a task force to run, and we had reached the limit of our command and control ability with the Rube Goldberg contraption we had bolted together at Sagrah.

Getting the outpost up and running and then sustaining it had been an impressive logistical effort. However, if anything was certain to be remembered, it would be the kinetics of the operation. In just a matter of days, the task force had prosecuted more than forty surface and aviation-delivered strikes in support of Qassim's forces. The toll on the enemy had been significant. By the end, we accounted for dozens of defending Islamic State fighters killed and many more enemy capabilities destroyed or neutralized: indirect fire and antiaircraft weapons, support equipment and vehicles, bed-down locations, and command and control nodes. Qassim's soldiers and the tribesmen had inflicted significant damage on the enemy as well. It was a high-water mark for Numan's 7th Division, which had the reputation as one of the least-resourced divisions in the Iraqi army. His unit did not escape the engagement unscathed, but with only six soldiers killed and fewer than thirty wounded, it was a pretty fair trade. And, as far as we could tell from the reporting, there was only one confirmed case of a wounded Iraqi civilian. After the volume of ordnance we had dropped into the city, I considered that a win. It was a testament to the care and precision of the task force's fires and intelligence teams back at Al Asad.

Twenty-four hours after our return to Al Asad, events in Anah convinced me the Sagrah firebase had outlived its utility altogether. With its swift victory on the battlefield, Qassim's Jazeera Operations Command was now a credible combat formation in the eyes of Prime Minister Abadi, and everyone was already looking to the future. The attack on Rawah would be a more complex problem than Anah, and so once I confirmed that Sagrah was no longer necessary, I gave the order to collapse the outpost altogether.

The Coalition headquarters staff couldn't provide a reliable timeline for Desert Lion's next phase. However, the nut roll we had experienced in the days and weeks leading up to Phase One reinforced one lesson: the Iraqis didn't care about our timelines, and we had to be ready to go at any moment. As much as I despised the phrase "Never make the Iraqis wait on us," our team's flexibility and agility had been its greatest attributes. That skill set would be vital during subsequent phases.

Before we could resume planning, there was one more crucial event to complete: an after-action review. We had made many mistakes—some critical—during Phase One's planning and execution. Were we to forego a debrief, we would undoubtedly make the same errors again. And so, as we retrograded people and materiel from Sagrah, the task force staff and key leaders from our adjacent and supporting units gathered for what was sure to be a painful debrief. My instructions to everyone crowded into the conference room were simple.

"We need to be brutally honest with ourselves and with each other if we want to do better," I said. Then, paraphrasing something a retired Special Forces operator named Eric Haney had once said, I added, "We won't get anything out of this if we use mistakes as weapons against each other. We're all on the same team here, and we need to make each other better—not worse." Then, remembering what one of my battalion commanders had told me many years earlier, I said, "It's okay to disagree . . . it's not okay to be disagreeable."

Bit by bit, we worked our way through the issues the task force had encountered. The most notable friction point, one that had tripped us up several times, was the separation between the command team at Sagrah and the watch floor at Al Asad. The challenges we had faced in communicating a common operational picture between the two command posts particularly agitated Major Julian. Despite his irritation, I still believed the friction was more a function of the Baghdad strike cell's glacially slow fires approval process than anything else. In the end, I reluctantly acknowledged that going forward with Qassim in future phases would mean relinquishing an even greater degree of control to the crew at the Main. It was a stark reminder about the difference between command and control: you are always in command of your unit, but you cannot always be in control. That was a hard reality to accept, not only for me, but also for an entire institution of control freaks and Type-A personalities.

To be sure, we had done ourselves no favors by failing to fully rehearse the fire support plan with Trident—a critical omission that manifested in a logjam once the Iraqis and their accompanying SOF teams converged on Anah. Throughout the planning process, we had understood that the operators would coordinate their fire support requests through our team at the Main. Instead, they had coordinated directly with the Baghdad strike cell, which frustrated our own battlespace and fires deconfliction efforts.

Despite the heated discussions that characterized the debrief, one thing stood out: the team members operating the Main command post were resilient, trustworthy, and more than capable of running the task force in the absence of the command team while we were forward with Qassim. With just a handful of telephonic and email touchpoints to guide them, they had operated almost entirely on my initial intent. As we leaned into planning for Desert Lion's next phases, their performance gave me the confidence I needed to commit to the basic model that had proved so successful during Phase One.

The exhilaration from the victories in Rayhanah and Anah didn't last long, and on September 27 we got our first glimpse of what possibly lay ahead now that we had ratcheted up the pressure on the Islamic State. That evening, in an attempt to disrupt the Iraqi army's rear area, an infiltrating formation of more than a hundred enemy foot soldiers and suicide bombers conducted a coordinated, large-scale attack in Ramadi. The local Iraqi SWAT (special weapons and tactics) team fought back against the assault while Damian Spooner's Task Force Spartan coordinated a series of strikes with armed drones and close air support. By evening's end, both Spartan and the SWAT team had accounted for more than seventy dead enemy fighters, but it was a Pyrrhic victory. The friendly toll included thirty-three Iraqi soldiers killed and sixty-eight wounded. Ten civilians also died in the melee.

The attack on Ramadi was not Spartan's problem to deal with alone. The enemy forces had infiltrated through a network of historic smuggling routes that ran through the maze of wadis and goat trails in the desert south of Al Asad. Locating the truck-mounted squads of fighters tearing ass through the night was like trying to find a needle in a haystack. For our part, we refocused our collection and targeting efforts along Pipeline Road after ISIS began probing the JaOC's defensive positions and attacking the soldiers with suicide vehicles and indirect fire. After a combination of persistent collection and observation—and sheer chance—our efforts to locate the infiltrating enemy forces paid off. Late in the evening of September 28, a sharp rap on my door awakened me.

"What's up?" I asked, wiping the sleep from my eyes.

"Convoy of pickups moving fast," the Marine said. "We're working the package with the strike cell right now."

I ran across camp to the COC, where Major Julian was directing the show.

"What do we got?" I asked, taking a seat in front of one of the television screens.

"Six *desh* Hiluxes to the southwest," he grunted. "Heading toward Hit and Ramadi."

On the screen, a column of Toyotas was hauling ass through the night. Then, in a moment of good fortune—for us—the convoy slowed to a halt.

"That's it," Julian said through the phone to his counterpart at the strike cell. "Convoy is halted; transient scans are clear. We need to hit them now; we won't get this chance again."

"Air is inbound," our JTAC called out. "Time to impact: thirty seconds."

"*Your ass is mine*, says Kong," I muttered.

The laser-guided bomb detonated in the center of the convoy, shredding the trucks and several passengers in an electron shower of sparks. The survivors darted from their stricken vehicles in all directions, and for the next hour we directed the orbiting aircraft onto them as they fled across the darkened landscape. When it was all over, the final casualty count was uncertain. Even after the Iraqi soldiers did their battle damage assessment at the strike site the following morning, the photos they proudly showed us were inconclusive. The relentless air strikes had scattered pieces of the enemy fighters all over the desert, and it was impossible to tell exactly how many we had killed.

Even to my untrained eye, it was evident from the satellite imagery provided by Major Kelly's S-2 shop that taking down Rawah would make Anah look like a cakewalk. A crowded, densely populated peninsular town, Rawah housed as many as 20,000 residents within its urban grid. As far as we could tell, all the Islamic State fighters escaping Anah had made their way there when the tide turned in the Iraqi army's favor. There was every indication they would defend the city to the last man. It was sure to be a challenging operation for Qassim's soldiers to execute, and possibly even more challenging for us to support.

With that in mind, we jumped into planning Phase Two. Anah, now clear of enemy holdouts and serving as Qassim's forward command post, would serve as a jump-off point for the attack on Rawah. We, in turn, would establish an outpost on the city's outskirts. The base would need to support many of the same capabilities as EFB Sagrah, but to do the job it could not be as austere as our first outpost. And it was looking like we would have to do it all ourselves again with no assistance from anyone outside of Al Asad. The paucity of resources in theater, as well as the shifting priorities of the Iraqi government, Abdul Amir's Combined Operations Command, and the Coalition itself led several of our team's more cynical staff officers to refer to Desert Lion as an "economy of force main effort operation."

By October 3, I settled on the location for Tactical Assembly Area Anah. But once we got eyes on it, I second-guessed my decision to support Qassim from that slice of real estate. Tucked into a plot of land near an old American outpost between Anah and the intersection of Routes Bronze and Hornets, the nascent assembly area presented many of the same problems Sagrah had in its initial stages. Anah's defending enemy forces had reengineered Hornets into an IED belt to barricade the city from the south and east, and an unknown number of hidden, unexploded devices remained—including one bomb buried next to the road that someone marked as a chemical weapons munition.

"Ah, man, this sucks," I grumbled to Awtry as we surveyed the scene. Our EOD techs were sniffing around the area with their metal detectors, and the other Marines who climbed down from their vehicle cabs stood close by the armored protection, not daring to leave the asphalt for fear they might trigger one of the concealed bombs lining the route.

"This is the only place the Paladins can range Rawah," he replied. "Everywhere else is out in the open. At least here the high ground gives us some reverse-slope protection."

"Good God," I muttered. "I can't believe we're about to do this to ourselves all over again."

"We're gonna need some more bodies to help this time. I'll have the list of requirements tonight."

"Yeah, good," I replied. "I need to prep everyone at 51/5 and MARCENT so they don't flip the fuck out when I start asking for more people."

The wish list wasn't as big as I had anticipated. Qassim's insatiable demand for intelligence products meant more analysts and production teams. Our persistent air coverage over Al Anbar's target-rich environment meant another JTAC to manage the expected air flow and provide terminal guidance support. We also needed to expand our communications capability. Major Falcon's S-6 shop was woefully undermanned for the intricacies of the coming operation, and he needed more radio operators, networkers, and maintainers to keep our overextended, shaky comm pipes open. But that was it; the total number of people we needed amounted to fifteen. It puzzled me, and while reviewing the requirements list, I convinced myself the staff had either underestimated the challenges confronting us, or they were supremely overconfident in their ability to execute an operation on a scale as grand as the one the Coalition expected us to undertake in Rawah. Neither was the case, as the team had internalized the lessons learned from Anah, and they had refined and optimized their own procedures to the point where they didn't require as much support and assistance as we initially estimated. It was impressive to watch their professional growth—proof that the task force had become a learning organization.

Equipment and personnel capacity shortages still faced the team, as did a looming logistics challenge. Above all else, we faced a time crunch once again. And so, on October 10, a large convoy pulled out of Hammer Gate and headed north toward Anah to begin the clearing effort. It was shaping up to be a significant lift. Staff Sergeant Brian and Sergeant Rioux had already worked their way around the assembly area's perimeter, and their grim assessment made me want to bang my head into a bloody pulp against the cinderblock walls of my office. Somehow, despite the lessons learned from planning and building the Sagrah firebase, the Anah outpost was also in the middle of the Hornets IED belt that stretched farther beyond Anah's western flank than we originally believed. What was tactically the best ground for our new outpost had also been good ground for the ISIS defensive plan. But there were no other real alternatives. The timeline was what it was, and with the experience of Sagrah behind us, this new challenge didn't seem to faze the Marines who would deal with it. Just as they had before Sagrah, the EOD team initiated their methodical clearance, with the 2120th Engineers waiting in the wings until the first slivers of the outpost were cleared for moving earth.

Most vexing was that the whole thing was not shaping up to be the team effort we had envisioned. As with Sagrah, the new outpost's clearance and construction would have to be an all-hands undertaking. Everyone needed to do windows, and we had planned for the clearance team to include the combat engineer squad from the Norwegian team. But Lieutenant Colonel Bruøygard pulled his engineers at the last minute. My growing frustration with him boiled over when I learned he had met privately with Qassim during a visit to Anah on October 9. It was the same issue I grappled with each time the Trident operators met with my partner without telling me. As Fridriksson had reminded me repeatedly, I owned the relationship with Qassim. When things went south, he expected *me* to honor any unfulfilled promises he had squeezed out of the others.

Still steaming after reading an email from Bruøygard—a missive where he had cited the Marine Corps planning process and Joint doctrinal definitions chapter and verse—I lost my temper when he came to see me.

"Listen, man," I said, forgetting my diplomacy skills. "I don't need the email lecture; I've been doing this shit for a while now. I'm well aware of my own service's planning process, and I'm also pretty well versed in what I can and can't do with TACON [tactical control]."

"Sir, with tactical control you cannot task elements of my force for missions other than what they have been assigned," he protested.

"You're goddamned right," I replied. "By the textbook definition, I can't. And you know what? According to the textbook, I don't have to resource you and your team, either . . . but I do it anyway, because it's the right thing to do, and there's no other way to do it around here. We get things done on this team because everyone is flexible; everyone is adaptable. Everyone works together to accomplish the mission. I thought you would have figured that out by now.

"So let me be clear," I said. "If you insist on doing things slowly, deliberately, and 'by the book,' you're gonna get left behind."

24

CHANGE OF PLANS

AS THE FIRST CONVOYS rumbled up Route Bronze to begin constructing the next outpost, I drove across base for a KLE at Camp Majid. Numan and Qassim were hosting Abdul Amir and the Anbar Operations Command's Mahmoud, and the event promised to be a real barnburner. It did not disappoint.

As he relaxed behind Numan's king-sized desk, Abdul Amir described a new plan. Rather than attack Rawah, the Iraqi army would instead jump ahead to Phase Three and push west as fast as it could toward Al Qa'im and the Syrian border. They would then double-back to the east for the final attack on Rawah. The new plan was a rehash of the Coalition's original, proposed scheme of maneuver. Abdul Amir also announced that Qassim would lead the operation, which he conceded would require significant reshuffling of Iraqi forces. That task organization would include reinforcing Qassim with 8th Division, a decision that riled Mahmoud. Before the conversation could get any more awkward, Abdul Amir gave his thoughts on the future of Al Anbar's military command structure.

"When this is all over," he said, looking at Qassim and Mahmoud, "There will probably be room for only one operational commander." Which of the two commanders it would be was anybody's guess.

We were hardly able to believe the turn of events. You would think we'd have learned by now. Abdul Amir's change of plans, along with his insistence that the operation begin two weeks later, turned everything on its head. I no longer knew what to think. The new plan was essentially what we had recommended to Qassim all along. However, the operation's acceleration and the wide geographic distances over which we would have to execute it gave me pause. As Major Awtry sent word to our team at Anah to cease work and prepare to return to Al Asad, Major Duesterhaus put on a pot of coffee and told his planning team to roll up their sleeves for the long nights ahead. The irritation felt by the Marines and soldiers dedicated to the Anah outpost's construction was palpable. The only thing I could tell them was to get some rest. They were going to need it in the coming weeks before we did it all over again.

Abdul Amir's decision caught Qassim off guard, and for several days he was silent. By October 14 we pried his plan out of him, and it became clear that Phase Three would be far more challenging than the tabled Rawah operation. Qassim was vocal about his preference for the Jazeera Operations Command's organic forces to execute the entire attack, and he grudgingly told me that both Abdul Amir and Prime Minister Abadi had insisted the Popular Mobilization Forces would play a major role. The idea of the PMF participating upset Qassim, and he was not alone in that sentiment. As he explained his plan to my team, we visualized the problem.

Qassim was adamant he would attack west along Route Bronze with Numan's 7th Division. Staff Major General Abdul Hussein Saud Suwadi, 8th Division's rail-thin, reedy-voiced commander, would likely lead the attack northwest along Pipeline Road. A collection of PMF units would circle around from the south, travelling parallel to the Syrian border along Route Silver. In effect, the two Iraqi army divisions would attack headfirst into the teeth of the enemy defenses in Al Qa'im while the PMF snuck in through a side door. Qassim was happy with his plan, which was to say he was comfortable with 7th Division's mission along the northern axis. He was less concerned with the details of the other two axes, including the Coalition resources necessary to support the movement up Pipeline Road. He was also convinced the elite Iraqi CTS forces would execute the final house-to-house clearance of Al Qa'im—an assumption my team and I weren't certain was valid.

Major General White emphasized that, while Qassim would be the operational Iraqi army commander responsible for all three axes of attack, I would have a similar responsibility as the Coalition ground force commander for the entirety of Phase Three. That meant coordinating with and supporting the Iraqis along both Bronze and Pipeline Road, but specifically *not* the PMF along the southern approach.

"Who's gonna keep an eye on them?" I asked.

"That's your partner's job," he grunted. "If Qassim really wants to be The Man, then he's got to control the whole deal. That includes the PMF. Abadi won't green-light this thing unless the PMF gets a part."

"And what happens when Qassim's forces and the PMF converge on Al Qa'im?"

"We're just gonna have to cross that bridge when we get to it."

White was correct: we had more pressing issues facing us at the moment than resolving the whole Shi'a-Sunni conflict in the Middle East. Questions abounded, and few answers presented themselves. How would we cover the Bronze axis with indirect fire support? The route was outside the range of our Paladins and, beyond a certain point, our HIMARS rockets. How too would we support the Norwegian and SOF units, who were keen to provide teams to accompany the same battalions they had supported in Rayhanah and Anah? It wasn't just a matter of the accompanying advisor teams being out of indirect fire range. Traveling with the Iraqis along Bronze meant they would out-range timely MEDEVAC coverage for most of the advance. At a minimum, we would need to establish at least one tactical assembly area on the way to Al Qa'im, and that outpost would have to be greater in scope and scale than what we had initially planned for the scuttled Anah outpost. And, in all likelihood, the mission would probably require one more outpost before the final push into Al Qa'im. Clearing, building, operating, and sustaining the Sagrah firebase had damned near wiped us out. Doing the same thing twice, and on a greater scale, seemed next to impossible—even with the support from the Coalition and SPMAGTF that was materializing as our planning efforts picked up pace.

After several map studies and consultations with Qassim, we settled on a tentative location for what would eventually become Tactical Assembly Area Fuhaymi. Located midway along ASR Tin's Pipeline Road, several kilometers southeast from the bombed-out Fuhaymi train station, the project site was a barren scab of desert with nothing around for miles. Unlike the Sagrah firebase, there was no nearby town for the Iraqis to occupy, and Qassim made no attempt to hide his disdain for the ground we had chosen. It was difficult to disagree with his assessment once we completed the bone-jarring, three-hour route reconnaissance along the crumbled asphalt of Pipeline Road. As site survey team members climbed down from their vehicles, nursing aching backs, knees, and hips, we collectively stared out into the emptiness before us.

"Well, Qassim was right," Sergeant Major Leibfried said. "There's a whole lot of nothing out here."

In truth, that whole lot of nothing was precisely what we needed. The area was more than big enough to accommodate two helicopter landing zones, artillery and rocket firing positions, and all the tents, containers, vehicles, and equipment necessary to support the operation. Equally important, the EOD techs determined the area around Fuhaymi was blessedly free of the IEDs that had plagued us at both Sagrah and Anah. It appeared even ISIS had had the good sense to leave the area alone. With the timely assistance of a U.S. Army route clearance platoon provided by the Coalition, the team completed its survey on October 17. The supporting assets White had promised were appearing, and as soon as we declared the area safe, Captain Thornton's 2120th Engineers went to work. Just as it had at Sagrah, the sunbaked crust of the desert floor dissolved into a quicksand of ankle-deep, powdery moondust as Thornton's bulldozers moved earth into the high berms that would surround the outpost's perimeter.

Not long after Abdul Amir announced the change in plans, White contacted me with additional news: he was working behind the scenes to get all the Iraqi commanders to show up at Al Asad for a mission rehearsal brief.

"Prep your partner," he told me. "If we're gonna get everyone in one room, Qassim's gotta own it. Otherwise, they're gonna steamroll him."

Later, in a green room session with Qassim, I echoed White's challenge.

"*Sayidi*," I said, leaning in close. "I know you know this, but this is *huge*. This is your moment. You are gonna be The Man. When this is all over, everyone will remember that General Qassim led the final attack to liberate western Al Anbar."

"With the Marines," he said, grinning and clapping me on the shoulder.

"That's right, *Sayidi*," I said. "We're with you all the way. But no one's gonna remember Task Force Lion; they're only gonna remember *you*. And it starts here, with all the Iraqi commanders at the table. You're gonna lead this thing, and this is your chance to show everyone in the room who's in charge. It's *you*; you're in charge. You are The Man."

He left the session beaming, and as he exited the command post into the afternoon light, he walked like he was ten feet tall. *Dude*, my inner cheerleader sighed. *Please don't jack this up, Sayidi.*

A parade of Humvees and SUVs descended on Al Asad on October 18, filling the command post with Iraqi officers of all shapes, sizes, and ranks. I mentally cataloged the different uniform styles and patterns before giving up; it was too difficult to count them all. The visitors crowded into the conference room, and our initial plan to establish some semblance of order vanished. The assembled commanders alternately chatted together and shouted their concerns about the coming operation, but throughout it all Qassim held his own. I stood to one side like an overly proud parent, not showing any visible signs of emotion apart from barely discernible nods whenever Qassim made salient points. As with the orders brief before Rayhanah and Anah, I wasn't certain the gathering accomplished much. But, as the crowd filed outside for a group photo, White put things into perspective.

"This is a big deal, Lion-6," he said, grinning. "This is the first time they've all shown up for something like this." He then pointed to a group of black-clad officers who stood out from the others dressed in camouflage. "Check it out: the *PMF* even came for this. It's gonna be a hell of a show."

Yeah, I thought, considering the overwhelming task facing us, *a hell of a show.*

The plan changed daily. Between that and the way the Iraqis were whipsawing us back and forth, we practically needed neck braces to alleviate the pain. The original October 25 date rolled to November 1, and in the days after the commanders met at Al Asad it became a moving target. All told, when Desert Lion's third phase finally kicked off, the plan had changed more than two dozen times. I received call after call from a frantic Qassim, describing new updates to the scheme of maneuver or a new timeline altogether. Whenever the team's frustration with the constant whiplash took root, we reminded ourselves we had built a plan based on maximum flexibility. But there were limits. Major Mathwick and her logistics team could only pre-coordinate so much contractor support through the PMNOC process. And planned rehearsals, like the MEDEVAC drill we hosted on October 19, lost some of their value with each slide of the operation to the right. Many of the enabling units that were arriving to support the effort had narrow timelines associated with how long they could assist us. At some point, they would turn into pumpkins, and their parent units would order them home or apply them to other problem sets across the theater. As it had before Phase One, the clock kept ticking, and we never knew for sure when the alarm would sound.

Exactly which Iraqi units would participate was also a guessing game. We went back to the drawing board after Qassim informed me 9th Division would play a major role by attacking along the Pipeline Road axis. A more heavily armored unit than Numan's 7th Division, 9th Division had made a name for itself in Iraq's north. By all estimations, Qassim would need additional firepower and mobility to deal with the entrenched fighters we expected inside and around Al Qa'im. He could stomach 9th Division joining the fight. They were, after all, another conventional army division—not a bunch of uncontrollable Shi'a paramilitary units.

The growing appetite to bolster Task Force Lion's efforts also extended to SPMAGTF. The day after Qassim informed me of 9th Division's imminent participation, Chris Gideons reached out to offer the headquarters of 2nd Battalion, 7th Marines—the infantry battalion assigned to SPMAGTF. He proposed assigning the battalion, which would be designated as Task Force Wardog, under my tactical control to serve as the rear area coordinator to help us manage all ground actions between Al Asad and our forward outposts. At first, the offer seemed like a solid idea. With each outpost we constructed—and the accompanying advancement of the Iraqi forward line of troops—our rear area expanded dramatically. As we moved closer to the Syrian border, our supply lines would become more vulnerable, and the requirements for outpost protection, route security, and a quick reaction force would similarly grow.

In many ways, SecFor personnel had become the coin of the realm in Iraq and Syria, and they were one of the first considerations any time planning commenced for a new outpost. Even though plenty of infantry capacity was available outside the borders of those two countries, getting approval to bring them forward was usually an exercise in futility. Requests for additional personnel typically encountered resistance from CENTCOM, who would tell the Coalition: *Use what you have in your AO* [area of operations]; *re-task and reallocate as necessary.* The bump in SecFor provided by Gideons' infantry battalion would be helpful. But as I reviewed the proposal, his final point gave me pause: *This is an opportunity to align all the other cats and dogs I have up there under a common SPMAGTF command structure, working TACON in support of you and TF Lion.*

I had initially thought there was some merit to his idea. Major General White had recently assigned the 5-25 Field Artillery (FA) battalion commander and his Task Force Thunder headquarters to support us. We then task organized 5-25 FA in a manner similar to what Gideons had proposed by designating the artillery commander as the coordinator of all the task force's growing indirect fire assets. But it seemed like Gideons had buried the lead, and the naturally suspicious part of me looked for a catch. Did he just want his infantry battalion to play a major role in Desert Lion? And what degree of control would *he* want to have?

Knowing I couldn't bite the extended hand, I carefully framed my response to ensure Gideons understood exactly what we needed. The tasks included, but would not be limited to, SecFor coordination and management (such as fixed-site and mobile security, QRF duties, and route security along Pipeline Road and Route Bronze), as well as overall base defense management of the outposts we expected to establish. As planned, TAA Fuhaymi would include many more assets than the Sagrah outpost, including a forward logistics element provided by an on-station MEU in the CENTCOM theater. It *would* be a lot of cats and dogs to herd. But I would not agree to roll all traditional ground combat element assets up under Wardog's command, to include Task Force Thunder's fire support assets and personnel. We had proven that a flattened command structure operating largely through commander's intent was both a workable solution *and* the most effective arrangement in the chaotic environment that characterized our partnership with the Iraqis.

To his credit—and to my great relief—Gideons accepted my position, and we agreed that the arrangement would be for a limited duration to support Desert Lion. I genuinely wanted it to work, but it still required Lieutenant General Beydler's blessing. SPMAGTF was MARCENT's baby, and time would tell whether the general supported the proposal or not.

The clock ran out on October 22. Late that evening, as I was closing up shop in my office, Amador appeared in the doorway with his cell phone in hand.

"General Qassim is on the line," he said. "He really needs to talk to you."

"Ah, Jesus," I said, squinting at my watch. It had been a long day, and the last thing I needed was another frantic call from Qassim. "Doesn't that guy ever sleep?"

"What's up, *Sayidi*?" I said into the phone.

"Prime Minister Abadi told Abdul Amir the army has to attack Al Qa'im now, with what he has," Qassim shouted. "Abadi won't wait until November 1. The operation must start on October 26."

"What about 9th Division and CTS?" I asked. "Aren't they part of the plan?"

"They won't make it here in time!" he yelled. The stress and agitation in his voice made him sound like an engine about to blow a valve.

"Okay, *Sayidi*," I said, taking a deep breath. "We're with you, man; let's go with what we got. How do you want to do it?"

"I want Numan's soldiers in the north on Highway 12, I want Hussein's soldiers to attack along Pipeline Road, and the PMF will attack on Highway 20."

I scanned the routes on the giant map papering my wall. *Bronze, Tin, Silver,* I thought, breathing easy. *No change; good to go.*

"Alright, man," I sighed, putting my head in my hands. "We'll be ready."

When the phone connection ended, I looked at Amador for his interpretation of our exchange.

"He's really nervous," Amador said.

"Yeah, no shit, man," I replied. "He ain't the only one. Let's just hope 9th Division and CTS can catch up with us soon. Otherwise, Qassim won't be going into the fight with much ass."

Amador looked at me with a puzzled expression.

"There are 2,000 ISIS assholes in Al Qa'im, my man," I said. "And they're all just waiting to die for the cause."

"Oh, shit," he replied.

"*Oh, shit* is right," I said. "Go find Major Awtry. We gotta get to work."

25

TAA FUHAYMI

WITH THE OPERATION just days away, the crew building TAA Fuhaymi went into overdrive. No one had any illusions that the outpost would be fully operational by the October 26 deadline. But, as with the Sagrah firebase, it didn't need to be. All we needed was a basic level of fire support, some degree of surgical capability, and a rudimentary communications node. The construction teams had brought their "A" game, though, and by October 23 Fuhaymi included a pair each of Paladins and HIMARS launchers, a counterbattery radar, a forward surgical team *and* a shock trauma section, a Marine SecFor platoon, and a ground sensor array to provide early warning of infiltrating enemy forces. Compared to where we had been at Sagrah at that point, the place was stacked.

Two days later, I was ready to move out to the assembly area. However, one crucial milestone remained: the deployment of Task Force Wardog's headquarters did not yet have Lieutenant General Beydler's approval. He had decided to fly to Al Asad for an in-person brief on the proposal, and by midafternoon he and his MARCENT team landed in one of SPMAGTF's Hercules transports. Chris Gideons and Wardog's command team had accompanied him from Kuwait, and once we piled into the conference room the general in Bahrain commanding Task Force 51/5 piped in by video teleconference.

All the confusion of the MARCENT reporting chain was present in one room. Task Force Lion, which was under the Coalition's tactical control, was operationally controlled by 51/5. SPMAGTF, meanwhile, was tactically controlled by 51/5 and operationally controlled by MARCENT. And even though 51/5 was a combined Navy-Marine task force, for Marine Corps matters it took its marching orders from MARCENT. We each had different bosses, but the bosses were all related to one degree or another. Above all, though, everyone knew the same thing: Beydler had the final say, and he was keenly interested in what our task force was about to undertake.

I remained silent as Gideons briefed the concept. The idea had originally been his, and I didn't want anyone to get the idea I was pushing for it. The 51/5 general chimed in.

"I support this," he said. "Seth's team will be vulnerable in the rear area. We need to buy down the risk for him and his Marines."

Beydler, whom I sensed had resisted the idea from its inception, turned to me.

"What do *you* think about this, Seth?"

I felt painted into a corner. I didn't particularly want the support, nor did I think we absolutely needed it. The Coalition was now contributing an additional Army infantry company from Kuwait to lessen the burden at Al Asad, and we had devised a plan to incorporate them and our existing Marine SecFor platoon into the outpost security plan. Also available to support the security effort was Lieutenant Colonel Bellamy's 2 Rifles, who had finally received British government approval to serve as the QRF in the battlespace several kilometers outside of Al Asad's wire. With all that in place, SPMAGTF's proposition felt thrust upon on me, but I knew it was an offer I couldn't refuse.

"We can use the support," I said, nodding at Gideons. "The more, the merrier."

As I drove Beydler to the flight line in my battered and dusty Chevy Tahoe, the general was the first to break the silence.

"Are you sure you want this?"

"Yes, sir," I said after a pause. Then I repeated my response from the conference room. "We can use the support."

"You know, there are a lot of people who want to see the SPMAGTF do what you're doing out here," he said. "But I'm not sure this is a mission for them. You and your team are truly demonstrating how 'by, with, and through' works out here. If you start to feel like the support you're getting from SPMAGTF is going the other way—if you start to feel pressured one way or another, or you start to feel like it's *you* who is supporting *them*—then you need to let me know, and I'll turn it off."

Beydler's vote of confidence was unexpected. It was difficult to get a true read on him, and I often wondered just how much he knew about what we were actually doing in Iraq. There were, after all, much larger issues afoot in CENTCOM to concern him than our team of has-beens and never-weres. And, truth be told, I wasn't so sure I was still on his Christmas card list. During one of our outpost convoys in early October, a piece of sensitive communications equipment had bounced out of a vehicle and gone permanently missing—a cardinal sin so egregious that it earned me my own personal video teleconference dressing-down from the MARCENT commander himself. After that debacle, I figured I was all but dead to him. Yet here he was, personally conveying how much trust he had in me and my Marines. As if to underscore his faith in us, the next day he sent me an email: "Please finalize and send me what SPMAGTF will send in the way of a 'support element' to support YOUR 'rear area ops and staff augmentation requirements' as the TF Lion advised, assisted, and enabled Desert Lion operation kicks off."

As Beydler's Hercules lifted off for its return to Kuwait, I drove back across base and reflected on our conversation. As far as I was concerned, between White and Beydler, I had all the top cover necessary to accomplish the mission. It was Task Force Lion's show once again. And, just as it had been for Phase One, it was ours to win or lose.

With the sun beginning its race toward the horizon, I threw together my gear for the Jump's convoy to Fuhaymi. The MARCENT visit had dashed any hopes of reaching the outpost before dusk, and as I scrambled to get out the door, the Wardog commander appeared.

"Do you have a few minutes?" the lieutenant colonel asked. "I've got some questions about this mission."

"I've got five, man," I said. "I need to get my ass on the road."

"I'm curious about how I will control fires once we assume the rear area security mission."

"Sorry, what?" I asked, dropping my gear.

"I'm going to need control of fires in my rear area AO."

"No," I replied. "You're not. That's not in your wheelhouse."

"But indirect fire support assets should be part of the GCE [ground combat element] . . . especially if I'm a battlespace owner."

"Hey, look," I said, irritation climbing in my voice. "You are *not* a battlespace owner, and you are *not* the head of the GCE. This isn't a MAGTF; we don't *have* a ground combat element. The task force command element—Major Julian and the FECC—will control fires the same way they did in Phase One. If you need fire support for some reason, request it through the Main COC."

"Well," he protested. "It was my understanding. . . ."

"Look," I said, heading to the door. "I don't really care what your understanding was; I'm out of time. *We're* out of time. I'll see you when you catch up with us at Fuhaymi."

As I lugged my gear out to the waiting vehicles, I was barely cognizant of the hypocrisy of my interaction with the lieutenant colonel. As a commander, he was insisting on fire support control in his AO, and as his higher headquarters, I was refusing. It was the same beef I had with my own higher headquarters, but I didn't recognize it as such at the time.

"Man," I grumbled to Awtry as I hoisted my equipment into the truck. "Where the hell did Wardog get the idea they would be controlling fires or owning battlespace?"

"I was afraid of this," he said, shaking his head. "They're gonna be a pain in our ass." He then looked at the case of Monster Energy, the carton of cigarettes, and the rolls of chewing tobacco resting at my feet. "You sure you have enough there?"

"Hey man," I said. "Who knows how long we'll be out there this time? I ain't gonna get fooled again."

Our shadows elongated as the Jump rolled out of Hammer Gate and toward Baghdadi. Iraqis of all ages crowded the shops and walking paths on both sides of the road, reminding me of my company's first foray into northern Baghdad in 2003. At first, I thought the people were there to cheer us on again. However, after moving through the town, we saw what the locals were *really* cheering for: cargo trucks, Humvees, and armored vehicles from 9th Division were lined up bumper-to-bumper along the route's shoulder. Throngs of Iraqi soldiers hung from the truck beds and milled about around their vehicles, proudly showing off for Baghdadi's curious onlookers. When the *jundis* saw our conspicuous file of tan armored vehicles approaching, they turned their attention to us with cheers, waves, and energetic thumbs-up.

There was a chuckle next to me, and I turned to my driver, 1stLt Ben Miles. An unexcitable armor officer who had joined our team from 1st Tank Battalion, Miles had assumed the role as my security detail commander and the Jump's leader. Between all the trips back and forth to Haditha to see Qassim, as well as the many hours of driving during Desert Lion's first phase, we had spent a considerable amount of time together in the cab of our vehicle. The long trips on Route Bronze made staying awake a challenge, and we had passed many hours talking about everything possible, including Frank Zappa's greatest hits. Despite our countless conversations, my most significant contribution to his professional development was no doubt introducing him to the "John Basilone"—a potent cocktail of Gatorade and Rip It named after the 1st Marine Division hero of Guadalcanal that my Marines had consumed nonstop years earlier in Afghanistan. Later, as the operation progressed, Miles would proudly unveil his own Marine Corps hero-themed drink: the "Dan Daly," which was a standard John Basilone with a Five-Hour Energy shot added to the mix.

"Man, that's a lot of hardware," Miles said, pointing to a column of BMPs parked along the roadside.

"Looks like 9th Division just might make it to The Show on time," I said. "Everyone loves a party."

The sun dipped out of sight as we turned off the Bronze hardball and onto the crumbling asphalt of Pipeline Road. Creeping along in the dark, our vehicles rattled and bounced as we navigated the wrecked trail, and well before we reached our destination my lower back was throbbing. Between the constant bouncing and the weight of my body armor, my spine had compressed into a tight coil. Even the trio of empty plastic water bottles I had taped together into a makeshift lumbar pad did little to ease the discomfort.

The Jump pulled into the darkened outpost, and Captain Jankowski met us as we climbed down from our cabs.

"How's it looking?" I asked, rubbing my aching lower back.

"The TAC is up and running," he said. "HIMARS are set, and the Paladins will start registering fires tonight. The forward surgical team and the shock trauma section are operational too. I think they're gonna regret putting their surgical tent right next to the LZ."

"How so?"

"No gravel out here yet," he said. "It's getting pretty messy."

I would understand what he was talking about the next day, when Major General White and a troop of straphangers visited us. Their giant Chinook kicked up a gargantuan dust cloud when it landed next to the medical tent, blanketing everything in its path. But by then it was too late to move anything, and each time I saw the doctors and medics afterward they looked permanently rusticated with the ochre-hued dust of Fuhaymi.

Jankowski walked me through the dark to the command post. Gone was Qassim's deluxe suite we had enjoyed at Sagrah. Instead, our forward command team now worked from a 305 tent—a small, modular tent the U.S. military had used widely since the early years of the Iraq War. Flat-screen televisions displaying Qassim's orbiting drone feeds lined the back wall, and the Marines had arranged three plastic folding tables in a U-shape facing the screens. Watch officers, radio operators, and clerks were wedged into their folding chairs around the "battle-U," and piles of gear, boxes of MREs, and cases of bottled water lined the nylon walls and filled every nook and cranny. A thick film of dust coated everything, and I wondered how long the humming server stack in the corner would survive before it gave up the ghost. It was a far stretch from the Sagrah command post, and after five minutes I missed the luxurious digs Qassim and his men had provided during the Rayhanah and Anah assaults.

"Alright, good," I said, looking around at the mess. "*Home Shit Home*. Where's the pisser? My kidneys are about to shut down."

"Out the tent, turn left, about fifty feet there is a slit trench cut into the hill," he said. "You can't miss it."

I inched my way through the blackness, moving past vibrating generators and side-stepping tent guidelines and their protruding stakes hammered into the earth. As I relieved myself in the hollowed-out slit trench, the ink-black sky turned to daylight. I jumped at the canvas-ripping shriek of a HIMARS volley screaming from the wheeled launchers several hundred meters away. As the rockets arced high into the night toward Al Qa'im, I looked down at my trousers to see if I had pissed all over myself.

Conditions were set. With little else to do, I lugged my gear to a cluster of folding cots that the Marines had arranged beneath a camouflage net. I dozed off in my bag, lulled to sleep by the rumbling of the Paladins registering their rounds. Phase Three was under way at last, and I needed my sleep. I had no idea what would happen next.

In what would become a daily ritual for the remainder of the operation, a booming volley of pre-assault artillery missions sounded reveille at first light on October 26. The morning volleys delivered the shaping fires that the Iraqis needed to soften up the defending enemy fighters, and the fire missions had the added benefit of motivating the hell out of the Iraqi soldiers. At 0700, with the Paladins continuing their barrage, Qassim's forces crossed the line of departure west toward Al Qa'im. Hussein's 8th Division stepped off from its assembly area across the road from Fuhaymi and advanced along

Pipeline Road toward its first objective: the Fuhaymi Train Station. Almost immediately, the soldiers destroyed a suicide vehicle hurtling toward them. Then, as Hussein's forces cleared the train station, they triggered a concealed IED, killing one *jundi*, wounding four, and totaling a Humvee. Undeterred, 8th Division's soldiers pushed toward their next objective, an oil pumping station and surrounding community designated on the map as "T-1." They were making impressive progress, pushing much faster and farther than we had anticipated, and by late afternoon 32nd Brigade had surrounded the pumping station. Before I could orient myself on the chart taped to the tent wall, Kiffa leaned over and said something to Amador.

"They're clearing T-1 from the southeast right now," Amador said. We shifted our attention to the video feed from the "Qassim bird" orbiting above the Iraqi soldiers. On the screen, a squad of enemy fighters was fleeing on foot from the pumping station. A quartet of tan Toyota Land Cruisers trailed them, bouncing up and down as they raced west across the uneven terrain.

"Who's that chasing them?" I asked.

"A'ali Al Furat," replied Kiffa, nodding and smiling.

The pursuit lasted just minutes. As the tribesmen closed the distance, the retreating fighters seemed to grasp the futility of running. They did an about face and fired their AK-47s wildly at the A'ali Al Furat trucks bearing down on them. A shootout erupted. The tribesmen gunned down their opponents one by one, and when the video feed panned out, the screen revealed a long trail of fallen, bullet-riddled bodies bleeding out onto the desert floor.

"Wow," someone said aloud. "That got dark quick."

"See what happens when you fuck around," I said, turning to Kiffa. "Good shit, *Sayidi*."

He stood and motioned for me to join him and Ahmed outside for a congratulatory cigarette. With Kiffa, it was *always* time to smoke a cigarette.

The operation was going precisely as planned. On the northern axis, 28th Brigade was attacking west along Route Bronze. They too discovered IEDs in their path, and before they reached the Shirwaniyah shark fin they had blown in place four of the massive, buried bombs. As 28th Brigade's battalions maneuvered into hasty blocking positions, the JaOC Commandos turned north and systematically cleared the settlements south of the Euphrates

River. Even Route Silver, the axis where the PMF was closing swiftly from the south, was quiet, with no reports of enemy activity. By late afternoon, as the sun retreated, the first wave of 9th Division forces occupied the empty assembly area at Fuhaymi, vacated by 8th Division earlier that morning. It was all coming together, but then I reminded myself that the first day of Phase One had gone pretty well too. I hoped Qassim's forces would be able to maintain the momentum.

26

THE SHAMAL

THE IRAQIS' RAPID MOVEMENT west ground to a halt on October 28. Had I listened to Major Kelly in the opening hours of Phase Three, I might have steeled myself better. But, like Qassim and his lieutenants, I was still feeling a contact high over the initial battlefield successes. On the second day, the two Commando units teamed up to clear a string of settlements between the Euphrates' southern bank and Route Bronze. At the same time, 28th Brigade continued its attack west, securing the bridges on Jibab peninsula's western edge. After volleys of enemy small-arms and recoilless rifle fire killed one *jundi*, wounded three, and destroyed a Humvee, a force of Mahalwi tribesmen rolled in to support the engagement with an impressive flanking maneuver from the south.

Along Pipeline Road, 32nd Brigade finished clearing the T-1 pumping station before noon, using it as a jump-off point for the attack on the cement factory southeast of the Al Qa'im District. Together with the A'ali Al Furat tribesmen, they rolled over a small defending enemy cadre in and around the installation. In the southwest, PMF forces enjoyed similar success, pushing north to within fifty kilometers of Al Qa'im. As the other units advanced, more armored vehicles from 9th Division rumbled into their assembly area next to our outpost, but the soldiers gave no indications they were planning to go anywhere. Each time I asked what the delay was, Kiffa would shrug and say, "They're awaiting further orders."

"Well, Jesus, *Sayidi*," I finally said. "Is General Qassim in charge of this lash-up, or isn't he?"

He shrugged again and excused himself to go outside for a smoke.

What the hell is going on? I wondered. *Do they know something I don't?*

They knew everything I did. I just hadn't listened when Kelly told me bad weather would roll into the area soon after the operation commenced.

The morning sky was a deep, cobalt blue. Splashes of wispy clouds that even Bob Ross would appreciate added a calming texture. All things considered, with Al Anbar's oppressive summer behind us, the desert wasn't a bad place to be. As midday approached, I found myself staring peacefully at a squadron of whirring dragonflies as they alighted on the guidelines of our radio antennas. I had never seen dragonflies in Iraq, of all places. Considering the peculiar circumstances, it was a pretty good view.

The view from inside the command post was pretty good too. Shortly after clearing the dilapidated cement factory, the soldiers of 32nd Brigade moved forward with the A'ali Al Furat tribesmen and secured the uncontested Al Qa'im rail yard closer to the district's heart. Along Route Bronze, 28th Brigade took the lead, with the two Commando units following and back-clearing the settlements that dotted the area south of the Euphrates. As 28th Brigade pressed forward, the soldiers reported finding several Iraqi families chained and bound in their houses in Al Hamriyah—an account that matched Islamic State's modus operandi. We had grown numb to reports of such brutality, and it alarmed me less than the message we received several hours later.

Just after 1400, an explosion ripped through a Humvee belonging to the JaOC Commandos. A string of confused reports followed. Some said an anti-tank guided missile had struck the vehicle; others said it was an RPG. After the battle at Anah, Staff Sergeant Brian and Sergeant Rioux had recovered the spent launch tube of a Russian-made Konkurs missile, which we later tied to the destruction of an Iraqi vehicle. The discovery confirmed our suspicions: the Islamic State forces possessed advanced weaponry that could reach out and touch not just our Iraqi partners but us as well. A properly aimed Konkurs could turn one of our armored vehicles inside out. In the weeks following the EOD team's recovery of the spent tube, we approached our movements outside the wire with a significantly greater degree of caution than we had before.

As Major Awtry and I debated what had hit the Iraqi vehicle, Sergeant Major Leibfried unzipped the tent flap and joined us.

"Man," he said, patting a cloud of dust from his clothes, "it's getting *shitty* out there."

The sun had disappeared behind a thick pewter quilt blanketing the sky, and the wind had picked up. The camouflage netting strung around the command post flapped in great bullwhip cracks. Team members ran back and forth, covering equipment, tying down loose ends, and securing guidelines. Many were wearing their dust goggles. Others had donned balaclavas or pulled neck gaiters up around their mouths and noses. As I looked around in the growing *shamal*, Awtry appeared next to me.

"This is gonna make movement tomorrow a problem," he said. "You still want to do the op order?"

The minor resistance the Iraqis had encountered in the previous two days had accelerated our timeline, and the Jump was supposed to be moving out the following morning to reconnoiter the next outpost. Now, with the weather getting bad, I was hoping for the best.

"Let's do it," I said, invoking Bill Murray in *Caddyshack*. "I don't think the heavy stuff's gonna come down for quite a while."

Our survey team—the Jump, the EOD techs, Thornton and her engineers, a Trident liaison officer, and a squad of SecFor Marines—gathered alongside a row of parked vehicles, and Awtry walked everyone through our movement to the next outpost. As the blowing wind worsened and the sun neared the horizon, the slate gray of the atmosphere warmed to a dull, dirty orange. Looking skyward, I took one last drag from the cigarette I was nursing and ground it into the dirt. The deteriorating conditions reopened the time portal of memory, and I was again a nervous young captain on the road to Baghdad with my company of Marines, wondering what the hell to do next as visibility dropped to zero. I snapped back to Fuhaymi and knew we wouldn't be going anywhere anytime soon. When he completed the orders brief, Awtry turned to me.

"Where are the Iraqis?" I asked.

"Twenty-eighth Brigade is halted at the 18 Easting," he replied. "Thirty-second Brigade is holding the T-1 pumping station, the cement factory, and the rail yard. Ninth Division has halted their movement west."

"Okay, everyone, now that you know what the plan is, the mission is now 'on order,'" I said. "In case anyone is wondering, this shit weather isn't gonna change anytime soon, and we're not going anywhere without MEDEVAC coverage. Time to go to ground."

The wind, which at first was merely a nuisance, soon reached gale force level. With the outpost still far from complete, decent shelter was hard to find. The men and women who didn't work in the command post or in its few small, adjacent tents hunkered down in the lee of parked vehicles or inside them. As I roamed the area to check on everyone exposed to the elements, Kiffa flagged me down and steered me toward a battered, dirty white Hilux parked next to our tents. He motioned to the driver's door, and as he opened it a billowing cloud of cigarette smoke wafted out and immediately dissipated in the swirling dust. Ahmed greeted me from the passenger seat with a warm smile, and Kiffa and I climbed inside. With the door sealed, the screaming wind outside eased to a low roar. Ahmed leaned over to light a cigarette for me, and I surveyed the vehicle's interior. Someone had really decked it out. Finely detailed ornaments and braids hung from the windshield, and a length of soft, intricately patterned material covered the dashboard. More of the same was affixed to the roof above us. The only thing missing was a pair of fuzzy dice hanging from the rear-view mirror.

"Nice," I said, taking it all in. "Sweet ride, *Sayidi.*"

"ISIS truck," Ahmed said in English. "*My* truck now."

I burst out laughing as I took a drag from my cigarette, and I promptly broke down into a fit of hacking, raspy coughs. I regained my composure and chuckled.

"Good to go, *Sayidi*," I said, patting the dashboard's soft material. "I like how you roll. Just let us know when you're gonna drive this thing outside the wire so we don't accidentally air you out."

I don't know how long we sat there together. Throughout it all, I wondered how I had wound up in such an absurd, comical position: hiding from a biblical storm inside a tricked-out enemy pickup truck, sucking down one heater after another with my two newest best friends in Iraq. It was a story so bizarre that no one at home would ever believe it. Even though the three of us had grown tight during the previous month, those moments laughing together and smoking each other's cigarettes in the ISIS hoopty cemented our friendship. I genuinely liked Kiffa and Ahmed; they were my dudes.

Hot-boxing inside the pickup eventually became too much for me, and by the time I excused myself the storm had reached apocalyptic dimensions. Visibility had left our world, and an impenetrable blackness overtook the camp once the horizon swallowed the last of the sun's muted orange glow. The curtain of dust particles drowned out even the brightest headlights shining from parked vehicles. I felt my way from tent to tent and stumbled into the command post, coughing uncontrollably, eyes watering, only to find the place packed with people hiding from the disaster outside. The air inside the tent was a haze—a dirty gauze filter some joker had placed over the camera lenses of our eyes. The micronized grit worked its way into my mouth, gently scouring the enamel from my teeth. I covered my mouth and nose with a filthy handkerchief, but it did little to protect me. With each breath, more and more of the Anbar desert staked its claim deep in my lungs.

The roaring wind rocked the tent back and forth, rustling and snapping the flimsy material in an ear-splitting staccato. As the storm's power grew, a team of Marines threw open the flap and heaved inside a young Iraqi interpreter shrouded in a grimy balaclava and dragging a dirt-encrusted blue sleeping bag. His eyes rolled around drunkenly in his head, which swayed back and forth as if detached from his spine. Completely disoriented, he had no idea where he was. The Marines pulled off his balaclava, and a wet blob of dirt dribbled from his mouth. They set him down in a corner, where he curled into a ball.

"What the hell happened to *him*?" Leibfried asked.

"We found him next to the ECP," one of the Marines said. "He's been out there the entire time."

"That," I said, shaking my head, "is a broken young man."

"Something tells me he didn't sign up for *this*," Leibfried said.

Awtry and I sat down together for our evening video teleconference with the team back at Al Asad. Drawing on lessons from Phase One, Lieutenant Colonel Merritt had begun convening routine staff synchronization meetings. Now, each morning and evening, our two teams cross-leveled information, and we set the plan for the next day. During the video conferences, Awtry and I had started sharing his headphones, which he plugged into the terminal's single audio jack. Between the cycling of the generators outside and the noise inside the tent, it was the only way to hear anyone on the other side of the video screen. With one audio bud plugged into his ear and one in mine, practically sitting in each other's lap, we struck an awkward appearance on a good day. Now, exhausted and covered in dust that accentuated the lines in our faces, we looked like a couple of ancient boozers leaning against each other to keep ourselves vertical. When the video connection went through and the staff appeared on the screen, genuine alarm filled their faces when they saw ours. A slight haze hung in my office where the staff had gathered, but it was nothing compared to what surrounded us inside the command post.

"In case you can't tell," I said, "we're having a bit of weather here. I blame you, John."

"Sorry, *Sayidi*," Kelly giggled. "I don't make the weather; I just report it."

As the meeting neared its end and we outlined plans for the next twenty-four hours, the young interpreter balled up on the floor had had enough. He sprang to his feet and started freaking out. As he thrashed around, a pair of Marines wrestled him to the ground, where he retched and then finally puked in the corner behind us. On the video screen, the staff's eyes fairly bulged at the commotion behind us.

"On that high note," I said, "we're outta here."

As we signed off, Leibfried sat down next to me.

"Brunson's lost," he said. "He went to take a piss and hasn't come back. Viking's master sergeant is missing too."

"You're kidding," I said, looking across the table for confirmation from the Norwegian liaison officer, who nodded grimly. The master sergeant was a tough guy, but the storm had become the great equalizer. Anyone who got lost outside would be equally screwed.

Staff Sergeant Rick and Staff Sergeant Brian walked in, wearing gas masks.

"We're heading out to find Brunson," Rick said, his voice a muffled shout inside his mask. "The Norwegians are looking for their man too."

"Don't get lost yourselves," Leibfried said, "or you're gonna be in for an even worse night."

"Don't worry," Rick replied, holding up a GPS receiver and a bundled wad of parachute cord. "We're tying ourselves together; we'll find him."

"Great," I said, pushing back from the table. "Now *I* need to take a piss. If I'm not back in fifteen minutes, send out the QRF to get me."

Guided by the weak blur of the parked headlights, I took my bearings and inched my way to the slit trench, counting my paces and sidestepping along the way. After about fifty meters I was cloaked in inky blackness, only halfway to my objective. The headlights were gone, and I was alone, the wind screaming in my ears and stinging every exposed inch of flesh with needling grains of dust. With my eyes squeezed shut against the blowing fury, I knew that continuing the rest of the way would most likely end with my picture on the back of a milk carton. I unbuttoned my fly, knelt as low as possible to the ground, and tried not to urinate all over myself in the swirling tempest. I was only marginally successful.

I backtracked my way to the tent, taking the same methodical, measured side steps. The faint glow of headlights shimmering in the darkness signaled that I was home free. I opened the tent flap and got an immediate "*Shut the fucking hatch!*" thrown my way from someone inside. Like the dust-blown young interpreter, everyone's fun meter was pegged. The tent's occupants had aged a hundred years in the few minutes I was away. An even thicker patina of chalky dust coated their faces, and the men and women inside the command post were now reanimated, mummified creatures from my childhood nightmares.

"They found Brunson and the Norwegian," Leibfried said. "Brunson was all the way over by the HIMARS. Viking's sergeant has something stuck in his eye; the Norwegians are trying to figure out how to get him out of here tomorrow morning."

"And the hits just keep on coming," I said, blowing off the new layer of grit that had settled on my computer's keyboard.

The air inside the tent grew so visibly thick that just breathing normally became a chore. Leibfried dozed off in the seat next to me, his elbow planted on the table and his head resting against his fist. My own breathing grew labored, and my skull throbbed. Chills rattled my body, and my stomach churned in acidic somersaults. *That's all I need now*, I thought, remembering the lunch Kiffa's men had delivered earlier. *A good old-fashioned case of food poisoning.*

By 2300, as I struggled to write the evening sitrep, I could take no more. With the night watch in place, Marines were filtering out of the tent. Once I hit "send" on the report, I moved toward the exit.

"Let's go," I croaked to Awtry. "Time to hit the rack."

The storm had died down, and the sky began to clear. We made our way to the nook Jankowski had carved out for us, only to find the camouflage net collapsed in a gigantic knot on top of our gear. Several Marines joined us as we wrestled with the netting, trying to untangle it and get it erected again, but it was a hopeless mess. My head shrieked with a stabbing pain behind the eyes, and my muscles and joints ached. Drenched in a clammy sweat and shaking like a withdrawing heroin addict, I was a bag of limp shit. The only thing I needed in the entire godforsaken world was to be nestled inside the warmth of my grubby sleeping bag.

"Man, *fuck* the net," I snapped at the struggling Marines. "Let's just get it off our gear; we'll put it back up tomorrow. Everyone, get your heads down now."

I collapsed into my bag fully clothed, my field jacket wrapped around me for good measure. Before I could think any more about my utter misery, I passed out cold.

27

THE HAUNTED
TRAIN STATION

AS THE DAY'S FIRST LIGHT filtered through the gunmetal sky on October 29, Fuhaymi's battered inhabitants roused themselves from the shelter of their sleeping bags. I pulled my rifle and pistol from my bag, where they had lain next to me all night, and I tested the action on each. The storm had power-sanded our equipment with grit, blanketing and injecting everything we owned with a thick glaze of dust and grainy debris. The weapons creaked with the nails-on-chalkboard sensation of sand against metal, now useless after the pounding they had taken. Keeping weapons clean and working properly in the desert was a chore on a good day; getting them back in working order would be an even greater challenge now.

Inside the command post, team members slumped in front of their terminals. It wasn't just our equipment that had taken a beating. The previous evening had topped all the *shamals* I had suffered through in earlier deployments—even the forty-eight-hour storm of the century my Marines and I had endured during the 2003 invasion. The dust storm was hard on the Iraqi army as well, bringing Qassim's forces to a standstill. The two Commando units were holding on the southern bank of the Euphrates River, and 28th Brigade hadn't moved from its coil along Route Bronze. Throughout the storm's lingering effects, which were keeping the soldiers from moving, the three units received sporadic enemy small-arms and indirect fire from the west. Along Pipeline Road, neither 32nd Brigade nor the A'ali Al Furat tribesmen had made any additional progress. They too were holding firm, occupying the cement factory, the rail yard, and the T-1 pumping station, where 9th Division had finally joined them. Even the SOF teams, whose recall I had urged to the Trident commander once the storm took hold, remained battened down at the rail yard, unable to operate because of the foul weather.

Inside the command post, Major Awtry and I sat down together for our morning video conference. When the connection went through, all we saw was Lieutenant Colonel Merritt sitting alone in my office. The place was normally packed with the primary staff officers and other straphangers.

"We ready to go?" I asked.

"Yes, sir," he said. "The staff's really been working their butts off. Since today is a resiliency day, I decided to let them all sleep in."

I looked at my watch: Sunday. At some point in the past, the Coalition headquarters had implemented "resiliency days" on Fridays and Sundays to ensure service members weren't working themselves into the ground seven days a week. To put a finer point on it, the policy was *really* designed to ensure bosses weren't working their people to death all day, every day. Before Desert Lion, we had taken full advantage of resiliency days. At one point, I even told the staff, "I don't want to see anyone in their office before noon unless something absolutely *must* be done." But now, with the operation in full swing, the team's absence on the other side of the screen ruffled my feathers. The weather was beating the shit out of us at Fuhaymi; the least the staff could do was show up for work. Then I remembered the weather was knocking them around at Al Asad as well, and they were working just as hard as we were at the outpost. As I fought to keep my body language from betraying my irritation, the entire staff jumped into the frame from their off-camera hiding place. They pointed at the two of us, laughing together in a hooting "*Gotcha!*" Any doubts I might have harbored about them being fully invested vanished. It was one of the hallmarks of a truly professional team: when the going got tough—when everyone was down and tired—they rallied with spirit and humor. I was so blessed to have them there with me.

The mystery illness that had floored me the previous evening perplexed me. I had fallen asleep wrapped in as many layers as I could find, sweating through my clothes and rattling with chills coursing through my body. Then, halfway through the night, my fever heat grew so bad that I threw off the extra layers and tossed and turned with my bag half-open until morning. I awakened with a dull tapping behind my eyes, but everything else—chills, shakes, aches—had disappeared. I probed the team members in the command post for comparable experiences.

"Man, I felt like hammered shit last night," I said.

"Me too," Sergeant Major Leibfried said. "I had a killer headache. Felt like someone beat the crap outta me."

"I was freezing all night," another Marine said. Others chimed in with similar tales of woe.

"Huh," I said. "I thought it was just me being a weakling."

The medical team's surgeon, an upbeat, prematurely graying Army lieutenant colonel, stopped by to check on everyone. I described our symptoms and asked what the hell had happened to us.

"Probably all the dust and God-knows-what-else getting blasted into your body," he said. "Your immune system went on high alert to protect it."

"Then how come I'm not sick anymore?"

He shrugged. "I guess you've got a strong immune system."

"Yeah, great," I said, heading for the door. "At least I got *that* going for me."

Outside, it was still a waiting game for our site survey team. With low-hanging cloud cover and a thin veil of dust suspended in the air, the MEDEVAC status remained "black," and everyone spent the rest of the day working on their weapons and equipment. Unable to clean their dirt-blasted bodies, the Marines disassembling weapons and scrubbing radio connections resembled a band of earthen trolls toiling in a desert foundry. Despite our best efforts, the information systems shut down piece by piece, and with each equipment failure the communications team went to work troubleshooting to get it back up and running. Somehow, though, our overworked Dell laptop computers remained functional throughout the entire operation. I wondered if it was the right time to buy stock in the company.

The weather didn't budge for the next twenty-four hours. The Iraqi units along Route Bronze held their positions, even with sporadic enemy fire from the west. Then, during a brief break in the weather, the units along Pipeline Road resumed movement. A'ali Al Furat and 4/32 attacked north toward the phosphate factory, where defending Islamic State forces opened up on them with small-arms fire and mortar rounds. Then, just when it looked like the Iraqi soldiers would take the phosphate factory, the weather deteriorated again and stopped the attack cold. Before the weather closed back in, 32nd Brigade's last act was to deploy a small force to monitor the PMF's advance along Route Silver. Even with the abysmal weather conditions, the PMF units had pushed until they reached their limit of advance, and they were now holding fast. My tacit mistrust of the PMF aside, I admired their ability to move and fight in such miserable conditions. They were an inherently lighter, more mobile force. If Qassim's army units didn't pick up the ball and run with it soon, the PMF was going to steal the whole game.

After a three-day shellacking, the storm dissipated on the morning of October 31, leaving unblemished blue skies in its wake. As I entered the command post tent, Awtry gave me some much-needed good news.

"MEDEVAC birds are flying," he said. "And I just confirmed with S-2: the weather is supposed to stay clear . . . at least for the next twenty-four to forty-eight hours."

"Good to go," I said. "Get everyone together, give them any updates to our patrol order, and let's get the hell out of here. We need to be at the train station before nightfall."

Weeks earlier, as we planned the series of outposts that would support Phase Three, we reviewed a product the Coalition planners had sent us. They insisted our next outpost objective after Fuhaymi should be a piece of ground alongside the T-1 pumping station. Relying on a grainy bit of satellite imagery, they claimed a small airstrip at the proposed site would support C-130s, which would further enable the sustainment effort. Awtry and Kelly reviewed the images with me, and we all agreed: the airstrip didn't look like much.

"My little birds say these points here, here, and here," Kelly said, pointing to a trio of faint lines, "are where the airfield has either been cut or bermed up. Either way, it's probably not immediately usable for C-130s."

"I don't know where the Hercules requirement came from," Awtry said. "The place just needs to support Chinooks, the same as Fuhaymi."

"T-1 is out in the middle of nowhere too," Kelly added. "Just like Sagrah was and Fuhaymi will be. It will take us just as much time to clear it and build it up."

"Time we don't have," I mumbled to myself.

"What about the train station?" Awtry asked, pointing to the Al Qa'im rail yard.

"AQ?" I asked, raising an eyebrow. In the war's early years, Camp Al Qa'im had housed numerous battalions that were operating in and around Al Qa'im, Karabilah, and Husaybah. By the time my advisor team showed up in 2008, it was a bustling hub with all the amenities FOBs were notorious for across Iraq: dining facilities, gyms, a PX—the list went on. Even the actor Gary Sinise and his Lt. Dan Band had made an appearance there while my team was working with 28th Brigade. The idea of reoccupying that particular outpost had never occurred to me.

"Oh yeah," Kelly grinned. "Taking it *all* the way back to 2005 . . . this is gonna be like playing *Oregon Trail*."

"Why don't we skip T-1 and just jump directly to the train station?" Awtry asked. "It will get us that much closer for the ISF's final push on the urban center."

"You and John just want to go visit your old stomping grounds," I said.

Both men shrugged, their faces filled with the sheepish expressions of two boys whose father had just seen through their hare-brained scheme. But Awtry had a point: speed was essential to support Qassim's attack, and the train station would get us closer to the final objective quicker than stopping to build another, intermediate outpost.

I held off making a decision until Kelly could produce better, more recent imagery. When he delivered it, what I saw did not impress me.

"AQ's still there," he said, pointing to a grainy overhead image of the train station. "But it's in a bad way. Looks like it's been bombed out . . . missing roofs, debris piles, you name it."

"What about the old graveled airfield there?" I asked.

"It looks clear."

"This area here looks cleared out too," Awtry said, pointing to an open space. "We could put the TAC on the concrete pad next to the HLZ [helicopter landing zone], and arty could position here and here."

"Okay," I said. "Let me know what it will take to secure this thing, then get with Amanda to see what her engineers can do. Once we have our answers, let Baghdad know T-1 is off the table. The next outpost after Fuhaymi will be TAA Al Qa'im—the train station."

⁂

With an 8th Division Humvee leading the way, our patrol pushed west along Pipeline Road. Several days earlier, as Trident's teams advanced with the Iraqi battalions, the SEALs reported a possible chemical IED in a building within the T-1 pumping station cantonment. Weeks earlier, we had received a similar report of a chemical IED on the main road leading into Anah, but it never amounted to anything. Now, as the Iraqis and their accompanying advisor teams closed in on Al Qa'im, it seemed more likely the withdrawing enemy forces would cross the threshold of employing chemical weapons.

We rolled to a stop in the cantonment. With the vehicle gunners in overwatch directing their machine guns outboard, our EOD team and an attached U.S. Army chemical, biological, radiological, and nuclear (CBRN) detection team geared up in their protective suits and tiptoed toward an abandoned building where the SEALs had spotted the device. As the two teams poked around with their metal detectors and chemical agent testing kits, I wondered whether my gas mask would still work after all the grit flying around in the storm. The men backed away from the building and returned to our waiting vehicles.

"Well?" I asked, watching the perspiring Marines and soldiers shed their bulky protective garb. "What do we got?"

"Definitely an IED," Brian replied. "Not sure how big it is. Part of it's under a tarp, and we couldn't get close enough to really tell."

"Is it chemical?"

"We got a verified reading," one of the CBRN soldiers said. "It tested positive for a high concentration of sulfur mustard agent."

"Sulfur mustard?" I asked. "Are you shitting me? What is this, World War I?"

"It's what the test said."

"We gonna wait around?" Awtry asked.

"No way," I said. "Who knows how long it'll take to get someone qualified out here. Mark it, report the location, and let's get the hell out of here. We're burning daylight."

Finding a chemical-laden IED was as much a game changer for us as it had been learning the Islamic State fighters were using Russian anti-tank missiles. All at once, our perceived bubble of safety shrank even more. Leaving the device for someone else to deal with was a risk, but screwing around with chemical explosives was not in our job jar. The mission right now was making our way to the train station and getting it up and running. Qassim's soldiers were on the move, making up for time lost in the storm, and we needed to keep pace with them. Along Route Bronze, the JaOC Commandos and 28th Brigade had finally secured Ubaydi peninsula, and they were clearing the intersection of Pipeline Road and Bronze. Once that was complete, they would be waiting on us. Farther ahead along Pipeline Road, 4/32 and the A'ali Al Furat tribesmen were clearing the phosphate factory and a nearby settlement. The resisting enemy soldiers were dying in place, and by all accounts the Iraqi forces were ahead of schedule, which meant our task force was about to be behind schedule. Someone else would have to tangle with the chemical device.

As our patrol pulled away from the cantonment, we caught a glimpse of the airfield the planners in Baghdad had clung to for so long. It was little more than a rocky dirt strip, and I was thankful Awtry and Kelly had pushed for us to leapfrog over T-1 and head directly to the rail yard. Finding the chemical IED made me feel even better about the decision to jump to the next outpost. I wasn't interested in setting up shop anywhere near it, and I hoped there would be no similar discoveries once we got to the train station. At the cantonment's outskirts, we also got our first look at some of the PMF forces participating in the operation. A procession of trucks flying Imam Ali Division banners had parked along the road's shoulder, and a gang of fighters glared as we edged by. We were all supposed to be on the same side for the moment, but you never would have guessed it from the chilly reception they gave us.

Pipeline Road, which was a bone-jarring stretch of broken asphalt to begin with, was in even worse condition on the final approach to Al Qa'im. Continuing west, we rattled past the moldering corpses of the ISIS fighters whom we had watched the A'ali Al Furat tribesmen gun down days earlier. Bloated and fly-blown, their flesh melting into a greasy black hue in Al Anbar's afternoon heat, they resembled piles of decomposing roadkill—not the invincible boogeymen everyone had built them up to be. Rolling by, I peered at the carnage from the cabin of my vehicle.

"Yep," I said, repeating my running commentary from the original engagement, "that's what happens when you fuck around."

As we passed the cement factory's towering silos and approached the growing silhouette of the rail yard, I grew nostalgic about my advisor tour a decade earlier. Each week, my team had convoyed to Camp Al Qa'im, our worn-out Humvees overloaded with dirty laundry. Our vehicles would be similarly overloaded with mail and pogey bait each time we returned to the barren outpost south of the district center that we shared with the Iraqis. In 2008, AQ had been a beehive of constant activity, with service members of all types shuffling back and forth, and aircraft landing and taking off at all hours of the day.

But that was then. What now stood of the train station was a hollowed-out shell of its former, glorious self. My nostalgia withered into dread, a feeling like returning to the scene of a crime. Leveled by air strikes many months before our arrival, the rail yard was almost completely destroyed. Some of the larger buildings had survived, but in most cases the roofs had collapsed, leaving pockmarked, crumbling walls. The only structures to weather the strikes relatively unscathed were dozens of laddered, fifty-foot-high observation towers and scores of arched, twenty-foot-high streetlights, which had ceased functioning long ago. The tree-trunk-wide towers, each topped by a lookout deck and dormant signal lights, ringed the rail yard like the spires of a flattened crown. Mountains of shattered wood planking, concrete rubble, and twisted, rusting knots of rebar littered the ground. Taken together, the smashed train station and the abandoned hulks of the phosphate plant and cement factory sketched the outline of what was once Saddam Hussein's Iraq before its showdown with the United States. Now the ruins represented little more than the fracturing of the country's once-respectable industrial infrastructure—the consequence of nearly three decades of war, strife, and instability. It was a depressing sight to behold. As we navigated through the smashed compound, I wondered if I had made a mistake by betting the farm on the train station as our final outpost.

The afternoon grew late, and as the light faded the shadows of the derelict rail yard bled across the desert. Awtry grabbed a radio and stood next to a makeshift landing zone alongside the concrete pad we had selected for the new command post. The same streetlights that lined the yard also surrounded the LZ's perimeter. Between the light poles and one of the aluminum observation towers blocking the western approach, guiding helicopters into the zone was going to be hairy. I wasn't certain *any* pilots supporting us would agree to land there at all.

As Awtry chatted with the crew of a circling Apache and the EOD team swept the immediate area around center camp, I walked around for one final survey. The sun's dying rays twisted my silhouette into a gangly creature skulking from building to building, a grave robber searching for treasures buried within the rubble. Purplish shadows stretched in ghostly fingers across the rail yard, and a cool breeze whistled in a moaning wail through the debris piles and the cavernous, gutted buildings. I looked at my watch: October 31. Halloween was my favorite holiday, one I enjoyed even more as the father of two young girls who seemed to appreciate it nearly as much as I did. I thought of all the holidays and birthdays and special occasions I had missed throughout the years—and the ones I would keep missing as long as I continued to serve. And, along with the sadness and grief that accompanied my homesickness, there was an underlying sense of regret and self-loathing. This assignment had not been thrust upon me; no one had ordered me to do it. I had volunteered. I had fought for the job, and in doing so I had chosen to leave my wife and children. I knew Ashley understood why I had to go, but I couldn't say the same for my daughters. All they really knew for sure was that their father simply wasn't there with them. There could be no doubt about it: I loved what I was doing with my team in Iraq, but I loved my family more. At that moment, alone in the empty rail yard, I missed my wife and daughters in a way I never had before. With only the spirits of the haunted train station to keep me company, I was suddenly conscious of the gaping, self-inflicted hole that filled my heart.

With the last of the light gone from the sky, I gathered the survey team's leaders.

"Alright," I said. "Give it to me."

"We can work with this," Captain Thornton said, looking at the wreckage surrounding us. "We'll make short work of all this junk once our heavy equipment gets moving."

"We've got some good high ground here," Awtry added. "The SecFor det [detachment] can secure center camp until we get more of Echo 2/7 out here, then we can expand the perimeter as needed. The MEDEVAC LZ is tight, but I think this place can work."

"It's gonna have to," I said. "Start calling the team forward; we've got a lot of work to do, and not a lot of time to do it."

The group dispersed into the darkness. As Awtry disappeared inside his vehicle to coordinate the next echelon's movement from Fuhaymi, I found a nearby perch to collect my thoughts. It had been a long day and, given the friction of the dust storm, an even longer op. And we were barely a week into it. With the sun gone, all that remained of the day was a narrow orange beam glowing on the horizon, which soon lit up with flashes followed by the booming echoes of explosions. Coalition airstrikes were softening up Al Qa'im for the Iraqi army's final push into the urban center, and we were about to have front-row seats. With the train station in our hands and the plan in motion, I could only hope the rest of the forward command team and the supporting assets would make it in time. As the thunder of Al Qa'im's bombardment reverberated across the darkened desert, I recalled my conversation with the survey team.

We've run out of time, I thought once more. *This has to work, or the shit's really gonna hit the fan.*

28

WRITING A CHECK

THE DIESEL STACCATO of heavy equipment belching to life woke the entire outpost on the first morning of November. Before I could wipe the sleep from my eyes, bulldozers from the 2120th were pushing aside the piles of rubble littering the rail yard. By the time the sun reached its midpoint in the sky, the engineers had cleared enough workable space on the concrete pad for us to place our tactical command post. They had also created additional room for the inbound Trident element and the forward surgical team. Meanwhile, crews from our route clearance platoon proofed artillery firing positions with their mine rollers and counter-IED vehicles. Across the rail yard, the SecFor Marines erected barricades from blocks of cement, and they scraped fighting positions into the hard-packed dirt of the outpost's perimeter.

The flight hazard posed by the observation tower at the edge of the MED-EVAC landing zone was still a concern, and I asked a nearby soldier steering a bulldozer what it would take to get rid of the obstacle. Our own EOD team was champing at the bit to demolish the spire with explosive charges—a measure

I wasn't keen to take for a variety of reasons, death and dismemberment by flying shrapnel being two of them. I didn't have to hold back the techs for long. After a quick survey, the engineer cut into the metal skin of the tower with his dozer's blade, scoring a pattern in the spire's base to weaken it. As everyone stopped in their tracks to cheer on the effort, the bulldozer grunted and groaned, spewing black smoke from its exhaust pipe. After a couple of pushes, the tower crashed down like an aluminum redwood, and the dozer shoved it off the side of an adjacent embankment. It was a small but important win: we now had a safe approach for inbound helicopters.

Early progress aside, the delay of our follow-on convoy delivering the people and guts of the command post aggravated me, and I stomped around in a black mood. Qassim's forces were picking up the pace in their push toward the district's urban center, and with each passing hour we were losing momentum. Along Route Bronze, 28th Brigade had cleared an area named Turayshiyah, which enabled 32nd Brigade to pass through them, continue pressing north, and finally clear the actual town of Al Qa'im. The JaOC Commandos, meanwhile, had cleared south from the Pipeline Road–Bronze intersection to the phosphate factory's tree-lined cantonment area. That action linked the two approach axes and set conditions for the Commandos and 28th Brigade to hold in place for a forty-eight-hour rest and refit before resuming the attack. Eighth Division had similarly reached its own limit of advance and was pausing as well. The Iraqis were now waiting on us, something they weren't supposed to do.

Inch by inch, the outpost was shaping up. Even as Marines and soldiers shed their body armor to work in the growing heat of the day, Captain Thornton remained suited up as she moved from crew to crew, her exposed skin again caked in a thick, cracking film of dirt and concrete dust. That broad smile never left her face, and I admired her ability to connect with her soldiers and be present no matter the physical hardship. I had never seen anyone maneuver heavy equipment with such shit-eating grins the way Thornton's soldiers did. There was no doubt in anyone's mind that her engineers worshipped the ground she walked on and would follow her anywhere.

Along with the debris littering the rail yard, there were other obstacles to address. After an exhaustive search of the train station's interior, our EOD team had found no surprises left behind by the withdrawing enemy fighters. Outside the wire was another story. Around 1500, Lieutenant Colonel Bruøygard's Viking team reported three platter-charge IEDs along Pipeline Road, just south of the phosphate plant's cantonment area. With little else to do besides watch the engineers push junk around, I loaded up with the Jump to escort the EOD team. As far ahead of our forces as we were, and as thin as our coverage was at the train station, I wasn't wild about the idea of the Jump cruising around the battlespace. But *someone* needed to deal with the threat posed by the IEDs. Employed properly, the projectile generated by a detonating platter-charge could potentially penetrate the armored plating of one of our Coalition vehicles. Just as important, the damage to one of the less protected Iraqi trucks would be catastrophic to both the vehicle and its occupants.

Daylight was fading fast, and as we sped north, we passed a wrecked bongo truck spun out on the shoulder. Weeks earlier, Major Julian and his Marines had guided an orbiting drone for a Hellfire strike against the truck and its ISIS passengers. A neat, round hole now pierced the thin skin of the stricken bongo's roof, and apart from the burned-out cab and the spray of glass shards surrounding it, the vehicle was otherwise unscathed. The occupants were nowhere to be found—either retrieved by comrades, or else blown to kingdom come and then picked apart by the desert wildlife.

We backed our vehicles away from the explosive charges concealed in a roadside berm, and Staff Sergeant Brian and Sergeant Rioux moved in. They made quick work of the IEDs, recording the find, collecting evidence, setting reduction charges, and detonating them remotely from the safety of their vehicle. With the sun gone, the explosion illuminated the sky around us, its overpressure shaking us in the safety of our cabs. Watching Brian and Rioux ply their trade never got old, which was a good thing. With the enemy now set back on its heels, the days ahead were certain to provide plenty more work for the two techs.

The convoy carrying the bulk of our communications equipment arrived in the middle of the night. At first light on November 2, we raced to get the command post operational before the assault into the district center resumed the next day. That afternoon, Qassim appeared, with Staff Major General Adil along for the ride. Abdul Amir's chief of plans, who was a regular face in CJOC-Baghdad, Adil was about as Western as an Iraqi officer could get. A dutiful chain-smoker who spoke fluent English peppered with profanity and American slang, he was unafraid to speak his mind—even if it cast doubt on his own army's plans. His American partners considered him a critical link in the relationship between the senior Iraqi leaders and the Coalition; when he spoke, I was getting the straight scoop.

The two generals presented the final attack plan, with Qassim emphasizing key points by tapping an index finger on a map laid out before us. With his forces set in their attack positions, he would launch the final assault the following day along four approaches toward Abu Kamal, Husaybah, Karabilah, and Sadah. On the map, the four approaches paralleled each other, and—at least as envisioned—the Iraqi forces would be generally abreast of each other.

"I want artillery," Qassim told the advisors huddled around the table. "*Lots* of artillery. And lots of ISR."

"You'll have it, *Sayidi*," I said, unsure yet again if I was writing a check my ass couldn't cash. There were plenty of armed and unarmed drones, and we were certain to have enough fixed-wing and rotary-wing air support. However, even though the howitzer battery from Task Force Thunder was setting its cannon into firing positions at the rail yard, the convoy ferrying their ammunition had not yet arrived.

To inject more friction into a plan already grinding with it, the arrival of the 9th Division and PMF commanders later that afternoon meant we were about to add another Qassim to the mix. Ninth Division's commander was a staff lieutenant general named Qassim Jasim Nazal, and he could hardly be more different than *my* Qassim. Lieutenant General Qassim had commanded his armored division through numerous skirmishes in the north, and he was one of the darlings of the Iraqi MoD. The Americans loved him too. As a colonel, Major General White had worked with him years earlier, before the 2011 U.S. departure from Iraq. He exuded an air of self-importance that made my Qassim's outsize ego pale in comparison, and he showed little interest in the coming attack—almost as if clearing the Islamic State from western Al Anbar was nothing but an annoying nuisance the prime minister had thrust upon him.

Thomas, the Danish SOF team's thickly bearded, ruggedly handsome commander, had no great love for either 9th Division's Qassim *or* the PMF commander. Bad blood had developed between Thomas' A'ali Al Furat partners and Staff Lieutenant General Qassim, and now the 9th Division commander was insisting our Qassim sideline the tribal fighters. At Thomas' urging, we had planned for the A'ali Al Furat force to attack into Karabilah, but now our Qassim was being muscled into consigning his once-trusted tribal fighters into a minor supporting role. Thomas—a cool, levelheaded guy who was equal parts Grizzly Adams and chill surfer dude, and upon whom we all had developed a serious man-crush—sat by my side throughout our session with the 9th Division and PMF commanders, uncharacteristically clenching his teeth and silently fuming. When the meeting was over, I stepped outside with him.

"Jesus, man," I said. "What is it with you?"

"I got it, right?" he grumbled. "What Qassim wants, Qassim gets."

"Yeah, right," I said, rolling my eyes. "Which one?"

"Doesn't matter. But man, that fucking PMF commander," he said, shaking his head. "I know who *that* motherfucker is; we all do. He's on everyone's shit list, man, and he's taking his orders directly from Muhandes and Soleimani. He is *not* on our side, dude."

General Qassem Soleimani was Iran's Quds Force commander, and Abu Mahdi al-Muhandes was the Iraqi PMF commander who had formed Kata'ib Hizballah years earlier. It was widely believed the two leaders had their fingers in much of what was happening in the counter-ISIS campaign, and hearing it again from Thomas made me bristle. But I also understood the reality of the position in which we found ourselves.

"Yeah, yeah, I got you," I said. "And I don't think we have a choice; we're in the minority here, my man. I think we're just gonna have to hold our nose on this one and press the 'I believe' button."

He stormed off to break the news to his teammates and their A'ali Al Furat partners, and I made my way through the darkness into the command post, which was finally coming online. Having outgrown the cramped, dusty tent we had used at Fuhaymi, we now worked from a larger, Quonset hut–shaped Alaska tent the SEALs had graciously loaned us. All we were waiting for was the artillery ammunition, which was on its way in the next convoy. It couldn't arrive soon enough.

Just when I thought we had left all the SPMAGTF drama behind at Al Asad, it reared its distracting head again when I logged into my weather-beaten laptop. An email was waiting from Chris Gideons, who wanted to discuss assault support options for personnel movement to Fuhaymi. Weeks earlier, the rotor wash from one of his MV-22s had kicked up a brownout as the aircrew attempted to land at FOB Shaddadi in Syria. The subsequent crash destroyed the tiltrotor aircraft, and MARCENT had grounded the entire squadron until they could demonstrate their ability to "return to flight." Gideons was now trying to get his Osprey crews back in the saddle.

"I can move all your remaining people tomorrow in four waves," he said. "51/5 wants to say 'yes,' but they are asking for a verbal or email approval or a support request from you."

His next point set me on my ear.

"I want/need to fly this mission," he said. "This is about precedent setting with MARCENT and 'return to ops normal' as it relates to MV-22s flying ops back into Iraq and Syria. I've been trying to work through your staff at Al Asad, but they don't feel empowered to ask for our help. They are working this request for assault support back through the Coalition."

The Shaddadi crash and the squadron's grounding had put Gideons' aviation component on its ass, and his note's underlying tone made it seem like he was just about at the end of his rope. The emotional part of me thought, *Oh, so* now *he needs me. . . . Where was he when I needed* his *support at the beginning of all this?* The suggestion that my staff lacked the confidence or authority to act in my absence similarly irked me. After a couple of deep breaths, I composed my response.

"I'm not trying to let the air out of you slowly," I wrote. "This is a procedural issue more than anything else. The world we live in out here, it's not as easy as me just asking 51/5 for support; we can't ask for external support (like your MV-22s) unless that capability is not available through the Coalition. We have to register all our requirements through CJFLCC's air shop, and they will source accordingly."

In effect—in Joint terms—we just needed to ask for a bus. The Coalition would decide what model and who would drive it. If no buses of their own were available, they would outsource. I really didn't care if it was Gideons' Ospreys or Task Force Normandy's Chinooks supporting us. We just needed *something* to get our people from there to here. And, while I told him that the Coalition headquarters would be the best entry point for the air support request, in the end I relented and requested the Ospreys from 51/5. Gideons needed help getting his aircraft back online, and I needed more people out west.

"We *do* need assault support to speed personnel transport from Al Asad to Fuhaymi," I wrote to the 51/5 commander. "Otherwise, we will deliver them in a trickle by surface transport. We have submitted our air movement request to the Coalition headquarters to register the requirement; they will determine who sources it. I am agnostic on the matter, whether it is MV-22s or CH-47s/UH-60s. We are just looking for whatever air transport will get the Marines to our outposts the quickest."

Apparently, that was enough. Within twenty-four hours, Gideons' newly certified aircrews were ferrying SecFor Marines to Fuhaymi, and all was right with the SPMAGTF world. Gideons seemed grateful, and I hoped he had gotten what he needed by getting his aircrews back into the fight. In some regards, I felt guilty about giving him the bureaucratic response. He truly believed that, as fellow colonels and commanders—as friends—we should have been able to solve the problem ourselves. And I didn't disagree with him; that was the Marine Corps we had both grown up in together. But that world had changed. It was hard not to feel like the system now pitted fellow commanders against each other, encouraging them to grapple for resources rather than work together. It was hard not to feel like our various higher headquarters were reluctant to embrace their collective responsibility to be the adults in the room.

Many months went by before the fissures in my relationship with Gideons healed. Over time, I realized how grateful I was for the support he provided during Desert Lion—the addition of the Ospreys had indeed accelerated the flow of people and supplies to the growing train station outpost—and I genuinely regretted the rift that had developed between the two of us. Although I never regretted my decision to stick to my guns and insist the task force lead the operation, I could see that, in many ways, Gideons had found himself in similar circumstances. He and his team had trained hard to go to The Show just as my team had. From their perspective, *they* were the correct choice to lead the fight. It just hadn't gone their way, and in the months and years that followed, I made sure to never throw it in his face. Eventually, we found ourselves working together again, and over time our friendship grew stronger than it had been before our final adventure in Al Anbar Province.

For my part, the circumstances in which I found myself in Iraq often left me feeling like anything *but* a battlefield commander. I was weary of the political maneuvering and constantly having to ask permission for everything. I believed, just as Gideons did, that I should have been able to cut through all the red tape to get it done. But it wasn't that simple. And, truth be told, in our short time in Iraq, Major General White and his staff had provided a greater degree of support—both tangible and emotional—to me and the task force than MARCENT, Task Force 51/5, SPMAGTF, or our parent command at I MEF. Now, as my team found itself in the thick of things, our loyalties were less with the Marine Corps that had birthed us and more with the Joint force that was supporting us in our effort to get the Iraqis to the five-yard line. Mulling the potential career consequences of my decisions, I wondered if I would still have a home left to return to in the Marine Corps when this was all over. Considering all our team had gone through, I wasn't certain I cared anymore.

29

A DISAPPEARING ACT

THE CLANGING OF METAL PLATES bouncing off concrete and the grunts of people belting out exercises jarred me awake at first light on November 3. The convoy transporting our artillery ammunition had arrived at 0200, and the howitzers took turns registering rounds throughout the night. Not long after the booms ceased, they were replaced by the grunting, banging, and clanging, which shook the concrete pad repeatedly. I sat up in my sleeping bag and saw the forward surgical team exercising while they put the finishing touches on a pretty respectable field gym. The day had barely begun, and my blood pressure was already climbing.

During our mission planning, the surgical team had insisted their shipping containers be among the first to travel by convoy to the rail yard, and we accommodated the request. It made sense at the time. As isolated as we expected to be, the medical capability would be necessary if anyone was wounded or injured. But no one had said anything about ferrying heavy, bulky exercise equipment, and so we had unwittingly prioritized those containers over the vital artillery ammunition. I later confronted the lead surgeon about the gym. He explained that his team had moved across the theater twelve times in nine months, but hearing that was no less irritating. The ammunition had barely arrived in time, but by 0700 the howitzer battery was belching rounds to the west as the Iraqis crossed the line of departure toward Al Qa'im's district center.

During our first evening at the rail yard, Major General White had informed me that Abdul Amir was taking control of the operation, and I would become his principal advisor. Qassim was no longer the overall commander, and he would now only need to focus on his Route Bronze axis with 7th Division. While hard to accept, it was easy to understand. All eyes in the Iraqi government were on Desert Lion, and Abdul Amir wanted to retain his place in the limelight. I wondered how Qassim felt. He said nothing to me about it, but I was fairly certain the demotion had hit him pretty hard. Or maybe it hadn't. He had always been more comfortable focusing on 7th Division and his own JaOC units, so maybe it was precisely what he wanted.

Abdul Amir decided to position himself at our command post, and I was not looking forward to it. He had come across as an asshole the first time I met him at Numan's office, and I doubted he had changed much since then. But I needed to make an effort, and that included cleaning myself up before he arrived. I hadn't bathed in nearly two weeks, and I was filthy. My hair was matted and heavy with dust. A thick scale of grime coated my skin, and my uniform was soiled and greasy. I reeked too. Even Qassim had politely told me that I needed to fix myself, touching my dirty cheek and saying, "We need to finish this operation so you can clean yourself up." Before Abdul Amir's arrival, I stepped away from the command post, poured a bottle of water over my head, and attempted to scrub at least one layer of dirt from my face. It was no use; I was a wreck.

A small helicopter touched down in the landing zone at 1000. From the moment Abdul Amir stepped out of the aircraft, he all but refused to speak to me. Irritated that I hadn't spent time with him before the operation, he sat in petulant silence inside our command post with a bored look on his face, casually flipping from screen to screen on his tablet. I sat off to one side to give him his space, and when I looked over his shoulder, I noticed the screen saver was a photo of himself striking a regal pose in his dress uniform. The more I learned about him, the more I thought he was a strange agent. Qassim and his senior officers never hesitated to talk trash about him in front of me. They insisted he still lived with his mother, and they often wondered aloud why he wasn't married. Months later, with the operation in our rearview mirror, I found myself in a private session with just Qassim, Numan, and Kiffa. As Qassim rattled on about Abdul Amir, Kiffa leaned over to me. A tragic look filled his face as he said, "He's a *gay*." Qassim and Numan nodded gravely, and I finally understood their bizarre obsession with Abdul Amir's marital status.

<hr />

The Iraqis were making great strides. The two Commando units raced north and then quickly secured the neighborhood of Al Sikak. In short order, 28th Brigade paired up with the 7th Division Commandos, and together they bypassed Husaybah and seized the border crossing into Syria. The CTS force and 32nd Brigade advanced toward Husaybah, broke into the town, and cleared close to a quarter of it before halting their movement and going to ground. Ninth Division, mounted in their armored fighting vehicles, was moving even quicker, and they broke into the town of Sadah early in the day. We knew that the attacking PMF units had cleared Karabilah, but apart from the position reports that Adil handed us, we had no true picture of what they were doing. All we really knew was that the PMF controlled the majority of Karabilah's urban grid, and they were looting everything in sight. It now made sense why 9th Division's Lieutenant General Qassim and his PMF counterpart had insisted A'ali Al Furat stay out of their way. Karabilah was A'ali Al Furat's old neighborhood, and no one wanted the tribals around to stop the PMF from doing as they pleased.

We stared at the ISR feeds all day, and Abdul Amir's boredom never wavered. Whenever the task force coordinated a strike, we would talk it up to him, choosing the exact moment a Hellfire left the rails to point to the screen and announce, "Here comes another one, *Sayidi!*" But each strike yielded little more than a passing glance from him, and he would immediately return to the fascination of his tablet. Even when we flattened an ISIS pickup truck and watched a mortally wounded fighter crawl away from the wreckage with two leaking red stumps where his legs once were, Abdul Amir yawned and fiddled with his phone.

Major General White had flown in from Baghdad as well, and he spent more energy than he should have singing my praises to Abdul Amir.

"*Sayidi*, this is *your* man," he said, echoing his endorsement to Qassim months earlier. "*Aqeed* Folsom knows what he's doing, and he loves to kill *Da'esh*."

We followed Abdul Amir to a tent his aides had erected outside our command post, and everyone sat down for lunch. Apart from the food Kiffa had delivered to Fuhaymi, it was my first prepared meal in weeks. After a steady diet of nothing but MREs, caffeine, and nicotine for many days, I wondered just how sick I would get afterward.

In the middle of lunch, Abdul Amir abruptly stood from his seat and headed to a waiting Humvee.

"There he goes," White said. "I told you; he likes to get out and about."

"Oh shit," I said, jumping to my feet. "Sorry, I gotta go."

"Have fun, Lion-6," he said. Then he called after me, pointing to the battery of recently arrived truck-mounted howitzers pulling into their firing positions. "Hey, I see the French finally got here with their Caesars. I wouldn't put them next to your COC if I were you."

I nodded absently and raced after Abdul Amir. "Hey!" I yelled to First Lieutenant Miles. "Get the Jump moving; we're leaving right now!"

The Marines scrambled to don their gear and get the trucks moving. I turned to Awtry, who had heard the commotion and was just now showing up.

"You coming?" I asked.

"I won't be ready in time," he said. "You better get moving; Abdul Amir is pulling out of the gate right now."

We chased the convoy across the desert to Qassim's command post four kilometers south of Husaybah. Abdul Amir climbed in the back of an MRAP and huddled around a map with Qassim, Numan, and Adil, and the four men chattered and gestured wildly through the thick cloud of cigarette smoke filling the cabin. It was impressive to watch them hash out their plan in the same manner I had seen American commanders do in similar circumstances. For me, it was a visual example of just how professionalized the Iraqi military had become over the years.

Once they stepped out of the vehicle, Qassim and Abdul Amir mugged for a swarm of waiting news crews. With video cameras rolling and shutters clicking like insects, I stepped aside, out of the frame. This was Qassim's moment, not mine.

First Lieutenant Miles walked over with a scowl on his face.

"The EOD truck won't start," he said.

"Shit, there he goes again," I said, watching Abdul Amir climb into his vehicle and speed away without us. I turned back to Miles. "We really can't get it up and running?"

"It's down hard."

"Fuck me," I said, looking at our barren surroundings. We were in the middle of nowhere, and Qassim's soldiers were mounting up. I turned to Amador and pointed to a nearby wrecker truck. "Hey, grab Qassim before he leaves."

"*Sayidi*," I said, trying to hide my embarrassment. "Our truck is broken. Can your wrecker tow it to the train station?"

"Of course!" he exclaimed, clapping me on the shoulder. He wasn't put out at all, but instead thrilled that he could finally do something for us.

It was dark when we pulled through the rail yard's control point. The crippled MRAP's rear axle had caught fire along the way, further delaying our trip home, and we were all beat. The train station was rattling from Task Force Wagram's artillery trucks hurling shells into the area beyond Al Qa'im, and the command post's occupants looked like they were about to lose their minds. Everyone had shoved foam plugs into their ears, and with the overpressure of each explosion the tent shuddered as though it might collapse around us. The maps, charts, and imagery mounted on the walls had long since fallen to the floor, and Marines were hunched over their terminals, heads in their hands. Awtry sat typing at his computer, a pissed-off frown turning the corners of his mouth downward.

"Jesus H. Christ," I said in between volleys. "General White wasn't shitting . . . that is the loudest goddamned thing I have ever heard."

"Yeah, we're moving them farther away from the COC first thing tomorrow," he said. "By the way, Prime Minister Abadi already declared Al Qa'im liberated."

"What? Are you kidding?"

"Nope."

Abadi had used the Iraqi army's rapid advance and the much lighter than expected enemy resistance to score a quick political victory. It really wasn't over, and everyone knew it. But the Iraqi soldiers were inside the district center now, and they were there to stay. There was mopping-up work to do inside the dense urban maze, and there was also the other side of the Euphrates River and Rawah to deal with. But all that would have to wait. No one was going to tell Abadi he had jumped the gun.

With the concussion from the French Caesars shaking our command post, I tallied the task force's contribution so far in Desert Lion's third phase. We had coordinated more than forty separate strikes, accounting for an equal number of Islamic State fighters killed and the destruction of numerous enemy vehicles, weapons systems, command and control nodes, and bed-down locations. But one thing stood out: by the time the Iraqis assaulted into the district center, the enemy had vanished. We didn't know what to make of it. Our earlier intelligence reports had indicated there might be upwards of two thousand fighters waiting inside the city, but that was no longer the case. If there ever were those kinds of numbers inside the district, ISIS had pulled one of the greatest disappearing acts of all time. *Where did they go?* I wondered. We had our suspicions, but nothing concrete to confirm them.

The kinetics of the operation and our support to the Iraqis aside, more impressive was the less exciting, less newsworthy feats our small outfit had accomplished in the previous three weeks. In addition to surveying and constructing the two tactical assembly areas, the team at Al Asad had run more than two dozen resupply convoys to the outposts at Fuhaymi and Al Qa'im—a one-way ground distance totaling more than 150 kilometers over truly hideous terrain. In total, before leaving Iraq six months later, the Marines, sailors, and soldiers would travel more than 11,000 miles along Iraq's roads to and from the different outposts. By my reckoning, Desert Lion was a logistical feat unlike any other the Marine Corps had executed since the invasion of Iraq nearly fifteen years earlier. I could not have been any prouder to be part of that team.

30

A MOMENTOUS OCCASION

DESPITE PRIME MINISTER Abadi's declaration to the contrary, the Al Qa'im District was anything but secure. There were still street-by-street, block-by-block searches for the Iraqi soldiers to conduct before they could officially declare the urban area safe—a process that could take weeks. To motivate the *jundis* and encourage them to keep moving into the city, we kicked off the morning of November 4 with an ear-splitting twenty-one-gun salute from the Caesars. Moving the battery away from our command post dramatically lessened the shock of the cannon's nonstop firing, and it was a good thing we had gotten it out of the way early. The French soldiers loved to fire their Caesars, and after the morning's initial volley they continued to shoot in soul-shaking episodes for the rest of the operation.

Inside the district center, the JaOC Commandos were back-clearing in Al Sikak, while 28th Brigade and the 7th Division Commandos were continuing to lock down the Syrian border all the way to the Euphrates River. Inside Husaybah, the CTS units were likewise back-clearing the town, but in Karabilah the activities of the PMF soldiers remained a mystery. They were determined to do things their own way, and no one was stopping them. Lieutenant General Qassim, already visibly bored, rushed 9th Division's search operations in Sadah, and as the day drew to a close, he declared the town secure. He had signaled his intent to leave Al Qa'im as quickly as possible, no doubt stemming from a desire to leave the tedious task of clearing the rest of the district to the other, lesser Iraqi army formations.

Clearing the district was proving to be more dangerous than the initial assault into it. The Iraqis had broken into the city without sustaining any significant casualties, but inside Al Sikak two enemy drone attacks killed three 7th Division commandos and wounded another three. The report placed the enemy quadcopter's origin somewhere across the border in Syria. Our earlier suspicions about the withdrawing enemy fighters' destination were coming true: they had fled out the back door left wide open by the Iraqi army and the PMF. The cross-border drone attacks would continue to kill and wound *jundis* searching the city for nearly a week, and it wasn't until the Coalition stepped up its targeting efforts across the frontier that the attacks subsided.

By the end of the day, the Iraqi units along the different approaches reported most of the district secure. I took a few moments to walk around the train station and clear my head. Weaving through a file of decrepit, rusting rail cars frozen in time, I found a platoon of Jughayfi tribal fighters celebrating with songs, dancing, and clapping. Three hapless goats stood off to one side, tethered to a railroad tie, waiting patiently to become a celebratory dinner for the raucous Jughayfi soldiers.

"Sorry guys," I said, strolling past the animals. "Wish I could help."

Armed quadcopters weren't the only threat from across the Syrian border. On November 5, the 7th Division Commandos reported two near misses by enemy anti-tank missiles. A SEAL team arrayed along the border west of Al Sikak was not so lucky. Earlier that morning, a missile volley had whizzed across the frontier and struck two of the team's trucks, wounding three operators and killing their military working dog. The warheads critically damaged one vehicle, warping and peeling apart its armored chassis, and so severely damaged the second that the Trident team would later call in an air strike to destroy the unsalvageable hulk. The cross-border attack on the SEALs signaled another concerning development: ISIS fighters were no longer reluctant to deliberately target Coalition vehicles, if they ever were in the first place.

Soon after receiving an order from the prime minister to move to a position ten kilometers south of the town, the PMF vacated Karabilah. Although new SMG units—among them Kata'ib Hizballah and Asa'ib Ahl Al-Haq Brigade—would roll into town days later, the PMF was gone for the time being. An eager force of A'ali Al Furat tribesmen swept in to fill the void, but the damage from the PMF was done. In addition to looting Karabilah for everything they possibly could, the departing paramilitary fighters had left scores of unit flags throughout the town and planted in the ground across the desert. The message for the locals was unmistakable: *The liberation of Al Qa'im was brought to you by the PMF.* You had to hand it to them: they had an effective public affairs program.

The PMF units weren't the only ones leaving. As expected, 9th Division would soon unveil its plans to return north—where the "real" fight was—and CTS wouldn't be far behind. With the eventual departure of those formations, the drudgery of stabilizing the district would fall to Qassim's soldiers. I sensed this was what he had wanted from the beginning—for everyone to just leave him the hell alone and let him run the campaign his own way—but I wondered if everyone was pulling chocks too quickly before the job was complete.

As a formation of Iraqi helicopters passed over our heads at the rail yard, we received a call that the prime minister was on board one of them. He intended to visit Al Qa'im himself to celebrate the liberation, and Qassim was sure to be with him. I hadn't seen my partner since his loan of the wrecker for the downed EOD truck, so the Jump team mounted up and raced out the gate to the phosphate plant. Abadi and his fleet of humongous Mi-17s had just touched down, and we chased a long caravan of blacked-out SUVs and up-armored Humvees into the district center.

Iraqi soldiers, government officials, and the district's inhabitants packed the town square. The prime minister's heavily armed security detail pushed through the crowd to a towering mast that dominated the square, and a black-clad CTS operator carrying an Iraqi flag scaled it. Hundreds of gathered soldiers shouted and chanted, waving unit standards and Iraqi flags. The energy in the square surged as the soldier neared the top. He secured the national colors to the mast and shouted, "This is our country! *Da'esh* will never take it back!" The crowd erupted in cheers and applause. Completely enveloped by the gathering, with Iraqi men of all shapes and sizes smiling, waving, and reaching out to touch me, I realized just how fortunate I was to bear witness to this momentous occasion.

As Abadi's convoy shot back to the phosphate plant and the waiting helicopters, Numan found me in the crowd and invited me to his command post south of Husaybah. With the prime minister gone and no one left to direct traffic, the town square collapsed into a glut of people and vehicles. Numan sped away, leaving us in the dust and confusion. With our escort gone, we crept west down Route Bronze as it snaked through the decayed neighborhoods of Karabilah and Husaybah, toward the sealed Syrian port of entry. We turned south, paralleling the unmarked border on our right and Husaybah's western edge on our left, and we passed the crippled Trident vehicle the enemy missile volley had struck earlier that morning. The operators were still on site, and as we approached their trucks, we stopped to coordinate with them before resuming our movement south. The radio crackled to life.

"Contact right, contact right!" a voice from the Jump's lead vehicle shouted. "We're taking fire from across the border!"

In the turret hatch above me, the gunner slewed his .50-caliber to the right, aiming toward the border. I peered through the passenger door's ballistic glass porthole. Tiny puffs of dirt popped on the ground far to our right, but as far as I could tell nothing was coming near us. There was no echo or report of our lead vehicle returning fire, either. I shouted up to the sergeant manning the turret.

"Hey, do you have a visual? Can you see the shooter?"

"I can't see shit!" he shouted over the electric whine of the turret slewing back and forth.

Our vehicles sat idling for an eternity as the two gunners searched for whoever was shooting at us. *This is stupid*, I thought, keying the radio's handset. *We're nothing but sitting ducks.*

"Vic-1, this is Six," I said. "Let's get the hell out of here. Keep pushing south."

"Copy, Six. We're Oscar Mike."

"Step on it," I told First Lieutenant Miles. "Whoever it was, they're gone. If they'd wanted to waste us, they would have done it by now."

I considered the brief engagement for the remainder of the trip to the 7th Division command post. I was already pissed off about our separation from Numan because it reminded me of a similar episode nine years earlier, when my Iraqi partner had abandoned me in the exact same stretch of road near Husaybah. But the tactical situation hadn't been as uncertain back then, nor had anyone been shooting at us. Now, here we were on the Syrian border, in a place we really weren't supposed to be, where a pair of enemy missiles had already taken out two SEAL trucks. With some asshole shooting at us from across the frontier—with us alone and possibly outgunned—we had come dangerously close to violating one of the Coalition's mandates: we had nearly become the main effort.

Weeks later, when we were back safe at Al Asad, several Marines who were with the Jump along the Syrian border would ask Sergeant Major Leibfried if they could get the Combat Action Ribbon for the engagement.

"*What* engagement?" I replied as he advocated for them to receive the decoration. "You mean the one where we never saw who was shooting at us, and where we never returned fire?"

"Having that award means a lot," he protested. "And it can help them get promoted."

"Forget it," I said, closing the case on the matter.

The event on the border, and the subsequent resentment several of my teammates harbored in the following years, would prove to me once more just how supercharged the Combat Action Ribbon had become. Over the course of the Long War, a growing movement of senior officers had begun to believe the award should be abolished. After my tours in Iraq and Afghanistan, I tended to agree. The issue had become too emotional—too divisive—and Marines were often willing to hazard themselves or others just to earn the coveted decoration. Countless others had been denied the award because of administrative negligence or oversight on the part of their leaders. The more I thought about it, the more I believed Napoleon may have been correct when he purportedly said, "A soldier will fight long and hard for a bit of colored ribbon." I wasn't so sure that was such a good thing.

By November 6, just three days after Abadi declared Al Qa'im liberated, the Iraqi army's search operation inside the district was old news. Everyone was losing interest. Abdul Amir wanted the area north of the Euphrates River liberated, as well as the long-sought-after Rawah, as early as November 11. But even he seemed to be growing bored of the operation, and it looked like Qassim was moving back into the operational command seat. And, as we had anticipated, from that point forward it would be a JaOC-only show. Ninth Division planned to depart as soon as possible, and CTS would only leave a small force in the district. Major General Hussein's 8th Division would continue to lock down the border and the district center, but I had my doubts. At a meeting in an opulent house across from the town square where the Iraqi flag now flew, I argued with him over his repeated lack of support for our daily supply convoys along Pipeline Road. He was unapologetic, and Qassim did nothing to intervene on my behalf. Later, Qassim privately conveyed his frustration to me. Even though Hussein now technically worked for Qassim, the 8th Division commander only answered to Abdul Amir. *Man*, I thought. *What is it with Abdul Amir? What does he have on these guys?*

To liberate the area north of the river, the Iraqis needed to get there first. They now faced the same dilemma we had considered before the cancelled Rawah operation a month earlier: the bombing campaign had destroyed or severely damaged all the bridges linking the river's two banks. On November 7, just one day after Abdul Amir announced his intent to launch the assault across the river into Rumannah, soldiers from 32nd Brigade initiated an uncoordinated repair of the cratered Abu Harden Bridge. Volleys of missiles and indirect fire slammed into the area around the working *jundis*, killing one and destroying a Humvee on the bridge, and crippling an Iraqi army bulldozer south of it. Three soldiers were still stuck on the bridge.

Watching all this develop on our screens, we called for immediate artillery suppression to support the soldiers in the beaten zone. When nothing happened for far too long, I picked up the phone and punched the numbers for the Main COC. A major who had joined us from Task Force Spartan to assist the FECC answered the phone.

"Hey man," I growled. "What the hell is taking so long?"

"We're waiting for strike cell approval."

"Are you fucking kidding me?!" I yelled. "This is collective self-defense; the ISF is getting hammered on the bridge. Get fires in there now! *Right . . . fucking . . . now!*"

Minutes later, a volley of smoke rounds landed across the river, obscuring the area and enabling the soldiers to recover their stranded teammates. Later that evening, 32nd Brigade made a second repair attempt, this time with our pre-coordinated artillery providing supporting fires across the river. After the first volley, the Iraqi liaison officer in our command post put his hand up and said something urgently.

"Cease fire, cease fire," Amador relayed. "It's too close to the *jundis*."

"Huh?" I said, looking at the video feed. "It's nowhere near them."

"They say it is."

"Fine," I replied, giving the signal to the watch officer. "Shut it down."

With the howitzers silenced, 32nd Brigade immediately received heavy small-arms fire from its flanks. Moments later, the radio in our tent lit up with the unnerving screams of someone shouting "*Shaheed* [Martyr]! *Shaheed!*"

"They've got five guys wounded on the ground," the watch officer announced. "They're bringing them back here for treatment."

"Man, what the hell is going on?" I asked. Kiffa motioned for me to join him outside for a cigarette.

"It was 9th Division who was shooting at them," he said.

"Huh? Are you sure?"

"They won't admit it, but it was them."

He was correct. We analyzed the geometry and the unit locations, and 9th Division was the only possible answer. They never admitted the error, and they never would. To do so would tarnish their sterling reputation. Friendly fire, it seems, is not a good look for *any* army.

To help us salvage that first disastrous attempt to secure the bridge crossing, the Trident commander offered an AC-130 gunship to soften up the far side of the river before the next attempt to repair the span. We stared at the video feed for hours, captivated by the footage from the circling gunship as it pumped round after round of 105-mm shells into obstacles and enemy defensive positions along the northern bank. Despite the motivation of the Ghostrider hosing down its targets, the first action at the bridge was a disappointment, and I had finally reached my limit with the Baghdad strike cell. Days earlier, I had made an angry call to the Coalition fires officer, grousing about the agonizingly slow process. The conversation ended with me telling the Army colonel I no longer had any confidence they could conduct timely fires in support of either Coalition *or* Iraqi forces. He promised to get the strike cell to do better, but they still fell short as we fought to support the soldiers on the bridge.

I didn't expect the situation would improve, and it never did—not even when Major General White was present in our command post on November 9 for the second repair attempt. Thirty-second Brigade had learned its lesson about going in without a plan during daytime, and they had asked us to support the effort with terrain denial, screening, and aviation-delivered fires on the northern bank of the Euphrates River. When the *jundis* finally approached the bridge, White saw firsthand how muddled the strike cell's process was. With his return flight delayed for hours by bad weather, he was stuck with us. He had succumbed to Al Anbar's mysterious upper respiratory infection, and he was doped up on meds. Sitting in a fog by my side, often resting his forehead on the cool plastic tabletop, he watched as the 32nd Brigade soldiers tried again to repair the bridge.

"Man, come on, Lion-6," he drawled. "You need to get some Joint fires and effects in there to support those guys."

"We've been trying for an hour. The strike cell won't approve it."

"Huh? An *hour*?"

"That's what I've been telling you, sir. The strike cell is ineffective. We can't count on them to do shit . . . even for collective self-defense."

"Shit," he slurred, picking up the phone. "I'll call them myself."

After a couple of minutes of pointed words, he hung up. I waited for the miracle to happen, for the process to accelerate. It never did. At that moment, I knew we would never see any measurable change in the strike cell's responsiveness. If the commanding general himself couldn't compel them to get their collective shit together, then no one could. My faith in CJOC-Baghdad, the strike cell, and the entire Coalition targeting and fire support process in Iraq dissolved, never to re-materialize.

In the years after my return from Iraq, I thought often about our persistent challenges with the strike cell. Had our team ever found itself in the shit—where our lives were truly in danger of being snuffed out—would the strike cell have risen to the occasion and given us the timely and accurate fire support needed to save our lives? Each time I pondered that question, I came to the same conclusion. The answer, unfortunately, would be "no."

31

HALLOWED GROUND

AS THE CLOCK STRUCK MIDNIGHT, turning November 9 into November 10, those of us still on watch celebrated the Marine Corps' 242nd birthday. Kiffa joined us, a puzzled look on his face, while we stood at rigid attention as the watch officer read Gen. John Lejeune's birthday message. The oldest and youngest Marines present each sampled an MRE pound cake adorned with burning paper matches. We then presented a piece of the dessert to Kiffa, our guest of honor. It was a tradition as timeless as the Corps itself, and carrying it out in the middle of the night on the edge of the empire gave the ceremony a new meaning for everyone.

Later that day, we continued the celebration with all the Marines present at the train station. To mark the occasion, some artistic soul had fashioned a full-sized cake from a stack of the small MRE desserts, slathering it with peanut butter and spelling out "Happy 242 B-day" with M&Ms. The Marines operating at the outpost—comprising men and women from our original team, SPMAGTF attachments, and the recently arrived 15th MEU forward logistics element—now numbered close to a hundred. They gathered in a semicircle as I spoke about the significance of Al Qa'im and our mission with the Iraqis.

"This is hallowed ground," I said, pointing to the rail yard around us and then west toward the district center. "Several of us have been here before and lost friends and comrades, Marines like Ray Mendoza and Rick Gannon. Jason Dunham earned the Medal of Honor here. There was a time when the streets here ran red with the blood of Marines and the enemy insurgents they were fighting.

"What we're doing here now is not just about supporting our Iraqi partners in their fight against the Islamic State. It's about our commitment to our brothers- and sisters-in-arms, and our commitment to being part of something bigger than ourselves. I am proud to be here, and I am honored to serve with each of you."

With the repairs to the Abu Harden Bridge finally completed, 32nd Brigade began crossing the Euphrates River at 0700 on November 11—this time under the fire support umbrella of Task Force Wagram's Caesars. During the Iraqi army's brief pause before launching the final assault into the district, Lieutenant Colonel Bruøygard and his team had returned to Al Asad to resupply themselves and work on their vehicles. The Norwegians made their way back to the outpost just in time, and they now supported 32nd Brigade from the river's southern bank as the Iraqis established a bridgehead on the northern bank and pulled 31st Brigade through. By sundown, 31st Brigade had established positions along the Syrian border, and the two Commando units turned east. With almost no enemy resistance, they cleared the urban areas of Rumannah, Abu Harden, and Dughaymah before consolidating for the night.

The next day, 31st and 32nd Brigades back-cleared in zone until Ar Rabit, Rumannah, and Abu Harden were secure. Despite the 9th Division commander's desire to leave, he had stuck around to support the advance of both 7th and 8th Divisions, who would become the lead units for the attack east against Rawah. Qassim laid out his plan during a KLE in a house next to an abandoned enemy aid station in Rumannah. The meeting place was near the location of a pontoon bridge that once spanned the Euphrates. My old team had traversed it several times during our forays across the river in 2008, but it had long since vanished.

During the meeting, I was surprised to see the senior PMF commander in Al Anbar Province. With the PMF's departure, we had believed they were done with us. Our subsequent intelligence assessments concluded that elements of KH and the Asa'ib Ahl Al-Haq Brigade had moved across the border and linked up with Syrian Hezbollah units. The more we learned about the PMF's actions in the area beyond our direct control, the less I wanted to have anything to do with them. The feeling seemed mutual, and they were keeping their distance from both the Iraqi army and the Coalition.

Qassim believed his forces would reach the midpoint between the "alien head" of Al Amari peninsula and the "humpback" of Jibab peninsula the next day, and they would reach the Shirwaniyah shark fin by November 13. The timeline he unveiled would posture the Iraqis in their attack positions by November 15, which would enable us to coordinate the shaping and pre-assault fires necessary for the final push. Abdul Amir even promised bridging assets in three days' time, but Qassim said he would keep going without them if necessary.

"And," he boasted, leaning forward in his seat, "I don't need CTS to liberate Rawah."

"You go, *Sayidi*," I said.

The lack of bridging assets to connect the two riverbanks and repair the damaged spans was more of a problem for the accompanying advisor teams than it was for the Iraqis. Qassim's forces attacking east would be split, with some units moving north of the river and others moving south of it along Route Bronze. Eager as ever to get kinetically engaged alongside their partners, both the Trident and Viking teams were pushing hard to accompany Qassim's battalions. I was not a fan of their plans.

"We're prepared to cross the river into Rawah with the ISF," Lieutenant Colonel Bruøygard told me.

"Yeah, well, I'm not so sure that's a great idea," I replied. "The bridge is shot, and I'm not comfortable putting your armored vehicles across it."

The bridge was indeed in bad shape; Major Julian and his team had seen to that during the final hours of the battle in Anah. But that wasn't the only reason I didn't support the Norwegians crossing the river. Despite all the intelligence Major Kelly and his team were collecting, we still had no idea what was waiting inside Rawah's congested urban grid. On top of it all, the damaged bridge would unnecessarily complicate the MEDEVAC process if the Norwegians had any casualties inside the city. I insisted the Viking team support the Iraqis from the river's southern bank, and I'm not sure their commander ever really forgave me for it. But I was content with my decision, and I stuck with it.

That night, a 7.2-magnitude earthquake that originated somewhere in Iran shook the ground around us. The wobbling made me reconsider my sleeping location. Late in our first evening at the train station, Sergeant Major Leibfried and I had set up a pair of folding cots alongside our truck, which was parked in the lee of a shattered building that listed precariously over us like a battle-damaged Leaning Tower of Pisa. Ignoring everyone's pleas for us to move out of the tilting structure's shadow for fear the whole thing would topple on us in the night, we had remained. It was a convenient place to sleep, as it kept us close to both our vehicle and the command post.

Despite the clangs and grunts of the surgical team exercising every morning, I had continued to sleep outside in the shadow of the sloping building for the first week at the train station. However, late in the evening of November 8, a cold rain fell, and I moved my belongings into a demolished shower and latrine facility behind the command post that became known as "the shitter." As a platoon commander in 2004, Awtry had quartered his Marines there. Now, many years later, he had moved back into it after we occupied the train station. Like every other building at the rail yard, the shitter had been struck by ordnance at some point, and it looked like a giant had picked it up and drop-kicked it. The roof had collapsed into the structure's eastern half, rendering that section useless. Awtry had set up shop in the corridor near the entrance, and his living conditions were bone-dry.

As I staggered out of the tent, my head spinning with vertigo from the tremor, I wondered if continuing to sleep inside the demolished shitter after an earthquake was such a good idea. But, in my fatigue-addled brain, the answer was clear: rubble and risk were better than cold and wet. If the roof caved in on us in the middle of the night, at least I would be warm and dry when it happened.

On November 13, the two Commando units moved east. They cleared settlements along the way with little resistance, and they eventually held fast at Al Bubiyah, three kilometers west of the alien head. Thirty-first Brigade followed the Commandos to secure their rear flank, and 28th Brigade positioned itself in Anah to provide artillery support from the Euphrates' southern bank. Still waiting for the much-hyped bridging equipment, 28th Brigade was planning to assemble a pontoon bridge crossing near the shark fin in the next twenty-four hours to connect Route Bronze with the Iraqi units north of the river.

Abdul Amir had announced his plans to attend a KLE at the train station, and Qassim appeared on scene first. He was jittery, and all I could pry from him was that the JaOC would continue its march east the next day. No 9th Division units would participate. Instead, Qassim's brigades would attack Rawah on November 16 with its two Commando units, 28th Brigade, and elements of 8th Division. After outlining the plan, he wasn't interested in talking about much else.

"Man, *Sayidi*," I asked. "What is it with you? What's going on?"

"Abdul Amir isn't happy," he said, fretfully smoking a cigarette.

I didn't press the issue; Abdul Amir *never* seemed to be happy. And, twenty minutes later, I understood why—at least for this time. A pair of circling Mi-17s and Abdul Amir's Bell Jet Ranger squeezed themselves into the landing zone, which we had designed for only one airframe at a time. As the three helicopters set down, they blanketed the camp with a choking storm of dust and debris, almost blowing down the nearby tents. I winced as the buzz saws of their spinning rotor blades threatened to rip into each other and the vehicles parked next to the pad. Amador ran to the nearest idling aircraft and banged on the pilot's window.

"You can't stay here!" he shouted over the rotor wash. "It's too dangerous!"

"We will accept the responsibility," the pilot snapped.

As Abdul Amir climbed from his Jet Ranger, Amador approached him.

"*Sayidi*," he asked. "Can you *please* move your helicopters to the big landing zone on the camp's east side?"

"This is my country!" Abdul Amir shouted. "I can land anywhere I want. And the Americans shouldn't be leaving their bases anyway!"

He sped away in his waiting Humvee without acknowledging me. I turned to Kiffa, who had stood next to me throughout the debacle.

"Man, what the fuck, *Sayidi*?" I said, fuming. "This is getting old."

"Don't worry about him," he said, handing me a cigarette. "Come on, let's smoke."

A curious friendship had blossomed between Kiffa and me. Qassim was my partner; we had a mutually respectful relationship, and the two of us had indeed grown close over the previous months. But Kiffa and I had forged an altogether different relationship. Qassim was always out and about, showing up at our position periodically for meetings and planning sessions. But, throughout the operation, Kiffa was always by my side. After we made it to the train station, he would often invite me to dinner at his trailer, where we would talk into the night about everything from our families to politics. He was not optimistic about his country's future, and I felt sad for him. Like everyone else, he just wanted a better life for his family, but he wasn't certain things would get any better now that the ISIS threat was waning. The problems, he insisted, were just beginning.

Qassim's units continued their eastward advance on November 15 and halted near Shirwaniyah, fifteen kilometers west of Rawah, to give 28th Brigade time to place the bridging assets that had arrived earlier in the day. The final assault, which was still on track for November 16, would hit from three directions: west, northwest, and north. As before, it would leave an open back door, but there was no convincing Qassim otherwise. He had made up his mind before sharing his plan with me.

At sunrise, I mounted up with the Jump and an attached team of SecFor Marines, and we drove from the rail yard to the new "Firebase Anah" to co-locate with 28th Brigade, Trident, and the Norwegian Viking team. The soldiers of Task Force Slugger were finally appearing in force at the rail yard, and their timing couldn't have been better. Originally assigned to Task Force Lion to partner with 9th Division during the attack on Al Qa'im, Slugger was the U.S. Army's 3-89 Cavalry squadron that belonged to 3-10 Mountain. The logistical realities of transporting heavy Coalition vehicles and equipment around the country with Iraqi contractors, coupled with the unexpected speed of the Iraqi advance, had made Slugger miss the entire push into Al Qa'im. Regardless, their commander, an enthusiastic, heavily mustachioed lieutenant colonel named Brandon Payne, was keen to get his team up and running at the rail yard. He was already prepared to take control of operations there, and his timely arrival had made my decision to move the Jump to Firebase Anah an easy one.

We headed east along Bronze, cruising past crumbling battle positions I hadn't seen since 2008. Mile after mile, as we drew closer to Anah, our vehicles passed over disarmed lollipop IEDs still embedded in the asphalt. Each time we approached one of the buried bombs I held my breath and prayed the Iraqi EOD teams had been paying attention to what they were doing. By noon we were pulling into the city limits, and I realized that, over the previous six weeks, we had made a full circle across a wide swath of western Al Anbar Province.

Our new home at the firebase was a bombed-out neighborhood on the city's outskirts. We surveyed our digs, but there wasn't much else to do except sit and wait until the rest of the force could arrive. Once Staff Sergeant Rick had set up security for our position, he disappeared to a nearby market. He returned thirty minutes later, carrying bags of souvenirs, eggs, and other snacks.

"The Iraqis said they'll get us anything we want," he said, doling out goodies to everyone.

A pack of mangy dogs and cats skulked around in the rubble, cautiously eyeing us, and curious locals poked their heads around corners to get a closer look at Anah's newest arrivals. Task Force Thunder's "Carnage" battery, with its soldiers and three M777 howitzers, had left Al Qa'im several hours after us, and with their arrival at last light the newly minted "Rawah Support Force" was officially in place. Our hastily assembled plan had come together without a hitch, and I wondered when the other shoe would drop. Nothing was supposed to be as easy as it had been to get Carnage's howitzers to Anah.

Later that evening, following the persistent requests by the commanders of both Task Force Wagram and SPMAGTF that their forces remain in the fight, a platoon of 2/7 Marines and a battery of French soldiers and their Caesar cannon left the wire of Fuhaymi and drove north across the desert to conduct an artillery raid on Rawah. It was an impressive display of maneuver and firepower. As volleys of high-explosive rounds sailed high above us toward the city, we sat in the dark and watched the stray dogs and cats chase each other around the shattered neighborhood. Fighting with each other and racing in circles around the empty lot, the animals kept us awake throughout the night—as did the shrieking volleys of Iraqi Grad rockets that intermittently screamed over our heads unannounced, illuminating the neighborhood and lighting up the sky with the brilliant orange fireflies of their exhaust jets. I wondered, for the thousandth time, how in the exact hell I had ended up in the middle of all this.

We awoke shivering on a noticeably colder November 16. The kiln of Al Anbar's summer was a distant memory, and we waited all day for the Iraqis to report that conditions were set for the assault. The previous evening, I had tried to convince Qassim to launch the attack on November 16, but he pretended it had been scheduled for November 17 all along. His adjustment sent Major Awtry and me through the roof, and we weren't the only ones. When word of the twenty-four-hour shift to the right reached our crew back at Al Asad, who had all worked their tails off to meet the original timeline, they threw their hands up in frustration. When he heard the news, even the proper, unflappable British army captain who was the Main's senior watch officer blurted out, "You have got be *fucking* kidding me!"

With his units in their attack positions, Qassim relayed his final plan to me. He then declared that much of the enemy's combat power inside Rawah had already departed, and he estimated his soldiers would secure the town within a day. I wasn't so sure. Between the fatigue dragging me down and the ever-changing plan, I no longer knew *what* to believe.

"Okay, *Sayidi*," I replied. "Viking is headed to their support positions on the southern bank, and our artillery here at Anah is ready to go."

Beginning at midnight, Carnage's howitzers fired hourly pre-assault missions, working over the approaches to Rawah. Just as I had gotten myself to sleep, reveille at Firebase Anah sounded at first light with a long, ear-piercing volley of Grad rockets screaming toward the Iraqis' final objective. And then, at 0730, the JaOC Commandos and the Ali Burgess tribal fighters stepped off from their attack positions and moved east. They penetrated the city and advanced quickly, securing Rawah's southern sector. Twenty-eighth Brigade and their Jughayfi partners pushed southeast, and the 7th Division Commandos and the Abdul Athir tribals swept in from the north and cleared their assigned zone. By 1400, Qassim's forces had seized Rawah—the last major urban center held by the Islamic State in the Middle Euphrates River Valley—at the cost of one Commando killed by a house-borne IED. It was a final middle finger from the withdrawing enemy. Concealed explosive devices would kill more soldiers in the coming days as they searched the town. Booby traps aside, the Iraqi army now owned Rawah, and the *jundis* were moving about freely through the town's maze of streets and alleys. The assault was over faster than anyone had imagined it.

An hour later, Abdul Amir arrived in Anah to meet with Qassim, and the two generals declared Rawah liberated. The prime minister followed suit, tweeting a congratulatory message to the Iraqi Security Forces for their swift victory. With his brigades holding their positions, Qassim outlined for me how his *jundis* would clean up shop in the coming days. Weeks later, after we had both returned to Al Asad, I would tell him, "You had a vision, and you made it happen. The campaign played out exactly as you described it to us months ago. We are honored to have supported you and played a role."

But that was still in the future, when we would have more time for pleasantries. Understanding he was busy and didn't need me wasting his time at that particular moment, I merely said, "Congratulations, *Sayidi*. You did it. You and your men did it."

"We couldn't have done it without the Liberators," he said.

"Huh?" I asked, puzzled.

"Your Marines . . . we call you the *Liberators* now."

"Liberators, huh?" I said, nodding and smiling. "Yeah, I can dig that, *Sayidi*."

It was an altogether anticlimactic end to the operation. As daylight faded, I turned to Awtry.

"Time to get the hell out of here," I said.

"Back to the train station?"

"No, home . . . Al Asad. Jankowski can hold down the fort at the train station until Slugger-6 is ready to take the con. Shit, he's probably ready *now*."

Awtry's look of unease told me he was not ready to go. Neither was I. But with the assault over, there would be many questions to answer, many briefs to give, and many reports to write. The Jump team needed to take a knee, get cleaned up, and prepare for who knew what would come next.

As we drove through the night, civilian vehicles zipped up and down the now-cleared highway of Route Bronze. It was as if the Islamic State invasion of Al Anbar Province had never occurred. The long ride gave me plenty of time to reflect on what had happened in the previous six weeks, what our team had accomplished. As proud as I was of Qassim and his *jundis*, I was even more proud of the men and women of Task Force Lion. Against all odds, they made Desert Lion happen, and they had given a pretty good account of themselves in the process. No one sitting in the cheap seats would ever be able to argue with the results.

Our convoy rolled though Al Asad's gates late in the evening. As we pulled into the staging lot next to CHU City-1, Marines from the task force greeted us with jubilant high-fives. After unloading my gear, I dragged myself to the nearby internet café. Despite the late hour, the place was packed. Many more people had arrived in the time we were away, and I had to wait in line for a phone to call home and talk with my family.

"Are you done partying with your friends?" Ashley asked.

"Yeah, we're back. The party's over."

"Well? How did it go?"

I paused, looking down at my filthy uniform and the dust and grit caked on my hands and embedded beneath my fingernails.

"It was a hell of a ride," I said. "And I'm glad it's over."

Of course, it wasn't over—the operation itself *or* the unending war in Iraq. And it's not over now; it may never be. But I wasn't thinking about that then. Instead, all I could think about was how happy I was, how fulfilled. And how much I missed my wife and two daughters. I walked outside into the chilly night air surrounding Al Asad. Stopping to let my eyes adjust to the darkness, I paused before making my way across camp to my CHU and the lumpy mattress inside that awaited me.

I hope the Liberators get some rest tonight, I thought. *They've certainly earned it.*

EPILOGUE
December 2017–April 2018

I am not afraid of tomorrow, for I have seen yesterday and I love today!

—William Allen White

Don't be dismayed by good-byes. A farewell is necessary before you can meet again. And meeting again, after moments or lifetimes, is certain for those who are friends.

—Richard Bach

I didn't ask for it to be over, but then again, I never asked for it to begin. For that's the way it is with life, as some of the most beautiful days come completely by chance. But even the most beautiful days eventually have their sunsets.

—Unknown

ON THE EVENING OF JANUARY 7, 2020—nearly two years after Task Force Lion parted ways with Major General Qassim and his Jazeera Operations Command—the Islamic Republic of Iran launched a volley of ballistic missiles at Al Asad Air Base. The Coalition base at Erbil received a similar, albeit smaller, volley. There were no U.S. or Coalition deaths at either impact site, but more than one hundred service members pinned down in concrete bunkers across Al Asad suffered the immediate and lingering effects of concussion and traumatic brain injury from the detonating warheads. The attack, which followed the U.S. assassination of Iranian Quds Force commander General Qassem Soleimani and Iraqi PMF commander Abu Mahdi al-Muhandes less than a week earlier at Baghdad International Airport, was a level of escalation for which few were prepared. Suddenly, after several weeks of tension that had begun with a Kata'ib Hizballah attack on the Coalition base at Taji and immediate U.S. retaliatory strikes against KH positions across Iraq, the United States and Iran appeared to be on the brink of a full-scale, hot war.

As my planning team in the 1st Marine Division G-3 labored through the night to develop potential deployment options to meet CENTCOM's renewed thirst for U.S. military deterrent power, my mind wandered. I thought back to 2017 and 2018, remembering my Task Force Lion team, remembering Qassim and his *jundis*. I knew that, although the events that had precipitated the U.S. drone attack against Soleimani and Muhandes—and Iran's subsequent retaliation—did not begin in the winter and spring of our deployment, they certainly had roots there.

✦

Once the adrenalin of Desert Lion and the Iraqi liberation of western Al Anbar subsided, life for our team settled into a somewhat predictable routine aboard Al Asad. But we had barely reached the halfway point in our deployment, and there was still much to do. Unsure of what lay ahead, we looked at our remaining five months with uncertainty and a fair degree of trepidation.

There was a lot to process after the operation wound down. The metrics and tangible statistics were the easy part. In total, by the operation's end the task force had coordinated more than four hundred strikes across western Al Anbar, expending thousands of rounds and killing more than two hundred enemy fighters. The team's logistics and sustainment efforts throughout the vast battlespace were even more impressive. Despite all those tactical victories, one question nagged us: *What had we really accomplished?* In a late-night bull session on Thanksgiving, stuffed with turkey and dressing from Al Asad's dining hall, four of the team's iron majors—John Kelly, Aaron Awtry, Chris Julian, and Roberto Falcon—sat in my office and chatted long after everyone else had retired for the evening. With the events of Desert Lion still fresh in our memories, the discussion turned to what had gone right and what had gone wrong.

"What would you have changed?" Julian asked me.

"Nothing significant," I replied after considering his question. And I meant it.

"At the end of the day," Kelly, ever the cynic, asked, "what did we really *do* here?"

"We gave the Iraqis confidence," I said. And it was true. Intelligence, logistics, fire support—that had all been us. But Qassim and his men had done everything else. The Iraqis had done the heavy lifting; they had done the fighting and the dying.

We continued running daily convoys to Fuhaymi and Al Qa'im until Lindsay Mathwick could put the finishing touches on an enduring contract solution for the Iraqis to take over the outpost resupply effort. Not long after Rawah's fall, I ordered Fuhaymi's closure and the retrograde of everyone manning it. Like the Sagrah firebase two months earlier, the post had outlived its usefulness. By November 22, Task Force Slugger assumed control at the rail yard to support 8th Division's holding force in Al Qa'im. Soon, Lieutenant Colonel Payne's cavalry squadron focused on what would eventually become its true mission: serving as Task Force Lion's primary sensors for Iraqi operations in western Al Anbar, which included working with a nearby SOF outpost in Syria to target Islamic State fighters across the border. A secondary, unintended mission Slugger assumed was monitoring the various Shi'a militia groups still operating in and around the Al Qa'im District—a task that grew more dangerous with each passing week as the SMGs' actions became more and more hostile.

Before long, 8th Division was screening displaced families and allowing them to return to their homes. Within the first three weeks, Slugger reported the successful return of more than 150 families. The district's repopulation was one measurable sign of a gradual return to stability in the border region. As we tracked the return of internally displaced persons, there were continued reports of the PMF screening returning residents for their political leanings—a process that amounted to a form of "reverse gerrymandering."

As November drew to a close, the Coalition concentrated on transitioning operations in Iraq. The focus of advisor operations by the task forces, including our own team, would shift to the operations command level, with less energy devoted to advising at the division level and below. The plan would have little impact on us, as my primary partner continued to be Qassim. After all, Qassim was all things JaOC, and the JaOC was all things Qassim—a reality the senior Coalition officers were not keen to acknowledge.

There would also be a renewed focus on the "building partner capacity" effort. For his part, Qassim finally indicated a desire for his forces to conduct refresher training via Lieutenant Colonel Momme's BPC program with his Danish soldiers aboard Al Asad. Lieutenant Colonel Bruøygard also leaned into the effort by transitioning his Norwegian crew to an expeditionary assessments team that would partner with 7th Division and evaluate its brigades across western Al Anbar. We would then feed that information to the Fantastic Four to inform their decisions regarding which units to pull off the line and enter the training pipeline.

And, as envisioned, Border Guard Force units under the Ministry of the Interior would eventually replace Iraqi army units along the frontier. Until then, a hold force from 8th Division would continue to improve positions and secure the region. The border guards were disorganized, untrained, and under-resourced. Despite our pleas, no one could provide a realistic timeline for when they would assume responsibility of the porous, volatile boundary between Iraq and Syria.

As Task Force Lion's advise, assist, and enable mission with the Jazeera Operations Command settled into a more static, advisor-focused role, we looked to the future. What would subsequent task force rotations look like? What would they do? What role would Qassim and his brigades play in the new post-ISIS world of Iraq? We weren't the only ones asking those questions.

Not long after Desert Lion's conclusion, MARCENT directed both Task Force Lion and Task Force Spartan to develop proposals for "optimized"—which is to say smaller—advisor teams to replace us once our deployments came to an end. With the immediate threat ostensibly out of the picture, the Marine Corps was no longer willing to foot the manpower bill associated with the task forces that had so successfully aided the Iraqi army's rout of the Islamic State invaders.

By mid-December, I feared Qassim was letting the momentum of Desert Lion slip away. At the conclusion of a KLE aboard Camp Majid, I had my most honest conversation with him since my arrival the previous August. Having grown tired of the usual roundtable of compliments with all hands present, I excused everyone so I could have a private, closed-door session with my partner. In carefully measured points, I conveyed my growing list of concerns about western Al Anbar. They included border security, stability in Al Qa'im, reintegrating the returning population, unresolved civil-military issues, the consolidation and reorganization of Iraqi forces in Al Anbar, and a creeping enemy resurgence—what everyone had begun calling "ISIS 2.0."

To be sure, Qassim had a basic plan to deal with ISIS 2.0. But my greater concern was all the other issues that, left unresolved, could reverse the Iraqi army's hard-won gains in the province. I urged him to coordinate a council meeting that would include his division commanders, the tribal militia leaders and sheikhs, and the Al Anbar governor. The council's purpose, I suggested, would be to address the civil-military issues we both acknowledged were hindering progress in Al Anbar. I challenged him to define his five-year vision for western Al Anbar, and as he started speaking extemporaneously, I urged him to consider it while he was on leave. When he returned, we could discuss it and begin laying the foundation for his vision.

I also addressed the PMF issue, reminding him the Shi'a militia groups were in Iraq to stay and would likely be an enduring part of the fabric of the Iraqi security apparatus—a fact that privately turned my stomach. Qassim's connection with Sistani and the PMF over the years meant they might have developed leverage over him, leading him to discount or outright ignore PMF activity in Al Qa'im. That had manifested in his frequent cancellations of partnered operations because of the potential optics and proximity to PMF forces. Regardless, and although the PMF's agenda still palpably agitated Qassim, I urged him to work with them as best he could. He admitted he was coordinating with Abu Mahdi al-Muhandes, the PMF's chairman who would later die in the same Hellfire strike that killed Soleimani. His revelation, alarming as it was, at least demonstrated signs of progress.

Finally, I discussed his ongoing challenges with the 8th Division commander. Although Qassim had overall responsibility for everything happening in his area, to include 8th Division's actions in Al Qa'im and along the border, he still had no authority over Major General Hussein. Qassim wasn't receiving the support he needed from his higher headquarters—Hussein still answered only to Abdul Amir—and that was hamstringing his ability to command. To this I had no response. I had command relationship issues of my own with *my* different sets of higher headquarters. I left that to Qassim to figure out by himself, just as I would.

Three days before Christmas, the Commandant of the Marine Corps visited Al Asad. A perpetually gruff introvert, he appeared unenthusiastic about being overseas during the holidays. Nevertheless, we spirited him and his team into the conference room, where we presented a brief that focused on Desert Lion and our assessment of the way ahead in Iraq. When Major Duesterhaus concluded the presentation, the Commandant slowly shook his head.

"All the generals in Baghdad don't know what's gonna happen next," he said. "When all is said and done, nothing we do here is gonna make any difference; nothing is gonna change. You *can't* get blown up out here."

There was no *Thanks for all the hard work*; no *We're proud of what your team did out here on the edge of the empire*. Instead, the message my officers took away from the general's blunt comments was that our efforts had been little more than a waste of time, material, and manpower. His remarks an hour later during a town hall with the Marines echoed his earlier words in the conference room: *You can't get blown up out here*. With that, it was as though some great, invisible vacuum had sucked all the air out of the tent, and the audience left the town hall confused and visibly upset. The Marine

Corps' most senior leader had essentially told them that their mission had been hopeless—that everything they had done was in vain. Months later, after reading one of my weekly sitreps, the Commandant openly questioned the wisdom of a successful strike we had conducted against an enemy weapons cache on behalf of the Iraqis. Reading his criticism of the strike in an email, I recalled his visit. *Geez,* I wondered. *Why does he even care?*

Still reeling from the Commandant's words, and now sick as a dog from the omnipresent Iraqi crud, on Christmas morning I hopped in a Blackhawk with Major General White for a flight to the Al Qa'im train station. Ten minutes out from our destination, high winds and hazy weather conditions turned the flight around. On the return trip to Al Asad, White and I discussed the precarious situation with ISIS 2.0 and the deteriorating relations with the PMF and its Shi'a militia groups surrounding Task Force Slugger in Al Qa'im.

"You guys need to watch yourselves, Lion-6," he grunted, seeming to echo the Commandant's earlier warning. "Force protection will always be my number one priority. There's nothing here worth dying for."

His guidance circled in my brain for the remainder of the flight. If our senior leaders were telling us this, I wondered just what the hell we were still doing there in Iraq. That brief exchange, coupled with my worsening illness, made the much-heralded visit to Al Asad by Gen Joseph Dunford and his traveling United Services Organization holiday road show later that evening a hollow, joyless event for me.

One thing soon became apparent: with the Islamic State militarily defeated, with no clear and present danger of a *physical* ISIS resurgence, the long political knives were being unsheathed in Iraq's halls of power. More than ever, Qassim openly feared for his job now that the government had dealt with the threat in Al Anbar. In our remaining months together, each decision he made seemed calculated to preserve his upward mobility. It was difficult to blame him. By April 2018 our team would be gone, back safe with our families in the United States. But he would still be in the thick of things, fighting for his life and his livelihood. He knew he had to survive, and so he began pulling away from me and my team of advisors.

There were moments when he revealed his true thoughts that he had buried deep within his brusque exterior. I cherished each one of them. One day before we conducted the transfer of authority with the next team, which would end up being Task Force Lion's final deployment rotation, Qassim and Numan appeared unannounced at our command post. As we sat down together for chai in the greeting room, Qassim leaned in close and placed his hand on my knee.

"You are my brother," he said. "I will not forget what you did for me. The people of Al Anbar will not forget what you and your Marines did for them. I hope you will return to us one day so we can know each other as friends and not as soldiers."

"This is not 'goodbye,' *Sayidi*," I said, clasping his hand. "This is 'until we meet again.'"

The next day, the two teams formed up in front of the command post for the transfer ceremony. As the guests took their seats, Qassim was nowhere to be found. I approached Numan.

"Where is General Qassim?"

"He had business to conduct at the border," he replied. I didn't need an interpreter to tell me he was covering for his boss. Our team's impending departure had so upset Qassim that he refused to attend the ceremony.

With the transfer of authority complete and Rotation-6 at the helm, I shook Numan's swollen, mangled hand one last time.

"It is as you said," he uttered, his eyes welling with tears. "I am not going to say 'goodbye'."

There were other frustrations to deal with after we returned home. Every now and then, team members would reach out for my assistance with end-of-tour awards. Given the challenges we had faced getting awards approved for those who deserved them while we were still in theater, I knew the requests would eventually surface. Going into the job a year earlier, the list of command authorities I specifically did *not* have included the ability to approve personal awards. Accordingly, anything beyond a letter of appreciation required the signature of Lieutenant General Beydler, who as a Marine three-star component commander was the sole approval authority for even the lowest-level awards for our team. While my peers commanding regiments were routinely taking care of their Marines by approving and presenting achievement and commendation medals, I was left trying to explain to my incredulous staff why I had less administrative authority as a task force commander than I did as a battalion commander seven years earlier.

Before our deployment, I had requested the MEF staff to get those administrative command authorities approved for me, but they were unsuccessful. When I protested, the answer was, "The operational commander at MAR-CENT gets to make the final call." Staff officers at MARCENT pointed the finger back to the MEF, saying it was the parent command's responsibility. Either way, MARCENT's strict awards quota policy, firmly dictated by their chief of staff, further impeded the process of getting my people recognized.

"Twenty percent," MARCENT's chief had insisted in February of 2018 after I asked about awards for the team. "That's all the commander will entertain."

Not satisfied with that answer, I confronted Beydler and asked for his guidance. His response seemed to dance around the issue.

"What is the right number?" he pontificated. "Twenty percent? I'm not sure."

But his message certainly *was* clear: 20 percent would be the magic number. With that limitation in mind, I could only nominate fewer than twenty team members. And I could be guaranteed that each award submission would be subject to intense scrutiny. Several units deployed to Iraq and Afghanistan prior to ours had allegedly nominated an unacceptably high number of people for high-ranking awards such as the Bronze Star. In doing so, they had apparently spoiled it for the rest of us. I never truly understood why the leaders at MARCENT and the MEF were so opposed to granting me and my other task force peers the command authority we rated. It was only after our team returned from Iraq that I gained a sliver of insight into Beydler's thought process.

"The colonels who have led the advise and assist task forces have routinely asked for O-6 command authority, and to be referred to as 'commanding officers,'" he told me in our final conversation in 2018. "But I have continued to hold them at the OIC level to keep them from getting out over their skis."

I respected Beydler. He had vocally supported me and my team perhaps more than any other senior leader in the Marine Corps, and I would forever be indebted to him for that. And yet, after commanding the task force for fifteen months and working with him twice in my career—a combined period totaling more than two years of my professional life—when he said that, I still had no idea what the hell he was talking about.

There was no doubt in my mind: many more than twenty of my Marines and sailors had earned personal awards. The degree of effort the team had exhibited during Desert Lion alone seemed enough to present a personal decoration to every single man and woman. But that would never fly. To ameliorate the situation, by the deployment's end I endorsed letters of continuity for all team members whom we had not nominated. Before leaving Iraq, I sent emails to parent units of the team members, hoping that the home station commanders would recognize the efforts of their personnel and present them with the awards they rated. Many commanders did the right thing; others did not. Some of the worst offenders were fellow colonels who either couldn't be bothered to go the extra mile for their people, or who had their own interpretation of the Navy and Marine Corps awards manual. Ultimately, just as it had been for those in positions of power who could have addressed the artificial limits placed on my targeting authorities, the issue of awards was, to everyone outside of my team, no big whoop.

To Lieutenant General Beydler's enduring credit, years after our return he personally involved himself in getting an award upgraded for one of my team members whose parent commander had refused to recognize the Marine's accomplishments overseas. But his endorsement, while genuinely appreciated, was merely a drop in the bucket. And so, as has likely happened since the first recruits left Tun Tavern in 1775, there were Marines and sailors on the task force who, in the shuffle of parent unit command teams, were lost in the system and never appropriately recognized for their efforts. It was just one more example of how skewed and haphazard the military awards system continued to be—a system where rear echelon commanders with little to no understanding of the circumstances on the battlefield could overrule commanders on the ground who had actually witnessed a Marine's actions.

Compared to my previous deployments to Iraq and Afghanistan in 2003 and 2011, our actions outside the wire in Al Anbar Province bore few resemblances to what I had come to know as combat. In many ways, my experience on the ground with Task Force Lion felt too sanitary, too clean to be considered actual combat. But the character of modern combat had changed over the many years of the Long War. In 2017, my Marines and I never confronted the ISIS foot soldiers face to face because that was not our role. That was not our mission. Rather, to support our Iraqi partners, we had killed our mutual enemies from afar, with the prism of drone video feeds creating a distance between us and the carnage on the battlefield that was as much emotional as it was physical. That emotional distance was alarming. With each ISIS fighter we killed, a growing numbness took root, and each successful strike that led to the enemy's destruction on the battlefield practically became a cause for celebration.

Perhaps we just didn't recognize that numbness at the time as we toiled from the relative safety of our command posts. Despite the constraints placed on us by our higher headquarters, the pace at which we conducted strikes and the physical distance from the carnage made it easy to lose our humanity. Recognizing my growing callousness, I periodically revisited the words of Friedrich Nietzsche. "Whoever fights monsters," he said, "should see to it that in the process he does not become a monster. And if you gaze long enough into an abyss, the abyss will gaze back into you." Just as it had in earlier tours in Iraq and Afghanistan, my mind often seemed to teeter on the edge of that abyss, and it wasn't until years after my return from Al Anbar that I came to grips with what I had done. As the deployment ended and we returned to our normal lives, each of us was forced to take stock of our actions. There could be no doubt about it: the ISIS fighters were the enemy, and our mission had been to help the Iraqis eradicate them. But we had not been merely "mowing the grass," as the saying went . . . we had been extinguishing human lives. To call it anything else would be obscene.

To be sure, there were a few uncertain, even harrowing, moments as we pushed west with the Iraqi troops, and the fog and friction of combat was always present for my men and women on the battlefield. But most of the friction we endured did not originate from enemy forces. Rather, we either generated it internally, or our multiple echelons of operational and administrative headquarters generated it for us. It was the externally generated friendly friction that would aggravate me the most—that was responsible for my simmering anger throughout much of the deployment and then long after we returned to our families and parent units in the United States. Whether it was the arguments over who would lead Desert Lion, the questioning of my authorities and abilities as a battlefield commander, or the tacit pressure from my various higher headquarters to "take one for the team" and relinquish my responsibilities to a more palatable Marine Corps force—all contributed to the greatest shock I felt throughout my time in Iraq: I never imagined the most significant threat I would face would wear the same uniform as me.

When all is said and done, nothing we do here is gonna make any difference. You can't get blown up out here . . .

There's nothing here worth dying for . . .

I didn't know how to reconcile what the Commandant and Major General White had told me that December after Desert Lion. On one hand, there was the Marine Corps' most senior officer implying that everything we had done—the time, energy, and resources we consumed, the risks we took, the personal and professional bridges we burned—was all for nothing. On the other hand, there was the commander of all Coalition land forces in Iraq, a genuine mentor and one of the finest battlefield commanders I had ever known, suggesting that there was no point in taking risks to accomplish our mission—in effect confirming what the Commandant had said days earlier.

Maybe the two men didn't really mean what they said. Perhaps the Commandant was exhausted from his holiday tour across the Middle East; maybe White was frustrated with the Iraqis slow-rolling operations and stymieing progress at the Syrian border. But words mean things, and subordinates look for that meaning—for guidance and direction—in the words of their superiors. Both men were career professionals, senior leaders at the top of their game, and neither had ascended to his position by being stupid or naïve. And so, as senior leaders of the organization, they were responsible for what sprang from their mouths.

What message had they been sending me? Like me, both generals had lost men in combat. Were they telling me there was no value in what we were doing? The most important lesson I had learned after my earlier experiences in Iraq and Afghanistan was that being in command is ultimately about making hard decisions. It is about prioritizing resources and managing risk—not avoiding it. Their comments implied that what we were doing was no longer worth the risk. If that were indeed the case, then I had to ask why we had left our families for Iraq in the first place. Serving in the military and deploying overseas—especially to a combat zone—is an inherently risky endeavor. So too was supporting our Iraqi partners in the way they needed it most: outside the wire, on the battlefield with Qassim and his soldiers.

I was not a reckless leader; I never had been. During previous deployments, others had accused me of hazarding myself too often, and maybe that was true. But it had always been in the spirit of not asking my Marines to do anything I wasn't willing to do myself. My Marines were always my most precious resource, and the young men and women who made up Task Force Lion were no different. As we entered each new phase of Desert Lion, and throughout the remainder of our nine-month tour, my final guidance to the team before any foray outside the wire was the same: *Do not sacrifice safety, security, or accountability for the sake of expediency.* The Marines and sailors took my mandate seriously, and the results were indisputable: every member of the team returned home safe, standing on two feet.

Accomplishing the mission in Iraq meant I had to take calculated risks, but by December of 2017 I sensed the organization's senior leaders no longer believed what we were doing was worth even that. I had to ask myself one simple question: *If they are unwilling to take risks, why should I?* If force protection had indeed become the number one priority above all others, then it was time to go home. As a result, in our final four months at Al Asad, I limited the team's activities outside the wire. Task Force Slugger's Brandon Payne was running a tight ship at the train station, and most of his squadron's logistical needs were being met by the contracted life support convoys Mathwick and her S-4 team had worked so hard to coordinate. I soon resisted Awtry's frequent, fervent suggestions that we conduct battlefield circulation trips across the desert to Al Qa'im. Instead, most of my visits to see Payne and his soldiers involved me catching a helicopter ride with the senior Coalition commanders from Baghdad and Kuwait during their routine tours across Iraq. There were still periodic expeditionary advise and assist missions to see Qassim at Haditha, but even those outings grew further apart as he spent more time on the frontier trying to lock down the situation at Al Qa'im's border with Syria.

In the years since my return from Iraq, I often think back to the shattered train station that became our home during Desert Lion's final phase. Inevitably, I remember the times I spent wandering around the rail yard alone, reflecting on all that had once occurred there in the early years of the war. Deep inside the shitter, where Aaron Awtry's Marines had once slept fitfully in between their bloody, never-ending patrols into Husaybah and Al Qa'im, young men whose names I will never know and whose faces I will never see had scrawled lines of graffiti throughout the chambers filling the rubbled building. The faded messages inscribed on the chipped tile walls were not what I had grown accustomed to seeing in the countless Port-A-Jons I frequented throughout my tours in Iraq and Afghanistan. There were no artful depictions of male and female genitalia, there were no proclamations about what someone named Wagner loved, there were no encouragements to eat the apple and fuck the Corps. Instead, I found messages of despair, messages of strength, messages of hope—messages from deep within the hearts of young men who perhaps did not plan on ending up where they did, but eventually understood that what they were doing had meaning, what they were doing was making a difference. The Marines and sailors of

Task Force Lion had made a difference too; what they did had meaning and purpose. In the end, and despite the words from my superiors that troubled me for so long, I realized there are some things that defy logic; there are some things worth the risk.

There are some things worth dying for.

S. W. B. Folsom
July 31, 2018–October 2, 2020

ACKNOWLEDGMENTS

Writing a book begins as a solitary project. Getting it through to actual publication, however, is a team effort. My eternal thanks go to my Task Force Lion teammates, who encouraged me to write this story before our 2017–18 deployment was even complete. They were similarly encouraging and enthusiastic when I began the arduous process of tracking down everyone to seek name usage and photograph permissions.

My thanks to Mike Andrews, Shannon Goans, Michael Durkin, Mike Doyle, Pauline Shanks Kaurin, and @cdrsalamander for taking the time and energy to read early drafts of this book. Their honest feedback as friends and colleagues greatly assisted me in making this a readable story. I am also deeply appreciative to Damien O'Connell, John Waters, John Ismay, @cdrsalamander, and @lawofsea for giving me the time, encouragement, and bandwidth on their different platforms to continue to tell my story in a public forum.

I am grateful to the publishing team at Naval Institute Press—including Adam Kane, Claire Noble, Padraic "Pat" Carlin, Susan Corrado, Ashley Baird, and Elena Pelton for finding merit in my work and committing the time and resources necessary to take this project from manuscript to finished product. My sincere thanks also to Pete McPhail for his skill, patience, and genuine collaboration . . . the results were the beautiful map illustrations for this book. I am also truly grateful to have worked again with Jehanne Moharram, whose skilled, painstaking, and thoughtful copyediting, as well as personal and cultural insights, aided tremendously in helping me get this story as correct as it could be. Simply put, this book would not be what it is without her contributions.

Most important, I am grateful for my family—Ashley, Emery, and Kinsey—and the enduring love and support they have provided over the years, especially during my long absences abroad and at home. Being the spouse and children of a Marine officer is an impossible burden—one my three girls shouldered for far longer than they should have. While I owe a debt of gratitude to the Marine Corps for the role it played in my adult life, I owe a greater debt to my family. Without them, I would have gotten lost long ago. But they showed me the way, and the way is home.

GLOSSARY

3/7	3rd Battalion, 7th Marines
A3E	advise, assist, accompany, and enable
Abu	Arabic for "father of"
AO	area of operations
AOC	Anbar Operations Command
Aqeed	Arabic for "colonel"
arty	short for "artillery"
ASR	alternate supply route
BMP	*boyevaya mashina pyekhoty* (Russian for "infantry fighting vehicle")
BOS-I	base operating support-integrator (pronounced *boss-eye*)
BPC	build partner capacity
BrigGen/Brig. Gen.	brigadier general (U.S. Marine Corps/U.S. Army)
Capt/Capt.	captain (U.S. Marine Corps/U.S. Army)
CAS	close air support
CBRN	chemical, biological, radiological, and nuclear (pronounced *see-bern*)
CDE	collateral damage estimate
CENTCOM	United States Central Command
CHU	containerized housing unit (pronounced *chew*)
circ	short for "circulation"
CIVCAS	civilian casualties
CJFLCC	Combined Joint Forces Land Component Command (pronounced *see-jay-flick*)

CJOC	Combined Joint Operations Center (pronounced *see-jock*)
CJSOTF	Combined Joint Special Operations Task Force (pronounced *see-juh-soe-tif*)
CO	commanding officer
COA	course of action (pronounced *koe-ah*)
COALSOF	Coalition special operations forces (pronounced *cole-soff*)
COC	combat operations center
Col/Col.	colonel (U.S. Marine Corps/ U.S. Army)
CONOP	concept of operations
CONUS	continental United States (pronounced *koe-nus*)
COPsO	current operations officer
CP	command post
CTS	Counterterrorism Service
Da'esh	acronym for Arabic name of ISIS (al-Dawlah al-Islamiyah fi l-Iraq wa-sh-Sham)
DANCON	Danish contingent
DANSOF	Danish special operations forces
det	short for "detachment"
DFAC	dining facility
dishdasha	long robe traditionally worn by men in the Middle East
DMR	digital mobile radio
ECP	entry control point
ECR	effective casualty radius
EFB	expeditionary firebase
EOD	explosive ordnance disposal
FA	field artillery
FECC	fires and effects coordination center
FedPol	Federal Police
FOB	forward operating base
FOC	full operating capability
FOPs	future operations

FOPsO	future operations officer
FSR	field service representative
GCE	ground combat element
GMLRS	guided multiple launch rocket system
GPS	global positioning system
Habibi	Arabic for "my dear"
HIMARS	high-mobility artillery rocket system
HLZ	helicopter landing zone
HMMWV	high-mobility multipurpose wheeled vehicle (pronounced *hum-vee*; also written as Humvee)
IA	individual augment
IED	improvised explosive device
I MEF	I Marine Expeditionary Force (also referred to as "the MEF")
IOC	initial operating capability
ISF	Iraqi Security Forces
ISIS	Islamic State of Iraq and Syria (pronounced *eye-sis*)
ISR	intelligence, surveillance, and reconnaissance
J-3	operations directorate or director of operations
JaOC	Jazeera Operations Command (pronounced *jay-ock*)
JOD-CENT	Joint Operations Directorat–Central Command Division
JTAC	joint terminal attack controller (pronounced *jay-tack*)
Jump, the	mobile command post to place the commander forward on the battlefield
jundi	Arabic for "soldier"
KBR	Kellogg, Brown, and Root
KH	Kata'ib Hizballah
KIA	killed in action
KLE	key leader engagement
LtCol/LTC	lieutenant colonel (U.S. Marine Corps/U.S. Army)
LtGen/LTG	lieutenant general (U.S. Marine Corps/U.S. Army)

LZ	landing zone
MAGTF	Marine Air-Ground Task Force
Main	main command post (also "Main CP" or "the Main")
Maj/MAJ	major (U.S. Marine Corps/U.S. Army)
MajGen/MG	major general (U.S. Marine Corps/U.S. Army)
MARCENT	Marine Corps Forces Central Command
MATV	MRAP-all terrain vehicle (pronounced *mat-vee*)
MEDEVAC	medical evacuation
MEF	Marine Expeditionary Force
MERV	Middle Euphrates River Valley
MEU	Marine expeditionary unit
MNF	Multinational Force
MoD	Ministry of Defense
MRAP	mine-resistant ambush-protected (pronounced *em-rap*) vehicle
MRE	meal, ready to eat
MSR	main supply route
MTVR	medium tactical vehicle replacement
NCO	noncommissioned officer
NOR TU	Norwegian Task Unit
NROTC	Naval Reserve Officers Training Corps
OCS	Officer Candidates School
OIC	officer-in-charge
OPCON	operational control (pronounced *op-con*)
OpsO	operations officer
OPT	operational planning team
optempo	short for "operational tempo"
PAO	public affairs officer
PGM	precision-guided munition
PID	positive identification
PMF	Popular Mobilization Forces
PMNOC	Prime Minister's National Operations Center

pogey bait	candy, snacks, and other similar food not generally available to service members in the field
PSD	personal security detail
PX	post exchange
QRF	quick reaction force
ROC	rehearsal of concept
Roto	rotation
RPG	rocket-propelled grenade
S-2	intelligence section or intelligence officer
S-3	operations section or operations officer
S-4	logistics section or logistics officer
S-6	communications section or communications officer
SATCOM	satellite communications
SAW	School of Advanced Warfighting
Sayidi	Arabic for "sir"
SEAL	sea, air, and land (U.S. Navy Special Operations Forces team member)
SecDef	secretary of defense
SecFor	security force
SgtMaj/Sgt. Maj.	sergeant major (U.S. Marine Corps/U.S. Army)
shaheed	Arabic for "martyr"
shamal	Arabic for "north" or "from the north;" used to describe sandstorms in Iraq
Shlonik	Arabic for "How are you/how's it going?" (literally translated as "What's your color?")
Sitrep	situational report
SJA	staff judge advocate
SMG	Shi'a militia group
SNCO	staff noncommissioned officer
SOF	Special Operations Forces (pronounced *soff*)
SOTF-West	Special Operations Task Force–West (pronounced *soe-tiff west*)
SPANSOF	Spanish special operations forces

SPMAGTF-CR-CC	Special Purpose Marine Air-Ground Task Force–Crisis Response–Central Command (referred to as SPMAGTF; pronounced *ess-pee-mag-taff* or *spuh-mag-taff*)
SUV	sport utility vehicle
SVBIED	suicide vehicle-borne improvised explosive device (pronounced *ess-vee-bid*)
SWA	Southwest Asia
SWAT	special weapons and tactics
TAA	tactical assembly area
TAC	tactical command post (also "TAC CP" or "the TAC")
TACON	tactical control (pronounced *tay-con*)
TCA	theater coordinated assistance
TEA	target engagement authority
TIC	troops in contact
TMF	Tribal Militia Forces
UAS	unmanned aerial system
UXO	unexploded ordnance
VHF	very high frequency (wavelength)
VIP	very important person
wasta	Arabic for "connections" or "clout"
XO	executive officer

INDEX

A'ali Al Furat tribal militia: and attack on Al Qa'im, 222, 224–25, 233, 235, 238, 246, 252; bad blood between Qassim and, 246; in Karabilah, 258; and planning of Desert Lion, 91; in Qassim's plan for Desert Lion, 115–16

Abadi, Haider Jawad Kadhim al- (Iraqi Prime Minister), 136–37; decision to delay Desert Lion, 119, 120; and JaOC credibility after Anah victory, 198–99; and liberation of Rawah, 273; and planning of Desert Lion Phase III, 206–7, 208; premature declaration of victory in attack on Al Qa'im, 254–55; strike approval authority give to Qassim, 167; visit to liberated Al Qa'im, 258–59

Abdul Amir. See Yarallah, Abdul Amir Rashid

Abdul-Zawbai, Numan (general): and attack on Al Qa'im, 207; and attack on Anah, 189; career of, 60–61; at celebration in town square of Al Qa'im, 259; as commander of Iraqi Army's 7th Division, 56, 60; described, 60–61; expressions of gratitude to author, 282; and "Fantastic Four," 63; four wives of, 61, 63; as General Qassim's shadow, 60; and gossip about Abdul Amir's sexuality, 252; and Lion March to TAA Sagrah site, 76; and meeting at Qassim's headquarters, after conquest of Arah, 191; meeting in office of, 106; meeting with author after approval of new Desert Lion timetable, 131–32; meeting with generals at Husaybah, 253; and

planning of Desert Lion Phase III, 206; plush office of, 103–4; preference for meeting in his office, 103; treatment at Camp Havoc medical facilities, 86

Abraham's Well, 33

Abu Harden Bridge, repair of, 261–62, 266

Adil (General): and attack on Al Qa'im, 252; described, 245; meeting with generals at Husaybah, 253; at TAA Al Qa'im for planning meeting, 245

Adnan Ali Mirza (Iraqi colonel), 162, 171

Afghanistan War: Awtry in, 19; IEDs in, 79; Marines put to work sweeping for IEDs, 147

Afghanistan War, author in: Afghanistan experience of battalion members, 26; and bathroom graffiti, 289; and earned trust as commander, 15; emotional scars from, 21, 286; and lesson on value of public recognition for soldiers, 173; lessons about command learned in, 288; living conditions, 42; and revulsion for war, 6; rough living conditions, 42; targeting authority given to, 127–28; wounded children witnessed by, 85

Ahmed (colonel): and attack on Anah, 170–71, 183–84; author's fondness for, 228; described, 63; family in Anah, 192; and "Fantastic Four," 63; and first day of Desert Lion, 160; friendship with Kelly, 63; friendship with Kiffa, 63–64; gift to author to celebrate Anah victory, 192; ISIS truck captured by, 227–28; management of relations between

257–58; attacks on Iraqi forces from Syria, 257; author's urge to defeat, 6–7; evolution of name, 6; infiltrating attacks in rear areas, 201–2; liberal use of IEDs, 78–80; mercilessness of, 186–87; resurgence as ISIS 2.0, 280, 282; use of drones, 257; use of grenade-armed quadcopters, 80. *See also* suicide vehicle-borne improvised explosive devices (SVBIEDs)

Jankowski, Robert "Bob": and attack on Anah, 180, 182; background and character of, 140–41; at EFB Sagrah, 157, 197–98; as S-3's plans officer, 141; and setup of EFB Sagrah, 140, 141, 148, 149; at TAA Al Qa'im, 273; at TAA Fuhaymi, 220
JaOC Commandos: and attack on Al Qa'im, 222–23, 238, 243; and attack on Anah, 183, 184; and attack on Rawah, 273; and street-by-street clearing of Al Qa'im, 256
Jasim Nazal, Qassim: bad blood between A'ali Al Furat tribal militia and, 246; career of, 245; character of, 245–46; as commander of Iraqi 9th Division, 245; departure from Al Qa'im, 257
Jazeera Operations Command (JaOC): and attack on areas north of Euphrates River, 10; credibility won by Anah victory, 198–99; as headquarters for Iraqi 7th Division, 10; and Iraqi attack on Al Qa'im, 207; Qassim as commander of, 56; reliance of task force for logistical support, 53. *See also* JaOC Commandos
John Basilone drink, 219–20
Joint Operations Directorate–U.S. Central Comman Division (JOD-CENT), author's work at, 5–6, 66
Jughayfi tribe: fighters celebrating fall of Al Qa'im, 257; in Qassim's plan for Desert Lion, 116
Julian, Christopher "Chris": and attack on Anah, 174, 175, 180–82, 185–87, 199–200,

268; career of, 68; and command centers for Desert Lion, 113–14; and debate on results of Desert Lion, 278; and delay of Desert Lion, 120; described, 67–68; and Desert Lion command center work, 165–66; and fire support planning, 167–68; as fires and effects coordinator, 67; hatred for ISIS, 68; and planning for TAA Sagrah, 73; and setup of EFP Sagrah, 144; and strike approval, 121–22; strike approval delays, frustrations with, 124–26, 167, 174, 175, 199–200; strike on ISIS truck, 244; and targeting packages, 123

Kata'ib Hizballah (KH): exchange of fire with Coalition forces, 277; in Karabilah, 258; link up with Syrian Hezbollah units, 267; unit at Al Taqaddum Air Base, 44, 45
Kelly, John (general), 28–29
Kelly, John (major): and attack on Anah, 183, 185, 268; background and career, 28–29; brother's death in Afghanistan, 82–83; career of, 72; and delay of Desert Lion, 120; friendship with Colonel Ahmed, 63; frustration with pre-deployment training, 29; General Qassim's views on, 60; management of relations between author and Qassim, 64; and meetings with Iraqi officers, 104, 107; and planning for next command post after TAA Fuhaymi, 235–36; and planning for TAA Sagrah, 73; and planning of attack on Rawah, 202; and preparation for Desert Lion, 151; Qassim's trust in, 63; responsibilities in Desert Lion, 165–66; and sandstorm at TAA Fuhaymi, 229; and setup of EFP Sagrah, 144; and targeting packages, 123; and travel to Iraq, 36–37; walk through minefield at Sagrah, 82–83; willingness to challenge author's assumptions, 29
Kestrel system, 34–35

ABOUT THE AUTHOR

COL SETH W. B. FOLSOM, USMC (RET.), served more than twenty-eight years in uniform. A graduate of the University of Virginia, Naval Postgraduate School, and the Marine Corps War College, he is the author of *The Highway War: A Marine Company Commander in Iraq*; *In the Gray Area: A Marine Advisor Team at War*; and *Where Youth and Laughter Go: With "The Cutting Edge" in Afghanistan*. He lives with his family in Southern California.

The **Naval Institute Press** is the book-publishing arm of the U.S. Naval Institute, a private, nonprofit, membership society for sea service professionals and others who share an interest in naval and maritime affairs. Established in 1873 at the U.S. Naval Academy in Annapolis, Maryland, where its offices remain today, the Naval Institute has members worldwide.

Members of the Naval Institute support the education programs of the society and receive the influential monthly magazine *Proceedings* or the colorful bimonthly magazine *Naval History* and discounts on fine nautical prints and on ship and aircraft photos. They also have access to the transcripts of the Institute's Oral History Program and get discounted admission to any of the Institute-sponsored seminars offered around the country.

The Naval Institute's book-publishing program, begun in 1898 with basic guides to naval practices, has broadened its scope to include books of more general interest. Now the Naval Institute Press publishes about seventy titles each year, ranging from how-to books on boating and navigation to battle histories, biographies, ship and aircraft guides, and novels. Institute members receive significant discounts on the Press' more than eight hundred books in print.

Full-time students are eligible for special half-price membership rates. Life memberships are also available.

For more information about Naval Institute Press books that are currently available, visit www.usni.org/press/books. To learn about joining the U.S. Naval Institute, please write to:

Member Services
U.S. Naval Institute
291 Wood Road
Annapolis, MD 21402-5034
Telephone: (800) 233-8764
Fax: (410) 571-1703
Web address: www.usni.org